On The Way
Toward A
Phenomenological
Psychology

DUQUESNE STUDIES
Psychological Series

5

On the Way Toward a
Phenomenological Psychology

The Psychology of William James

by

Johannes

HANS LINSCHOTEN, PH.D.

edited by

AMEDEO GIORGI

Duquesne University Press, Pittsburgh, Pa.

Editions E. Nauwelaerts, Louvain

DUQUESNE STUDIES

Psychological Series

Adrian van Kaam, Ph.D., editor

Volume One—*Stephen Strasser*, PHENOMENOLOGY AND THE HUMAN SCIENCES. *A Contribution to a New Scientific Ideal.* XIII and 339 pages. Price: $6.00.

Volume Two—*Aron Gurwitsch*, THE FIELD OF CONSCIOUSNESS. XIV and 427 pages. Price: $5.25.

Volume Three—*Adrian van Kaam*, EXISTENTIAL FOUNDATIONS OF PSYCHOLOGY. XIV and 386 pages. Price: $7.95.

Volume Four—*Joseph J. Kockelmans*, EDMUND HUSSERL'S PHENOMENOLOGICAL PSYCHOLOGY. *A Historico-Critical Study.* 359 pages. Price: $7.95.

This work is a translation of
OP WEG NAAR EEN FENOMENOLOGISCHE PSYCHOLOGIE,
© Erven J. Bijleveld, Utrecht, Holland

Library of Congress Catalog Card Number 68-20279
© 1968, by Duquesne University
PRINTED IN THE UNITED STATES OF AMERICA
BY KINGSPORT PRESS, INC., KINGSPORT, TENNESSEE

To the memory of
Hans Linschoten

PREFACE TO THE ENGLISH EDITION

Probably not many American psychologists have
heard of Hans Linschoten, but surely many more would have
had he not died at the relatively young age of thirty-eight. While
his academic career was brief, it was an active and a productive
one. At the time of his death, Linschoten had written or col-
laborated on approximately thirty articles and six books. However, it was not just the sheer bulk of his works that brought him
his recognition, but also the quality and the viewpoint. While
his viewpoint may have been controversial (for the most part it
was phenomenological), everyone acknowledged his brilliance
and his scholarship, and in the end, it was these latter qualities
more than the viewpoint that enabled him to become one of the
leading psychologists in Holland, and to a certain extent, in
continental Europe as a whole.

Hans Linschoten was born on September 21, 1925 in
Utrecht, The Netherlands. He attended grammar school in
Bandoeng, Indonesia, but his studies were interrupted by World
War II, and after spending three years in a Japanese concentra-
tion camp, he finally was able to complete his studies in
Bilthoven, Holland in 1946.

In the same year, Linschoten enrolled at the University of
Utrecht and completed his studies in approximately one-half the
time normally required. He joined the staff of the psychological
laboratory of the University of Utrecht as a research worker, and
he received his doctorate (cum laude) in 1956 when he completed
his thesis on "The Structural Analysis of Binocular Depth Perception". In the following year, he succeeded Prof. Dr. F. J. J.

Buytendijk to the chair of experimental and general psychology at Utrecht University, when only 32 years of age.

In his years as a research worker he was deeply influenced by phenomenological philosophers, especially Husserl, Heidegger, and Merleau-Ponty. He was an expert on Husserl and he devoted many of his lectures in psychology to working out the implications of Husserl's thoughts for contemporary psychology. Many of his publications were also concerned with the relationship between phenomenology and psychology.

In the spring of 1961, Linschoten came to Duquesne University as a guest lecturer and one of his courses was a course on James based upon this book which he had completed in 1959. It was at this time that I first met Linschoten and it was also at this time that arrangements were made to translate his book into English (a German edition was also published in 1961). Linschoten himself was to do the translating from Dutch into English, and I was to "smooth" the English. He realized that he could not complete the translation by the end of the semester, so further arrangements were made whereby I would be his guest at the University of Utrecht during the summer of 1961 where we could complete the translation. Unfortunately, Linschoten became seriously ill towards the end of the semester, and he had to spend most of the summer recuperating and his working schedule was severely limited. At the time of the onset of his illness, Linschoten had translated approximately one-third of his book. Actually, it would be more appropriate to say that he rewrote these pages. As is often the case with authors, he was not satisfied with what he had said earlier, and began to reformulate and re-interpret his own ideas. Undoubtedly, this is probably one of the reasons that his progress with the translation was not faster. At any rate, during the summer we were only able to go over the pages he had completed before he became ill, although I did enjoy many conversations with him and members of his staff that were invaluable in helping to understand his thought.

Linschoten never did finish the translation. Because of his illness he had to keep taking more and more time off from work, and the pressure of his other duties and new interests prevented him from returning to this task again. He died on March 17, 1964, but not before finishing another book *Idols of Psychology*, which appeared posthumously, and which deals with certain psychological fallacies and the methodological problems to be worked through to overcome these fallacies. This latter book reveals more than anything else the theoretical struggle that Linschoten was going through during his last years. He seemed to turn more and more towards positivism, but whether this was merely to correct certain phenomenological biases, or to start once again a new systematic outlook, it is difficult to say. The one thing that we can be sure of is that he had a continual interest in the methodological problems of psychology, and this undoubtedly helps to account for his simultaneous interest in phenomenology and positivism. His perennial methodological concern was also an important factor for his interest in psycholinguistics which was his major research preoccupation at the time of his death.

Consequently, the task of translating his book had to be begun again. As implied before, Linschoten himself had stopped just a few pages short of completing Chapter III. It was at this point that Rev. Walter van de Putte, C.S.Sp., who accepted the assignment of completing the translation, began the basic translation from Dutch into English, and once again the task of "smoothing" the English and checking for psychological interpretations and accuracy was left to me. We were aware that there were some discrepancies in the first three chapters between the Dutch text and the English because Linschoten had rewritten some parts, but we decided to let his own English expressions remain rather than to revert back to the expressions of the Dutch text itself. Nevertheless, it was still necessary to make some grammatical modifications of Linschoten's own expressions.

As usual, many people contributed to the completion of this task, and I would like to thank E. P. Köster of Utrecht University for his invaluable aid in supplying sorely needed information at various critical times; Paul Colaizzi for his helpful comments on the English text; and Rev. Henry Koren, C.S.Sp., Rev. Franz van Doorne, C.S.Sp., and Rev. E. van Croonenberg, C.S.Sp. for their technical help. Lastly, I would especially like to thank Thomas

Cloonan for his painstaking reading and editing of the text and for his patience in pursuing literally hundreds of references. While Rev. Walter van de Putte, C.S.Sp. translated the Dutch into English, I was responsible for all final expressions, and consequently all errors and omissions must ultimately be attributed to me.

Amedeo Giorgi

Duquesne University
Pittsburgh, Pa.

TABLE OF CONTENTS

INTRODUCTION

William James' *Principles of Psychology* is a classic. It seems that only a few psychologists of the younger generation have read the whole work and, according to Allport,[1] this holds even for American psychologists. Those who have read the *Principles* generally agree with John Dewey's judgment that whatever one may think about it in the light of our vastly more differentiated psychological knowledge of today, this book is as much a classic as Locke's *Essay* or Hume's *Treatise*.[2] It is one of the few truly original conceptions of psychology. James not only summarizes nineteenth century psychology but his personal style and vision transcend the limitations of the concrete data known to him in his lifetime. In as much as a new edition of the *Principles* has appeared recently, it seems proper to bring to light once more the originality of James' ideas.

However, to review all the analyses and insights contained in the 1400 pages of the *Principles* would be an impossible task. No completely systematic exposition of this work is possible. The decisive reason for this must be sought in James' approach to the problems he was interested in. Being enthralled by the phenomena he so vividly portrays and describes, he never felt a need for developing a methodically closed system. On the contrary, by nature and habits of thought he felt a repugnance for a too strictly defined system. In his view the closed system was a strait jacket imprisoning the mind; an artificial net in which one vainly tries to trap the ever changing phenomena that slip through it. It is not surprising that James lands in a paradox every time he tries to solve a problem, but then it proves to be what Allport[3] calls a *productive* paradox. James' abhorrence of closed systems certainly is a weakness, but it is also the source of his strength. The reason for this is shown in his own description of Bergson, with whom he kept up a correspondence dating from 1902: "That he gives us no closed-in system will of course be fatal to him in intellectualist eyes. He only evokes and invites; but he first annuls the intellectualist veto, so that we now join step with reality with a philosophical conscience never quite set free before."[4] These same words apply to James. They could have been a description of his own character by Bergson. These two contemporaries were congenial spirits. We are not surprised to find a passage in Bergson's correspondence which states that a summary of James' lectures brings to the foreground one central theme: the necessity to transcend the concepts, the simple logic and the approaches of a *too* systematic philosophy that postulates the unity of all things.[5] In opposition to this tendency to unity, James called one of his books *A Pluralistic Universe.*

The principles that form the base of his psychology are also pluriform and changing. He was never frightened when he met with some contradiction in his endeavor to formulate direct experience and connect it with objective knowledge of physiological processes. James felt perfectly at home in the midst of paradoxes. His psychology often appears paradoxical in the original sense of the word; that is, uncommon, running counter to common opinion among psychologists. Here is a man who never allowed himself to be shackled by his extensive knowledge of psychological data and systems. Unceasingly he traced new ways of formulating more adequately the things that are proper to psychology. Quite often this made him come near to a phenomenological psychology. In the following chapters we shall explicitly emphasize this affinity. To express it in the terminology of the *Principles:* James' psychology is the *topic* of our study. This we shall discuss in the light of phenomenology and try to show that James' ideas moved in a phenomenological direction.

This is not an arbitrary interpretation. James repeatedly paved the way for a phenomenological psychology, although it must be said that sometimes he blocked it again. We shall try to show both his phenomenological orientation and his non-phe-

nomenological leanings in developing his lines of thought. In
this context it is interesting to note what Husserl wrote in his
diary in connection with a course he taught in psychology.[6]

> Although I was able to read only a few things and too little of
> James' Psychology, it brought some lightning flashes. I saw how
> a courageous and original man did not let himself be shackled by
> any tradition but endeavored effectively to hold on to and describe
> what he saw. This influence was not unimportant for me. . . .[7]

Later on, Husserl mentioned James as the only one who noticed
the phenomenon called "the horizon."[8] A. Metzger recalls some
favorable remarks Husserl made about James in Freiburg, but
that author is mistaken in his supposition that James' psychol-
ogism and empiricism might have annoyed Husserl.[9] On this point
Husserl gave his opinion unequivocally.[10]

Do the affinities between James and Husserl exist only in the
details of their thought? Only a more thorough investigation
than has been made to date can decide to what extent James
influenced the development of Husserl's phenomenology. This
question does not belong to the purpose of the present study.
Even without any data on the factual relations between the two
thinkers, the connections between their systems are unmistakable.
I came across them for the first time in 1952, while reading the
Principles. Some studies on this point made at that time remain
unpublished. They found their way into this book, together with
materials from a course about this subject, given in 1957-58.

Dr. W. Biemel and Dr. R. Boehm, from the Husserl-Archives
in Cologne and Louvain, gave some useful indications of this
relationship. I want to express my sincere gratitude for their help.
I also feel very grateful for the permission Fr. Herman Van
Breda, O.F.M., director of the Husserl-Archives in Louvain, gave
me to study Husserl's copy of the *Principles*. The marginal notes
Husserl made, contain some indications about his evaluation of
James' thoughts.[11]

The strong affinity between James and Husserl is also emphasized by Gurwitsch in his recent book.[12] Gurwitsch has repeatedly
made use of James' views for his own phenomenological analyses.
Hence some of Gurwitsch's more important themes are also taken

up in the present study, but it was not possible to enter into
lengthy discussions of these views.

NOTES

1. Gordon Allport, "The Productive Paradoxes of William James,"
Psychological Review, vol. 50, 1943, p. 95.
2. John Dewey, "The Principles," *Psychological Review,* vol. 50,
1943, p. 121.
3. Allport, "The Productive Paradoxes of William James," p. 97.
4. William James, *A Pluralistic Universe,* (New York, 1936),
pp. 265 f.
5. Henri Bergson, *Écrits et Paroles,* (Paris, 1957), p. 198.
6. Unfortunately, the notes for this lecture, which Husserl as a
Privatdozent gave in Halle in 1891-92 have not been preserved so far as
the Husserl Archives in Louvain could ascertain.
7. Edmund Husserl, "Persönliche Aufzeichnungen, hrggb. von W.
Biemel," *Philosophy and Phenomenological Research,* vol. 16, 1956,
p. 295.
8. Edmund Husserl, *Die Krisis der Europäischen Wissenschaften,*
(The Hague, 1954), p. 267.
9. A. Metzger, "William James and the Crisis of Philosophy," in *In
Commemoration of William James,* (New York, 1942), p. 209.
10. Edmund Husserl, *Logische Untersuchungen,* Bd. 2, (Halle,
1901), p. 206.
11. We find marginal notes, key words and translation of terms
especially in Part I, ch. 4-9, 11, 12, 14-16; Part II, ch. 17-22, and 26. Most
of the other independent publications of James appear to be present in
Husserl's personal library. None of these showed any sign of being
studied except the abbreviated edition of the *Psychology.* Of the two
reprints which James sent to Husserl, "The Knowing of Things Together" shows such signs; "A World of Pure Experience" does not.
12. Aron Gurwitsch, *The Field of Consciousness,* (Pittsburgh,
1964), p. 7.

I SOME BIOGRAPHICAL DATA ON WILLIAM JAMES

William James was born in New York in the year 1842.[1] He was an American and an American he remained in sentiment in spite of the many ties that bound him to Europe. His parents were of Scottish and Irish descent and there were frequent changes in the scenery that surrounded him in his early years; he lived with his parents in Newport, New York, Paris, London, Geneva, Boulogne, and Bonn. As a student James followed courses at several European universities and he acquired extensive knowledge of European philosophy and psychology. He often, and with pleasure, visited Europe because he felt as much at home there as in his own country. He gratefully accepted much that the Old World offered him, while he critically sifted it. James met Europe with a spirit that had been formed by the youthful élan of the United States. He himself however, more formed by Europe than he realized, analyzed this élan with a sharp feeling for its weaknesses. In this way he was able to accomplish what no one after him was able to achieve, namely, he integrated European and American thought in his psychology.

The smaller circle of his own family also played an important part in the formation of James' mentality. His father, Henry James, had written on religious subjects in a way that showed how greatly he was influenced by Swedenborg; and these works William published after his father's death. William's own work *The Varieties of Religious Experience* which is still unique in its kind, shows him as a true son of his father. Then there was his brother Henry who won renown as a novelist. William's works reveal his talents as a writer and they can be read with pleasure because of their literary excellence.

In his youth William took up painting for a year, displaying some talent, and he even conceived the idea of becoming a painter. A painter he did become but the pen was to take the place of the brush. Religious and artistic impulses mingled with scientific interests in the work of his life.

At the age of nineteen, William enrolled in Lawrence Scientific School at Harvard University where he studied chemistry and comparative anatomy, changing to medicine in 1864. One year later, in 1865, moved by a spirit of adventure, he accompanied the biologist Louis Agassiz on a then famous expedition to the Amazon. William James did not contribute to the purposes of the expedition but it certainly helped him to develop his interest in biological problems. When, at a later time, he incorporated the theory of evolution in his psychology, he must have remembered the objections that were expressed against the theory, for Agassiz, who taught at Harvard, was a fervent opponent of it. But James made another discovery during that expedition to the Amazon; he became convinced that he should become a philosopher.

It is true that after his return to Europe in 1867 for further study (one and a half years in Germany: Dresden, Teplitz, Berlin), he applied himself to medicine and physiology, but he also began reading the great philosophers. It was then also that his slumbering interest in psychology crystallized. He writes in 1868 that

> I have been reading nothing of any interest but some chapters of physiology. There has a good deal been doing here of late on the physiology of the senses, overlapping perception, and consequently, in a measure, the psychological field. I am wading my way towards it, and if in course of time I strike on anything exhilarating, I'll let you know.[2]

And he had written before that, in 1867:

> It seems to me that perhaps the time has come for psychology to begin to be a science—some measurements have already been made in the region lying between the physical changes in the nerves and the appearance of consciousness—at (in the shape of sense perceptions), and more may come of it. I am going on to study what is already known, and perhaps may be able to do some work at it.[3]

Then follows a sentence that clearly shows that psychology was still in its infancy when James became acquainted with its first results: "Helmholtz and a man named Wundt at Heidelberg are working at it." Hermann von Helmholtz, who was later characterized by James as "a fine looking old fellow, but with formidable powers of holding his tongue, and answering you by a friendly inclination of the head,"[4] already enjoyed a world-wide fame. In 1868 James called him "the greatest scientific genius extant."[5]

On the other hand, it can be seen that "a man named Wundt" was still unknown at that time, though later he would be called the father of experimental psychology. In 1867 this scientist who for many years would be the undisputed grand-master of European psychology was still at the beginning of his career. Nevertheless, though only ten years the senior of James, he was already part-time professor at the University of Heidelberg in 1864.

Psychology increasingly absorbed the attention of James. He was deeply impressed by the accomplishments of this new experimental science. Around 1860 some important works like Fechner's *Elemente der Psychophysik* (1860) and Wundt's *Beiträge zur Theorie der Sinneswahrnehmung* (1858-62), appeared, and these marked the beginnings of physiological psychology, in the narrow sense of the term. Five years later Helmholtz' *Handbuch der Physiologischen Optik* (1867) was published, a work that quickly became famous and was printed again in 1920.

James thus found himself in the midst of that upcoming movement and enthusiasm for the new branch of science. For this was generally greeted as the fulfillment of what had only been projected and sketched in previous centuries, namely, the scientific study of the human mind. Here arose a science that had great promise for the natural scientists as well as philosophers. These expectations were strengthened by the universal optimism about science that had constantly grown stronger in the second half of the previous century.

In those years the sciences attained unprecedented splendor and glory and the public was filled with respect and hope: "this

Science was coming, a spirit of light and order, to the rescue of a world groaning and travailing in muddle for the want of it."[6] This is also clearly expressed in many passages of the novels of Dostoevski, but do we not find the expectation of a proximate achievement by science in the words of Helmholtz when he wrote: "Its task will be fulfilled as soon as the reduction of the phenomena to simple forces is completed and, at the same time, it can be proved that this is the only possible reduction the phenomena allow."[7]

This self-assured Messianic science now took possession of the man's inner experience by subjecting it to the experimental method. Taine expressed such a confidence in science when he wrote:

> Science at last is coming nearer, it comes nearer to man; it has passed beyond the visible and palpable world of stars, stones, plants where it had disdainfully been confined; it now tackles the soul, armed with precise and piercing instruments of which three hundred years of experience have proved the exactness and measured the range.[8]

It is not possible to understand the most profound problems, and also the conflicts, with which James' psychology confronts us, without a knowledge of the spirit of that time. James was, from one standpoint, animated by that spirit and it has left its mark on his psychology. On the other hand, he tried to free himself from the implications which he considered to spell the death of psychology, namely mechanism, the instrumental analysis of that which does *not* have the structure of stars, stones and plants.

The text continues further:

> Thought and its development, its rank, its structure and its ties, its profound corporal roots, its infinite growth through history, its high flowering at the summit of things, this now is its object, the object it has had in mind for the last sixty years in Germany and which, by means of slow and sure soundings and the methods used in the physical world, will be transformed before our eyes as the physical world has been transformed.

James vigorously fought the self-conceit and the partiality with which a certain type of natural science, anticipating a synthesis, tried to explain what was still unknown together with the known, reducing *all* phenomena to the same principles. The progress of science is so enormous, he was to say later in a speech, that it is no wonder that the worshipers of science lose their heads from time to time.

> In this very University, accordingly, I have heard more than one teacher say that all the fundamental conceptions of truth have already been found by science, and that the future has only the details of the picture to fill in. But the slightest reflection on the real conditions will suffice to show how barbaric such notions are. They show such a lack of scientific imagination, that it is hard to see how one who is actively advancing any part of science can make a mistake so crude.[9]

Statements of this kind, however, never hindered James in his conception of psychology as being a "natural science." But before we accuse him of inconsistency on this point, we ought to consider whether this inner conflict is not at the root of the fruitfulness of James' psychological thought. However, we are not that far yet. We must first follow the course of his life and development.

During his studies in Europe, James made plans for starting a career as a teacher of physiology; this he thought the best way to serve his interest in psychology. Was this a strange way? Not really, because in those times a considerable part of psychological experimentation was done by medical scientists and the investigations were strongly directed towards physiological problems. That is why experimental psychology began as physiological psychology.

We said already that it was all in the spirit of the times. Stanley Hall wrote the following concerning the formation of Wundt:

> In the dozen years of apprenticeship, he was in hot pursuit of the problems of physiology, the modern development of which is one of the great achievements of German science and which has lifted medicine throughout the world to a higher plane. Physiology brings various other sciences to a focus. To know it has well been called a liberal education as well as an excellent practical discipline in logic and in manipulation. . . . It rests upon the great ideal of

applying physics, the most exact of all sciences, and more recently
chemistry, to the study of the functions of living tissue and of the
human body. . . . Thus, to apply these methods to the senses
and to the elementary intellectual processes was the inevitable next
step and behind it was all the momentum of the physiological
Renaissance which was itself of great cultural significance.[10]

In 1869, having returned to America, James earned his medical degree at Harvard but he never practiced medicine. He had
delicate health and several times had tried to improve it while in
Europe, but he now became quite ill. A serious inner conflict
made him become self-centered; a feeling of the uselessness of his
life brought on a state of mental depression and more than once
he was tempted to commit suicide. Thirty years later he described
one of his most pathetic experiences of that time in the chapter
entitled "The Sick Soul" of his "Varieties of Religious Experience":

> Whilst in this state of philosophic pessimism and general depres-
> sion of spirits about my prospects, I went one evening into a
> dressing-room in the twilight to procure some article that was
> there; when suddenly there fell upon me without any warning,
> just as if it came out of the darkness, a horrible fear of my own
> existence. Simultaneously there arose in my mind the image of an
> epileptic patient whom I had seen in the asylum, a black-haired
> youth with greenish skin, entirely idiotic, who used to sit all day
> on one of the benches, or rather shelves against the wall, with his
> knees drawn up against his chin, and the coarse gray undershirt,
> which was his only garment, drawn over them inclosing his entire
> figure. He sat there like a sort of sculptured Egyptian cat or
> Peruvian mummy, moving nothing but his black eyes and look-
> ing absolutely non-human. This image and my fear entered into
> a species of combination with each other. *That shape am I,* I felt,
> potentially. Nothing that I possess can defend me against that
> fate, if the hour for it should strike for me as it struck for him.
> There was such a horror of him, and such a perception of my
> own merely momentary discrepancy from him, that it was as if
> something hitherto solid within my breast gave way entirely, and
> I became a mass of quivering fear. After this the universe was
> changed for me altogether. I awoke morning after morning with
> a horrible dread at the pit of my stomach, and with a sense of the
> insecurity of life that I never knew before, and that I have never
> felt since. It was like a revelation; and although the immediate

feelings passed away, the experience has made me sympathetic with the morbid feelings of others ever since. It gradually faded, but for months I was unable to go out into the dark alone.

In general I dreaded to be left alone. I remember wondering how other people could live, how I myself had ever lived, so unconscious of that pit of insecurity beneath the surface of life. My mother in particular, a very cheerful person, seemed to me a perfect paradox in her unconsciousness of danger, which you may well believe I was very careful not to disturb by revelations of my own state of mind. I have always thought that this experience of melancholia of mine had a religious bearing.[11]

Probably in connection with this frustrating experience of his own existence, James, in 1869, made the following remark:

I feel that we are Nature through and through, that we are wholly conditioned, that not a wiggle of our will happens save as the result of physical laws; and yet, notwithstanding, we are *en rapport* with reason. —How to conceive it? . . . It is not that we are all nature *but* some point which is reason, but that all is nature *and* all is reason too.[12]

This theme, this same thread runs continuously throughout his psychology. There is a fundamental anxiety in James about this ambiguity in human existence. For him, the problem of the relations between free will and determinism was not a purely intellectual problem, but primarily a lived ambiguity.

This problem too, defines one of the fundamental conflicts in the very foundation of his psychology. James never could decide which stand to take. He maintains at one and the same time that human experience and behavior are determined by physical laws, *and* that they are the spontaneous expressions of a free agent. And yet, there is no inconsistency in his views, as we shall see in the following chapters of this book.

After finding his way out of his crisis, James, in 1870, noted in his diary that he wanted to believe in the resistance of the Ego to the outer world, that life must be built upon activity, endurance, and creativity. It was the beginning of the creative period of his own life. In 1873 James became an instructor in anatomy and physiology at Harvard, the one university to which he was to consecrate his entire academic life. Then came his chance to realize what he had set out to do: teaching psychology via physiology, interesting some students in this matter, creating with them a new psychology in his home country; a renewed psychology, freeing itself from the theological and philosophical context in which its problems had been confined up to that time. Roback, in his *History of American Psychology*,[13] gives a vivid description of psychology in America at that time.

James was made an assistant professor in physiology in 1876. He then introduced a course in physiological psychology and became, in a way, the rival of James Walker, a colleague and professor of philosophy since 1838, who had always been interested in psychological problems. Walker regularly lectured on these problems, showing preference for the views of Scottish associationism, especially for Dugald Stewart and Thomas Reid. These men represented a school of moderate associationism, taking a stand against David Hume's scepticism and consistent sensationalism. The Scottish school defended the validity of *common sense,* holding that the real world is much like the way we perceive it. Their views had an affinity with the opinions of William James. But psychological thought had progressed since the theorizing of those Scotchmen. In 1878 the youngest of them had already been dead for fifty years. Associationism had evolved in the meantime, and James introduced some of the newer systems, like that of Hippolyte Taine, whose book *De l'Intelligence* had been the decisive break-through of associationism in France; or that of Herbert Spencer in England. Hume and Stuart Mill are cited repeatedly by James. On the other hand, his own discussions of association reveal that James was keeping at a cautious distance from the fundamental conceptions of the associationist group. He eagerly took in whatever food he found useful for his psychological research but he was not able to digest all of it. James was constantly on the lookout for new ideas in the books of his time hoping they would confirm his opinions and express them better than he could. And yet he always felt obliged to fight the systems proposed in these books, because they did not bring out what he himself had to say, and said well, notwithstanding his doubts about his own ability.

It would be difficult to determine exactly what influence all these men exercised on James. He sometimes borrowed fundamental concepts, or again only a small detail. The title of his book he may have borrowed from Spencer, who also wrote a *Principles of Psychology* in two volumes and influenced James' thought in a more important way.[14] It was Herbert Spencer who introduced evolutionism into psychology. Like Darwin, Spencer took his inspiration from Lyell's *Principles of Geology* (1832), but unlike Darwin, he did not accept Lyell's refutation of Lamarck. Spencer founded his theory of evolution on the hypothesis that acquired characteristics may cause hereditary changes. He published this theory in 1852, seven years before *The Origin of Species* appeared (this work won him over to Darwin's views).

In Spencer's opinion, associations may lead to hereditary tendencies like instincts. Instincts, which urge animals to certain useful patterns of behavior, he interprets as the slowly acquired deposit of the experience of many generations. Such instincts then form the basis of mental life. Even the highest activity of the human animal, thinking, rests on this foundation. The notion behind this theory is that psychology is, in fact, a biological science. Only by studying animal behavior, by finding its origin, by reducing human experience and behavior to its animal origins, may we come to understand man. A bio-psychologist looks at animal life to find the roots of human mental characteristics.

Without adhering to the full content of Spencer's notions on this point, James did adopt the bio-psychological approach. The continuity between human beings and animals is one of the principles he defended. James never considered his medical training as a hindrance in his psychologizing. On the contrary, he recognized it as an advantage.

It was in this spirit that he took up his activities at Harvard. He was fully alive to the importance of experimental investigation as a source of knowledge. In 1876, or maybe a year earlier, he fitted up a room for experimental research. History has its ironic twists. James' room preceded the official founding of the world's first psychological laboratory by some years. Wundt opened the later famous Institute at Leipzig in 1879.

It is true that much experimental work had been done before that. It is also a fact that James' lab was not very impressive. G. Stanley Hall describes it as a "tiny room under the stairway of Agassiz Museum . . . with a metronome, a device for whirling a frog, a horopter chart, and one or two bits of apparatus."[15] But there is a slight suspicion that the undertone of depreciation in this description might be professional jealousy. Stanley Hall founded the first official psychological laboratory in the United States in 1881, at Johns Hopkins University. Whatever the exact status of James' enterprise may have been, he was the first American to use psychological apparatus in psychology. In psychical research too, he wanted facts. Let us keep free of theories, he said, we need *facts*.[16] But James' enthusiasm about experiments does not imply that he himself accomplished much in that line. No important experiment was ever published under his name. Some lesser investigations are recorded in the *Principles:* a few experiments on transfer of training in memorizing (I, 666 ff.), and some work disproving the theory of feelings of innervation (II, 511 ff.). A more extensive investigation of the sense of dizziness in deaf-mutes[17] met with the approval of Ernst Mach.[18]

In 1890 he confessed to his friend Münsterberg that he hated experimental work and always felt inclined to postpone it. His experimental room grew up into a real laboratory in 1891, but James never made a home in it. However, he did much to stimulate experimentation. The year 1878, when James Walker retired, saw William James signing the contract for a handbook of psychology. He hoped to complete it in two years. He accomplished it in twelve years; the *Principles of Psychology* was published in 1890.[19] The book caused him much concern and it continuously occupied his attention. If there is anything good in it at all, it is the product of much work, he said.

He wrote and rewrote everything four or five times. Many parts were published separately. They appeared as articles in several journals, especially European journals, as unnoticed in the States at that time as they are now. His fame rose in Europe, while in the States, as Santayana tells us, "until the return wave of James's reputation reached America from Europe, his pupils and friends were hardly aware that he was such a distinguished man."[20] With some pride James wrote in a letter to Münsterberg in 1896: "A Berlin paper has been sent me with a letter from Munich, which said that the 'psychological pope of the old world, Wundt, and the psychological pope of the new world, James, were both distinguished by their absence.' I am becoming illustrious!"[21] His absence from the third international congress of psychology was the reason for this gratifying comment.

But James was not at all satisfied with his *Principles* once the work was finished. This he expresses clearly in some of his letters. To his editor he wrote, even before the printing was completed, that his work proves two things: "*1st,* that there is no such thing as a *science* of psychology, and *2nd,* that W. J. is an incapable."[22] No sane man would repeat the last statement. It goes to show, however, the uncertainty James experienced in regard to his own accomplishments. On the other hand it shows his courage and openness of mind to reject his own work after twelve years of labor. He proves this openness once more when, after having based the *Principles* upon the theme of the "stream of consciousness," he comes to the simple question: "Does consciousness exist?" This question is the title of a paper he published in 1904. James admits in this paper that he has had his doubts about the existence of consciousness for twenty years. This period stretches back for half the time he worked on the *Principles.* The question itself already makes him one of the forerunners, if not one of the founders, of behaviorism. In the meantime he had become an assistant professor of philosophy in 1880, a professor in 1885.

In 1889 his mandate was changed again and James became professor of psychology, one of the few bearers of this title. But in his kaleidoscopic life the arrangements never got a chance to settle. From 1890 onwards he directed his attention more and more towards the philosophical problems of pluralism and pragmatism. Earlier, on receiving an invitation from James, Hugo Münsterberg, a young and promising scholar from Freiburg in Germany, came to Harvard in 1892. He stayed for three years, then returned to Germany. Having thought it over for two years,

Münsterberg came back to Harvard as James' successor, and James' title was changed back into professor of philosophy. James now devoted his efforts to philosophy and more and more confined his publications to this field. The ideals, discovered on the banks of the Amazon, came true, although his psychological interests never disappeared. He retired in 1907.

James was an uncommon man who stood for an unusual psychology. The *Principles* met with a strong response. At the end of the century public opinion rated him as the most important scholar in the United States, the scholar *par excellence*. But James rejected his own work, probably on the same grounds that drove him to deny the existence of any "new psychology." In one of his *Talks to Teachers* he declares:

> So I say at once that in my humble opinion there *is* no 'new psychology' worthy of the name. There is nothing but the old psychology which began in Locke's time, plus a little physiology of the brain and senses and theory of evolution, and a few refinements of introspective detail, for the most part without adaptation to the teacher's use. It is only the fundamental conceptions of psychology which are of real value to the teacher; and they, apart from the aforesaid theory of evolution, are very far from being new.[23]

In those words James judged a psychology he himself had helped to develop. His attitude certainly looks complicated, and is confusing now and then. The same man who tells us that every conscious experience goes back to some happening in the brain, that we have to look into neurophysiology to solve psychological problems, also tells us that:

> Many persons nowadays seem to think that any conclusion must be very scientific if the arguments in favor of it are all derived from twitching of frogs' legs—especially if the frogs are decapitated —and that, on the other hand, any doctrine chiefly vouched for by the feelings of human beings—with heads on their shoulders— must be benighted and superstitious.[24]

Are we not obliged, then, to consider as the most essential part of James' thinking those opinions that have *not* been formulated in so many words in his works? These opinions lie in the distinct phenomenological undercurrent that runs through all his writings: the endeavor to trust direct experience, to create a psychology out of man's everyday awareness of his own doings.

But we must not overlook the fact that many a school in psychology referred to James as one of its precursors; and that, on the other hand, as many have denied him this role, even where we notice unmistakable affinities. Dewey took him for a behaviorist in intention.[25] According to Judd, it is James' theory of emotions that rings in the era of behaviorism.[26] Watson, however, did not agree at all; he states that his theory is a regression from which behaviorism recovered only with some difficulty[27] (mainly through the contributions of J. B. Watson). Kantor, too, accuses James of having failed in despiritualizing psychology.[28] These denials of James' behavioristic tendency, although not in agreement with James' writings, at least agree with the judgment of Perry, according to whom James, who saw himself as a "strict positivist," would have been a fervent opponent of positivism today.[29]

In Europe, the Leipzig school of "Ganzheitspsychologen" claims James as one of its early heralds.[30] Boring considered him to be a phenomenologist,[31] and Allport held almost the same view when he said:

> Radical empiricism has never become integrated with modern psychology. It might have served as the foundations for an American school of phenomenology, but it did not. Instead, the examination of the intent and constitution of experience was left largely to Husserl and his associates in Germany. . . .[32]

Had James known all this, it would have amused him. "Yes, I *am* too unsystematic and loose!" he tells us.[33] In the precise thought and consistency of a man like Wundt he suspected "a terrible flavor of humbug."[34] In a letter to Stumpf, 1887, he wrote the following about Wundt:

> But surely you must admit that, since there must be professors in the world, Wundt is the most praiseworthy and never-too-much-to-be-respected type of the species. He isn't a genius, he is a *professor*—a being whose duty is to know everything, and have his own opinion about everything, connected with his *Fach* . . . was there

ever, since Christian Wolff's time, such a model of the German Professor?[35]

Is this an expression of envy? It would be understandable, seeing that systematical Wundt, as Boring tells us, published an average of 2.2 pages per day between 1853 and 1921.[36] But we have no reason to suspect James of envy.

All the aspects and tendencies on account of which he is claimed by diverse psychological schools are indeed present in his works. James never wanted any fertile notion removed from his thought. As Santayana said:

> Philosophy for him had a Polish constitution; so long as a single vote was cast against the majority, nothing could pass. The suspense of judgment which he had imposed on himself as a duty, became almost a necessity . . . Experience seems to most of us to lead to conclusions, but empiricism has sworn never to draw them.[37]

Open empiricism or radical empiricism James branded his own kind of thought. He always went back to direct experience for a guide to the facts, but not to "facts" in the generally accepted sense. To James fact is the given itself, the reality we experience, and not some artificially reduced relations in which he could only see arte-facts. He did not want any "facts" the facticity of which had already been determined *a priori* by positivistic reasoning. His "open empiricism" is essentially the endeavor to describe the phenomena that interest him without presuppositions or prejudices, without being bound by any theoretical system, but to take as his guide the concrete reality of pluralistic experience. Of course, there is one difficulty in this position: open empiricism, too, is a theoretical system.

William James did not enjoy an easy life. Cosmopolitan, at home in two worlds, accustomed to their different spiritual climates, he often felt his own broadness and open-mindedness as a dissension. He gave vent to this feeling to Stumpf, in a letter of 1894: "One should not be a cosmopolitan, one's soul becomes 'disintegrated,' as Janet would say. Parts of it remain in different places, and the whole of it is nowhere. One's native land seems foreign. It is not wholly a good thing, and I think I suffer from it."[38]

The whole of it is nowhere: these words may be characteristic of the content of his life and thought; they certainly do *not* describe its form. That form possessed a unity, implied in his description of the pragmatist attitude: to live on the basis of uncertified possibilities in which one has confidence.[39]

William James died on the 26th of August, 1910, only a few days after his return from his last European voyage. Back home, he sank in his chair saying, "It's so good to get home."

NOTES

1. Here we limit ourselves to a short sketch. More complete information can be found in the following works: Henry James (ed.), *The Letters of William James*, 2 vol., (Boston, 1920); R. B. Perry, *The Thought and Character of William James*, vol. 1, (Boston, 1935), and vol. 2, (Boston, 1936); and R. B. Perry, *In The Spirit of William James*, (New Haven, 1938). Cf. also "A List of the Published Writings of William James," *Psychological Review*, vol. 18, 1911, pp. 157-165. (Boston, 1920), p. 127.

2. James, *Letters*, vol. 1, p. 127.

3. *Ibid.*, pp. 118 ff.

4. Perry, *Thought*, vol. 2, p. 188. Cf. James, *Letters*, vol. 1, p. 347.

5. Perry, *Thought*, vol. 1, p. 283.

6. H. G. Wells, *The New Machiavelli*, (Baltimore, 1964), p. 30.

7. Herman von Helmholz, "Über die Erhaltung der Kraft," in *Wissenschaftliche Abhandlungen*, vol. 1, (Leipzig, 1882), p. 17. Although some other things still need to be proved, he already gives a more definite expression of the final goal (p. 15): "The phenomena of nature will be reduced to motions of materials that have unchangeable powers of movement, which depend only on spatial relations (Die Naturerscheinungen sollen zurückgefuhrt werden auf Bewegungen von Materien mit unveränderlichen Bewegungskräften, welche nur von den räumlichen Verhältnissen abhängig sind)."

8. Hyppolite Taine, *Histoire de la Littérature Anglaise*, T. IV, (Paris, 1911), p. 388. The text continues further: "Thought and its development, its rank, its structure and its ties, its profound corporal roots, its infinite growth through history, its high flowering at the summit of things, this now is its object, the object it has had in mind for the last sixty years in Germany and which, by means of slow and sure soundings and the methods used in the physical world, will be transformed before our eyes as the physical world has been transformed."

9. William James, *The Will to Believe*, (New York, 1898), p. 53.

10. G. Stanley Hall, *Founders of Modern Psychology*, (New York, 1912) , pp. 313 f.

11. William James, *The Varieties of Religious Experience*, (New York, 1902) , pp. 157 f. Cf. James, *Letters*, vol. I, pp. 145 ff.

12. James, *Letters*, vol. I, pp. 152 f.

13. A. A. Roback, *History of American Psychology*, (New York, 1952) .

14. Cf. for the significance of Spencer in the development of James' thought: Perry, *Thought*, vol. I, pp. 474 ff.

15. G. Stanley Hall, quoted by Roback, *History of American Psychology*, p. 129. Also by Perry, *Thought*, vol. 2, p. 14; cf. pp. 6 ff.

16. James, *Letters*, vol. 1, p. 250.

17. William James, "The Sense of Dizziness in Deaf-mutes," *Amer. J. Otol.*, vol. 4, 1882.

18. Ernst Mach, *Die Analyse der Empfindungen*, (Jena, 1906) , p. 122.

19. Cf. regarding the historical development of the *Principles:* Perry, *Thought*, vol. 2.

20. George Santayana, *Character and Opinion in the United States*, (New York, 1921) , p. 94. Perry, *Thought*, vol. 2, pp. 91 ff.; *ibid.*, pp. 104 ff., a selection of malicious comments of James' American colleagues.

21. Perry, *Thought*, vol. 2, p. 145.

22. James, *Letters*, vol. 1, p. 294.

23. William James, *Talks to Teachers*, (London, 1920) , p. 7.

24. Perry, *Thought*, vol. 2, p. 30.

25. John Dewey, "The Vanishing Subject in the Psychology of James," *J. Phil.*, vol. 37, 1940, pp. 589-59.

26. Letter to Roback, quoted by Roback, *History of American Psychology*, p. 224.

27. J. B. Watson, *Behaviorism*, (New York, 1925) , p. 108.

28. J. R. Kantor, "Jamesian Psychology and the Stream of Psychological Thought," in *In Commemoration of William James*, (New York, 1942) , p. 147.

29. R. B. Perry, "James the Psychologist," *Psychol. Rev.*, vol. 50, 1943, p. 124.

30. H. Volkelt, "Grundbegriffe," *Neue psychol. Stud.*, vol. 12, 1934, pp. 9 ff.

31. E. G. Boring, "Human Nature vs. Sensation: William James and the Psychology of the Present," *Amer. J. Psychol.*, vol. 55, 1942, pp. 310-327.

32. Allport, "The Productive Paradoxes of William James," p. 101.

33. Perry, *Thought*, vol. 2, p. 96.

34. *Ibid.*, p. 55.

35. James, *Letters*, vol. 1, pp. 263 f.

36. E. G. Boring, *A History of Experimental Psychology*, (New York, 1929), p. 34.

37. Santayana, *Character and Opinion in the United States*, p. 82.

38. James, *Letters*, vol. 1, p. 347.

39. William James. *Pragmatism*, (London, 1907), pp. 297 ff.

II THE SCOPE OF JAMESIAN PSYCHOLOGY

1. The Definition of Psychology

Psychology is "the science of mental life." These words mark the beginning of the *Principles* (I, 1).[1] The psychologist wants to study the phenomena of consciousness, such as feelings, strivings, thoughts, reasoning, decisions, etc., and the conditions in which they appear. But how do we know whether we meet with such phenomena? There is no great difficulty regarding our personal life. Introspective observation, a return to what we have experienced, teaches us that various situations appear in our consciousness. Joy is a totally different mode or experience from listening attentively or longing for things. With respect to others, other men, other living beings such as animals, we have no direct experience of their experiences. But that all of us have some sort of experience is something that *cannot be doubted*. This we believe. And James looks upon this belief as the most fundamental postulate of psychology (I, 185). This means that the psychologist simply does not *want* to doubt that others have experiences. He *presupposes* that this *is* the case; his scientific work is based on that presupposition.

Having taken this stand, James accepts the validity of the notions of *common sense* on this point. Many other psychologists have not followed him in this but have tried to find *proof* for the fact that others have experiences that are similar to their own. They were thus led to wonder about the possibility of persons transmitting and making known to another what they have experienced and the way of that experience. Behaviorism has told us that no such possibility exists. Interior experiences are, by definition, subjective; there is no means to ascertain what goes on in other people's minds. So behaviorism discarded these questions altogether, and even denied what James took for granted. We shall see later that James' "uncritical" acceptance of common sense has an important function in the construction of his system.

Studying his work, we find that this is only one of James' approaches to psychology. Introspective description under the assumptions we just heard, defines a psychology in the *first person*. There is also a psychology in the *third person*. James uses this approach in the beginning of the *Principles* to make clear on what grounds we may speak of mind and mental life in general.

In observing animal activity, the assumption that animals too have interior feelings or states of consciousness cannot be guaranteed by the experience of our own human minds. In the case of both animal and human behavior, however, we can say that they are expressions of psychic (mental) life that manifest *purposiveness* and also *variability* in respect to the choice of means for attaining various ends. (I, 8 ff.) Behavior of this kind cannot be mechanically determined by the structure of the organism; it betrays "mind," the ability to attain an end by having the body at its *command*.

> Romeo wants Juliet as the filings want the magnet; and if no obstacles intervene he moves towards her by as straight a line as they. But Romeo and Juliet, if a wall be built between them, do not remain idiotically pressing their faces against its opposite sides like the magnet and the filings with the card. Romeo soon finds a circuitous way . . . (I, 7).

As one of the German philosophers, from whom James repeatedly took inspiration, tells us: "We have already mentioned the point where thinking in mental development begins, viz. at the place where the drive leaves its anatomically prescribed reflex path, choosing another one."[2] Mind manifests itself where the organism does not act like a simple machine, but shows the ability to make *detours*.

Now there is one interpretation James does not want us to make here. The mind that moves the body is not an independent entity like a soul inhabiting the body. Although James is not always clear on this point, he certainly rejected any spiritualist theory. "Mind," in his writings, seems to be a descriptive characteristic of living bodies, a term to catch that which distinguishes the organism from non-living things.[3]

The first-person and the third-person approach lead up to a second definition of psychology as the science of finite and individual minds. This science "assumes as its data (1) *thoughts and feelings,* and (2) *a physical world* in time and space with which they coexist and which (3) *they know*" (I, 6) .[4]

These data, says James, determine the psychologist's view of reality. They trace a *picture* of reality that is naturally subject to debate. But it is no subject for a *psychological* discussion. The data assumed by psychology must eventually be overhauled, but that is the task of metaphysics, not of psychology. One may ask whether such concepts as "the physical world in time and space" refer to a reality we really know, or to what degree thoughts and feelings know such a reality adequately. But such curious inquiries about the validity of knowledge are no part of psychology as such (I, VI; I, 185) .

James did not uphold this positivistic position in later times. In the preface to the Italian edition of the *Principles* (1900) he tells us: "I confess that during the years which have elapsed since the publication of the book, I have become more and more convinced of the difficulty of treating psychology without introducing some true and suitable philosophical doctrine."[5] When writing the *Principles* it may have looked like an easy way out to refer to metaphysics for the solution of fundamental problems. But it is not safe to avoid these problems that come in as implications and presuppositions affecting psychological statements. In a later chapter we shall see that James, in his theory of the stream of consciousness, cannot and does not detour around the problem of knowledge. But right now, we must follow him and leave the problem out of the picture. The assumptions and the irreducible data of psychology comprise four categories (I, 184) :

(1) the psychologist;
(2) the thought studied by him, the psychic phenomenon;

(3) the thought's object, or the object of the psychic phenomenon in general;

(4) "the psychologist's reality" which must be clearly distinguished from the physical reality.

The relation between these four categories can be described in the following way. The psychologist (No. 1), believes Nos. 2, 3, and 4, which together constitute *his* total object, and are realities. It is the psychologist's task to describe these realities and examine their mutual relations as best he can, but he does not trouble himself with the problem of how he has the ability to describe them.

The categories (1) and (4) of that schema are of special importance. James makes the statement that the *psychologist himself*, and the *psychologist's reality* belong to the irreducible data of psychology. This can mean but one thing: the presumption that the observer is an active factor in the constitution of the processes he observes. Psychological description then is not the objective description of an absolute reality. The psychologist himself is mixed up in it in much the same way that the point of view determines the foreshortening in a drawing.

One way in which this finds expression is what James calls "the psychologist's fallacy," the confusion of one's own standpoint with that of the phenomenon of consciousness one is recording (I, 196). Speaking of a thought, the psychologist stands outside of it. Both the thought *and* its object form the object for the psychologist. Now, if this thought is a cognitive state like a percept or a concept, the psychologist ordinarily has no other way of naming it than as the thought-of-that-object. But knowing the same object in *his* way, he supposes easily that the thought, which is *of* it, knows the object in the same way *he* knows it. Herein lies one of the grounds for the trend in classical psychology to conceive consciousness as a complex of discrete *contents,* leaving mental *acts* out of the picture.

Another variety of this fallacy is the assumption that the mental state studied must be conscious of itself as the psychologist is conscious of it (I, 197). The thought sees only its own object. The psychologist, being aware of this thought from without, sees not only the thought's object, but also the thought itself, plus possibly all the rest of the world. He may fall easily into the trap of describing his point of view as that of the mental state he thinks he is describing. Let us cite a passage to illustrate the point James is making here.

> If, for example, the thought be 'the pack of cards is on the table,' we say, well, isn't it a thought of the pack of cards? Isn't it of the cards as included in the pack? Isn't it of the table? And of the legs of the table as well? The table has legs—how can you think the table without virtually thinking its legs? Hasn't our thought then, all these parts—one part for the pack and another for the table? And within the pack-part a part for each card, as within the table-part a part for each leg? And isn't each of these parts an idea? And can our thought, then, be anything but an assemblage or pack of ideas, each answering to some element of what it knows? (I, 278) .[6]

Such errors can be eliminated, but a question remains. James does not refer to it in his treatment of the psychologist's fallacy. But we may very well suppose that this fallacy has a deeper meaning. Is there not a perspectivity in the whole of the psychologist's reality? Is it not so, for instance, that certain things like a superiority complex, or intelligence, or even mind, exist only in the psychologist's way of looking at everyday reality?[7] When James comes to speak about the various orders of reality (II, 287 ff.) , when he tells us that thought in general *transforms* and extends reality, does he not imply that the psychologist's reality is, at least partly, the creation of the psychologist? In that case, the psychologist's fallacy would only be a special case of human perspectivity in general.

2. *Thought and Feeling*

Psychology wants a general term to designate all states of consciousness, whatever their particular quality or nature may be (I, 185) . Of course, looking for such a general term only makes sense when the different mental states have something essential in common. What is it, that the feeling of joy, a sensation such as a "sweet taste," a memory, and a decision have in common? By putting them together in one general category, by giving them a common general name, the psychologist creates a specific perspective on reality. He supposes that all these different things can be conceived as particularizations of one fundamental form. Anticipating a later development in James' thought, we'll use the term *experience* to designate this fundamental form. In an experience a person who is able to designate himself as "I," is conscious of something he can distinguish from himself.

It is only in his later works that James uses the term experience. In the *Principles* he proposes two terms: *thought* and *feeling*. Looking over several terms used in classical psychology, he feels obliged to reject them. "Mental state," "states of consciousness," "conscious modification," "subjective condition," all these terms are cumbersome to use, and, more important, they have no kindred verbs. This last remark has an interesting implication. James is in search of a term that does not only suggest a *state* of mind, or a mental *content;* he wants it to express the *active* qualities of mental life, too. Consciousness is not just a passively being aware of something, it is an active taking-cognizance-of, an ongoing *stream*.

Taking "feeling" as a general term, we avoid some of these difficulties. "Feeling" is convenient because it has the verb "to feel," and such derivatives as "feelingly," "felt" and "feltness." It is a disadvantage that the word is already in use for specific mental states in the emotional sphere, and for sensations of touch. In using it we may therefore imply connotations that were not meant. On the other hand, "feeling" brings back into our terminology some aspects of mental states that got lost in the development of psychological theorizing.

Descartes, whose philosophy is at the origin of the development of psychology during the last three centuries, called the phenomena of consciousness *cogitationes;* their object he called an *idea*. When we describe a perception like "I see a bird," or "I think of my father," "seeing" and "thinking" are *cogitationes;* "a bird" and "my father" are *ideas*. John Locke adopted the term *idea*. To him this meant everything that is the object of the understanding when a man thinks.[8] In the then starting tradition of British association psychology the active aspect of the *cogitatio* did not come much to the foreground. There was interest in the ideas, in the *contents* of consciousness.

In David Hume's opinion, Locke made a too general use of the term idea. Hume thought it useful to distinguish an idea, the experience of an *absent* object, from *impression,* the experience of something given to the senses. Hartley later changed impression into *sensation,* and so it remained. Sensations and ideas, in German psychology *Empfindung* and *Vorstellung,* being the most important *contents* of consciousness, defined the central interest of (philosophical) psychologists who were primarily concerned with the function of knowledge (perception, imagination, thought). In fact, modern psychology of cognition, and the philosophical theory of knowledge, developed since Kant, have these early British systems for a common root.

We shall have to keep in mind that the terms "sensation" and "idea" have become imbued in their history with several implications James wanted to get rid of.

(1) In emphasizing sensations and ideas the notion of their being complements of mental acts got lost.

(2) Parallel with that, sensations and ideas, not being objects of an activity any more, became *contents* of consciousness, to be split up into their constitutive *elements.* Finally their character of contents was taken for granted and then became a "self-evident" matter. Thus there is nearly complete identification of content and activity in a passage like the following, taken from John Stuart Mill: "A Feeling and a State of Consciousness are, in the language of philosophy, equivalent expressions: everything is a feeling of which the mind is conscious; everything which it *feels . . .*"[9]

(3) The concepts "sensation" and "idea" have too long been used in the context of a theory of knowledge. There is no connotation of feeling in them any more. Now we saw that James too, considered the *cognitive* relation between the thought and its object to be the most important one (I, 184). On the other hand, he chose "feeling" as a second general term for mental states. So we might suppose that he wants to emphasize also the

importance of affective relations in consciousness. James was well aware of the fact that words tend to evoke implied connotations, even when these are not meant explicitly (I, 194 ff.). Later on we shall see that our supposition about his reconsiderations of affective tone in consciousness has other good grounds, too.

It is true, however, that according to James "thought" would be the most adequate general term, if it were not for the character of certain sensations. Thus he points out that the expression "thought of a toothache" can never suggest the actual present pain itself (I, 186). And so he decides to use both words, in a wider sense than usual, and in a sense that fits the context.

3. Mental Elements and Integral Experience

Which properties and qualities we ascribe to reality, depends upon the perspective in which we view reality. Reality is mute, it says nothing about itself, but *we* speak about reality.[10] We are creative in our knowing as well as in our acting. Lotze is right when he calls our descriptions extensions of reality.[11]

So likewise do the description and designation of mental phenomena, and the connection of meanings evoked by that designation broaden and mold mental reality. In another chapter we shall consider the relations between language and reality. It will give us the opportunity to discuss fully James' notions concerning those relations. Here we shall examine how these ideas are expressed in James' rejection of the doctrine of mental elements.

"But the whole historic doctrine of psychological association is tainted with one huge error—that of the construction of our thoughts out of the compounding of themselves together of immutable and incessantly recurring 'simple ideas' " (I, 553). But our experiences are certainly not compounds in the sense given to them in association psychology. They cannot be broken up into discrete, thing-like, elementary contents. "I have therefore treated our passing thoughts as integers," James (I, VI ff.) tells us "as *integral experiences.*"[12] Although James does not always cling to this view, it runs like a thread through his thought.

The assumption that mental states are composite in structure, that they are made up of smaller conjoined states of consciousness, he calls one of the most obscure and baffling of psychological assumptions (I, 145). We do not hesitate to accept this statement. At the time it was made, however, this assumption was still dominant in psychological thought. Thus Wundt still declares:

> Because all contents of mental experience are composite in nature, *mental elements,* in the sense of absolutely simple and indivisible components of mental processes, are the results of an analysis and an abstraction that are possible only because the elements are really joined in diverse ways.[13]

Suppose we are looking at a matchbox. Of what elements is the content of this visual perception composed? We have a number of color sensations. I see a *blackish* side, a *blue* piece of paper with *red* and *yellow* designs. Or, more strictly, the simple sensations of black, blue, red and yellow are joined together in a *spatial* connection for they are arranged in a definite order. And they are joined together because they appear at the same time. My visual perception is a temporal and spatial organization of elementary sensations. These same elements, however, can be organized in other ways, as they are when I look at other objects. I can recognize the color of a hat as being the same color, the very same elementary sensation as that which was a part of my perception of the matchbox.

According to Wundt, it is one of the tasks of psychology to discover all the different mental elements, and all the different ways they combine. Wundt devotes six hundred fifty pages of his *"Physiological Psychology"*[14] to the description and analysis of mental elements and their properties, and he distinguishes two kinds. The elements composing the objective content of experience (the things seen, heard, smelled, etc.) he calls *sensations* (for instance, a sensation of a light, sound, heat) . A second kind is formed by the mental elements that contribute to the subjective aspects of experience, namely, the elementary *feelings.* Every mental content is built up out of these elementary data, associated in different ways.

This conception of mental life as a mosaic, or a chemical compound, consisting of thousands and thousands of elementary ingredients that combine into everchanging complexes, James vigorously rejects.

To illustrate his point of view, it will be useful to quote him at length.

> Most books start with sensations, as the simplest mental facts, and proceed synthetically, constructing each higher stage from those below it. But this is abandoning the empirical method of investigation. No one ever had a simple sensation by itself. Consciousness, from our natal day, is of a teeming multiplicity of objects and relations, and what we call simple sensations are results of discriminative attention, pushed often to a very high degree. It is astonishing what havoc is wrought in psychology by admitting at the outset apparently innocent suppositions, that nevertheless contain a flaw. The bad consequences develop themselves later on, and are irremediable, being woven through the whole texture of the work. The notion that sensations, being the simplest things, are the first things to take up in psychology is one of these suppositions. The only thing which psychology has a right to postulate at the outset is the fact of thinking itself, and that must first be taken up and analyzed (I, 224).

We have to treat our thoughts as integers.

We should try to get a clear understanding of James' argument. The quoted passage might be interpreted as being a *methodological* argument. Granted that experience can be analyzed as to its elementary constituents, it can be approached better by starting with the integral experience. Is this what James meant when he wrote those words? Certainly not. He definitely and plainly rejected the theory of mental elements in his chapter on the "mind-stuff theory" (I, 145 ff.).

Among other things, James tells us in that chapter about some experiments by means of which the German physiologist Fick tried to prove the summation of elementary sensations into more complex feelings. Fick held the view that the feelings of temperature and of contact consist of the same elementary sensations summed in different ways. He found that patients made frequent mistakes in discrimination between the feelings of warmth and touch when only a small part of the skin was excited through a hole in a card. Fick argued that evidently the too few number of elementary sensations in this case prevented their summation into either of the qualities of warmth or touch. Now it has been known for a long time that the sense of touch and the sense of warmth really are different sensory systems. But that is not the point here. Let us suppose that there is only one warmth-touch system, and further, that the distinction between these two feelings indeed arises from the different gradation of the units of feelings in this system, as Fick would have it. Even in that case, James stated, the summation is not a *mental* fact, belonging to the field of psychology. Such a summation would be a *brain-fact*. The stimulation of many nerve endings at the same time may set up a complicated brain process, or even a series of processes. Even then a single integral experience corresponds with the mutliplicity of events in the brain. Because this notion of psychophysical correspondence is very important in the psychology of James, it is worthwhile to examine it more fully.

In the palm of our hand we find points that are sensitive to touch at a distance of 0.1 mm. from each other. This means that quite a different number of these points are stimulated when we touch our hand either with the point of a pencil, or with its blunt side. The sensation resulting in these two cases is clearly different. But the difference is in its quality, not in any experienced compositeness. On the contrary, whether many or few points are touched, we always have an integral feeling. There is no *mental* summation involved. The classical theory of mental compounding, on the other hand, would state that the stimulation of every separate sensitive point results in a separate simple sensation. These sensations, simple data on the level of conscious experience, would then have to be summed up by association on this same mental level. Nothing in our experience supports this view. If there is summation, or integration, it happens in the brain. Separate stimulations do not correspond in a one to one relationship to simple sensations. All *integration* occurs below the threshold of consciousness. Above this threshold, on the level of thought and feeling, integral experiences correspond wholly and totally with the most complicated and diversified brain events (I, 156). "The consciousness, which is itself an integral thing not made of parts, 'corresponds' to the entire activity of the brain, whatever that may be, at the moment" (I, 177). Imagine the stimulation of the millions of simple receptors in the eye setting up a collection of millions of elementary sensations in the mind, to be combined and organized in our conscious experience. No mind would be able to find its way out of this confusion. Instead of the unintelligible notion that an integral experience like hatred may really be ten thousand elementary feelings summed up (I, 175), James prefers an approach that takes the entire thought as the minimum with which to deal on the mental level (I, 177).

Looking at the same problem from another side, one must ask what or who is supposed to sum up the mental elements. Or do they do it themselves? But the *self-compounding* of mental facts is inadmissible. On this point James agrees fully with this statement of his friend Royce: "No summing up of parts can make an unity of a mass of discrete constituents, unless this unity exist for some other subject, not for the mass itself" (I, 159).[15] The sum itself exists only for an "onlooker." Now our experience tells us that we do not integrate mental elements in our conscious activity. The hypothesis of a soul, or spirit, inhabiting man, has been rejected in psychology. How then, could an integration take place? The simple answer is that it cannot and does not take place. In a sum, every constituent remains what it was; but together, the constituents may affect some other entity. An observer may overlook the units and apprehend the sum as such. The sum of our sensation can never, in itself, produce the unity of our experience. Neither is Stuart Mill's chemical analogy of any use. Because even in the case of chemical compounding the properties of the composite actually are the effects of the units, said to be combined, upon some other medium. In water, the old units H_2 and O have no new properties in themselves; water is nothing but the old atoms in the new position H-O-H; and its "new" properties are the combined *effects* of these atoms, when in this position, upon an external medium (I, 159).

In fact, James' rejection of mental elements is at the same time a rejection of the idea that all things have a double existence: in the real physical world *and* in a mental container called "consciousness." Things can be divided into parts. By a process of abstraction, man can also distinguish between different qualities and properties of one and the same thing. Man can even think of this abstraction as if it were a mental decomposition of experience into mental parts and elements. But these do not exist within his mind. His analysis pertains to the real thing, not to atoms of consciousness. Perception is not inner representation, but perceiving things that are *there,* in the world around us.

4. Psychology as a "Natural Science"

When James tells us that thinking is the only thing that psychology has the right to postulate at its beginning (I, 276); that the entire thought is the minimum with which to deal on the mental level (I, 177); and that we should cling as closely as possible to the actual constitution of thought (I, 276), do these statements designate him as a mentalist? They certainly do, in so far as this term signifies a psychologist who maintains that mental states exist, and that it is the function of psychology to study them. But the term "mentalist" has several connotations. In a narrower sense it refers to a purely *introspective* psychology. An example of this kind of mentalism is the definition of psychology given by Heymans, the first Dutch professor in psychology. Psychology, Heymans tells us, is interested in "everything we experience immediately in our consciousness (thoughts, emotions, strivings, etc., and of course also the sensations and perceptions that furnish us with the immediate data for our knowledge of the outer world)."[16] Psychology "is in search for laws that are brought to light in the mental life of every individual human being."[17] The true mentalist confines himself to this introspective investigation. James certainly did not confine himself in this way, and he is not a "mental psychologist" in this sense. We already saw that he called psychology a "natural science," namely, that it is concerned with the mental phenomena of distinct individuals who live objectively in space and time amidst other objects (I,

183) .[18] Minds are temporal beings yoked to bodies through which they express and manifest themselves (I, 199). Such statements suggest a mentalist attitude, but James goes on to explain that bodily experiences and, more particularly, brain processes, have their place among the conditions of the mental life that are investigated by psychology. A certain amount of brain physiology must be included in psychology. One can safely lay down the general law that no mental phenomenon ever occurs which is not accompanied or followed by a bodily change (I, 5).

This shows that James is not a mentalist in the narrow sense, and it proves no more than that he, like many others, accepted *psychophysical parallelism*. A mentalist psychology in the wider sense certainly does not exclude parallelism. But a strict parallelism makes no specific statement about the concrete relationship between mind and body. James went further than that. He excused himself for the way he mixed the physical and the mental, talking in the same breath about reflex acts and reminiscences. But language lends itself so easily to this mixed description and James did not want to abandon the implied common sense position (I, 24 n). Although different in appearance, mind and body are intimately related. Brain states must be supposed to condition mental states (I, 14). The cortex is the organ of consciousness (I, 66). One is even tempted to suppose that brain-centres themselves *have* consciousness: their essential function is that of "intelligent" action, they feel, prefer one thing to another and have "ends" (I, 79).

The reader of James' works is easily confused by his seemingly contradictory statements in these matters. In one place James speaks about a causal efficacy of consciousness (I, 141 ff.); in another he tells us that we never get a *feeling* in the skin, however strongly we imagine it, until some actual change in the condition of the skin itself has occurred (II, 69). What then is meant by the causal efficacy of consciousness? The relations of the mind to its own brain are of a unique and mysterious sort (I, 216). But that is no solution for our problem. And it does not help when James, after his remark about the common sense point of view in mixing the mental and the physical, asks why and how such disparate things like thought and brain are connected at all (I, 177).

But then it is one of the aims of the present study to clarify the meaning of James' endeavors to solve the psychophysical problem. Perhaps the inconsistency arises from an inability to formulate clearly precisely where his own view differs from the then traditional systems. Most schools in psychological thought, behaviorism included, presuppose the Cartesian notion of *dualism*. Taking it for granted that mind and matter are mutually exclusive substances that have nothing in common, the parallelist view has been the most logical inference. The philosophers who disliked the idea of a twofold universe now had their choice: they could deny the reality of the physical world, or deny the reality of the mental world. In philosophy, the first choice came to be known as idealism, the second as materialism. Both presuppose Cartesianism in so far as they deny one of its two worlds. James is one of the few who has tried to give up the dualist position completely by starting anew from common sense. And that is the most important reason why we cannot call him a mentalist, precisely because this term and its implications presuppose Cartesian dualism.

5. *Neurophysiology and Behaviorism*

The same reason that prevented James from being a "mentalist" made it impossible for him to become a behaviorist. There is no doubt that his works reveal a strong tendency towards behaviorism. But then, James is not "a scientist who investigates the behavior of animals objectively and who attempts to relate his observations together in a theoretical system that does not include concepts borrowed from introspection and mental philosophy"[19]—and so he was no behaviorist in the sense of this definition.

There are good reasons, however, to speak of at least a tendency in the direction of behaviorism. Let us examine James' comments on some of Wundt's reaction experiments (I, 88 ff.).[20]

The Dutch physiologist F. C. Donders initiated a type of experiment which consisted in asking the subject to repeat, as quickly as possible, a syllable given as stimulus by the experimenter. The reaction takes a measurable amount of time. According to Wundt the reaction time in this simple situation is about 197 milliseconds. When the set-up is a little more complicated, as when the experimenter calls out one of five syllables and the subject, knowing the five syllables, has to repeat the right one, the reaction takes a longer time; it now becomes 285 milliseconds. In other words, the more complicated task requires a longer reaction time. To Wundt this suggested the possibility of measuring the time taken by higher mental processes. In the case of a simple predetermined reaction like the repetition of a known syllable, the subject has only to prepare himself for this reaction. In the case of five syllables, however, he must notice which one is called out, and he has to decide with which one to respond. The subject has to discriminate and choose. Wundt's assumption now was, that the increase in reaction time is due to these processes of discrimination and choice, and that the time taken by them is added to the simple reaction time. If we now calculate the answer, $285 - 197 = 88$ milliseconds, we have found the exact time required for the higher mental processes in this experiment. Of course, it is questionable whether Wundt's assumption is valid.

James, commenting on this type of experiment, distinguished five stages in the total reaction process, each of them taking some time.

(1) The excitation of the sense organ needs a certain time for setting up a current.

(2) The sensory nerve is traversed.

(3) Somewhere in the brain, the sensory current is transformed into a motor current.

(4) The motor nerve is traversed.

(5) The responding system is excited.

The third stage is the most interesting one when we want to understand what happens inside of us, either in the brain or mind, or perhaps in both. For this is the *psychophysical* stage in which, according to Wundt, some conscious events are bound to take place. Especially in the more complicated type of experiment, the subject must perceive the stimulus syllable, turn his attention to it, and "apperceive" it, that is, he has to identify which one of the five possible stimuli has been used. He then has to decide that he will respond with the same syllable, and give the proper command to his motor system. Wundt believes that all these processes are conscious activities. This is the point where James disagreed. He personally believed that no/ such succession of conscious feelings takes place:

> Feeling of the impression, attention to it, thought of the reaction, volition to react, *would*, undoubtedly, all be links of the process *under other conditions,* and would lead to the same reaction—after an indefinitely longer time . . . *The reaction whose time is measured is,* in short, *a reflex action pure and simple, and not a psychic act* (I, 90).

If there is any feeling at all in stage 3, it certainly is not an articulate perception, but maybe, the mere awareness of a reflex discharge. There is no evidence in direct experience that all the complicated mental processes described by Wundt do take place. Indeed, no sprinter who is prepared to start promptly when he hears the shot sits back to think and decide what to do once he hears it. When he is asked to describe his experience at the moment he comes into action, he will likely tell us that he just acted— like any machine. It is a reflex, James said, although a foregoing psychic condition may be a prerequisite. Today it would be called a conditional response, proceeding automatically, without interference by conscious thought processes, or by any consciousness at all. This behavioristic interpretation is clearly indicated by James. He even made the remark, that "from the radically physical point of view it is easy to conceive of the chain of events amongst the cells and fibres as complete in itself, and that whilst so conceiving it one need make no mention of 'ideas'" (I, 24). But he added that he suspected that his view might be an unreal abstraction.

This is not the only place in his work where he suggests that the chain of events between stimulus and response might be a closed chain. James repeatedly used neurophysiological models to explain conscious experience. But he never came to a one-sided, materialistic interpretation. He never developed a strictly behavioristic system.

6. The Biopsychological Approach

James felt free to make any sallies into zoology or into pure nerve-physiology that could be useful for his purpose. The theory of evolution had convinced him of the relationship between animals and human beings. Because they are linked together by evolution, certain principles apply to both categories, not only in reference to organic structures, but also with regard to functions. Although very vague as to its precise meaning, Spencer's statement that the essence of both bodily life and mental life are one, namely, "the adjustment of inner to outer relations," has done real service in psychology (I, 6).[21] Consciousness has been given to man to help him to adjust himself to his environment.[22] Consciousness is dependent on the brain, which serves behavior.[23] The whole neural organism is a machine for converting stimuli into reactions (II, 372). And the brain evolves from ancestor to descendant (I, 79). The evolution theory does good service by reducing all mentality to the type of reflex action.[24]

The foregoing statements are evidence of James' biopsychological approach. Psychology has to do with living beings, not only with consciousness as such. Mental phenomena must be seen in the context of the adjustment of the living being to its environment. In American psychology it is customary to call this type of psychology *functional*. One of Dewey's early statements characterizes this trend: "The idea of environment is a necessity to the idea of organism, and with the conception of environment comes the impossibility of considering psychical life as an individual, isolated thing developing in a vacuum."[25] Angell defined functionalism as the psychology of mental operations, and as a theory about the *utilities* of consciousness as it intermediates between the environment and the needs of the organism.[26] It is opposed to the structuralism of Wundt and Titchener. In structuralism, the psychologist tries to find the mental elements and their relationships. He may easily overlook the fact that the mental make-up has to do with the functioning of an organism adjusting itself to its environment. It is precisely in such a case that what Dewey mentioned may take place; namely, that psychology considers consciousness as such and analyzes the "inner man," as has been the case in the Cartesian tradition. Under this condition, mind or consciousness is easily taken as an isolated thing, or even existing *per se.* The "gulf" between mind and body is then not easily bridged. Mind and body appear as discontinuous entities. James felt a danger here. He explicitly stated that psychology must postulate a continuity between mind and body: "We ought therefore ourselves sincerely to try every possible mode of conceiving the dawn of consciousness so that it may *not* appear equivalent to the irruption into the universe of a new nature, non-existent until then" (I, 148). He even adds the opinion, going in another extreme direction, that consciousness in some shape must have been present at the very origin of things (I, 149). We shall consider this statement in a later chapter. Here we must content ourselves with the conclusion that it is his biopsychological approach that prevents James from considering consciousness as an isolated entity, developing in a vacuum.

7. *The Inner Discord in the Psychology of James*

It is quite clear by now that there exists an inner dissension in the psychology of James. He accepted a variety of opinions that seem to go in completely different directions. But the attentive reader of his works feels that this is but one side of the picture. The apparent eclecticism, the many sudden changes in approach, although producing some irreconcilable statements, are signs of a basic openness which is systematically maintained. To get at the core of this, one must consider the central problem in Jamesian psychology, namely the problem of consciousness. Consciousness exists. It manifests itself in purposive behavior, in the intelligent pursuance of ends, in the choice of proper means, in being aware of a situation. The mind gets at the meaning of things and events, it has the relation of knowing in dealing with the environment. The mind knows things and this seems to imply that it differs from the things known. Knowing is a property of mind only; thought has an active relation to its objects.

Now all this could just be a way of describing characteristics of behavior, without implying that mind or consciousness exists as an independent thing that has substantiality. But then, James tells us, "if we postulate the fact of the thinking at all, I believe that we must postulate its power as well" (II, 571). Or take another apparent mentalist statement: "The *particulars of the distribution of consciousness,* so far as we know them, *point to its being efficacious*" (I, 138). Somewhere else James mentions the "*causal* efficacy" of consciousness (I, 142). In his opinion, then, consciousness is not just an epiphenomenon, but an active and efficacious factor in behavior. On the other hand, he considered consciousness to be determined by processes in the brain. And the brain is an organ that, like all other organs, has been developed during evolution. The brain functions for the good of the organism; it cannot be the organ of a free floating spirit. Psychology is a biological science. But, on the other hand, integral experience is irreducible; it cannot be deduced from the structure and the function of the brain. The particulars of the stream of consciousness require an approach independent of the biological approach. Psychology, as the science of human experience, must begin with the description of this experience, and not try immediately to explain it away by reducing it to brain processes.

What then, does it mean that integral experiences correspond with, and are determined by, brain processes? Ladd openly criticized James' opinions in this matter. The correspondence between mental processes and brain processes, postulated by James, is not quite evident, he said. *We do not know anything about it.*[27] Consciousness experiences *meanings,* and even today the problem of meaning still stands unsolved.[28] McDougall stated succinctly and forcefully that "meaning has no immediate physical correlate in the brain."[29] The solution given by Gestalt Psychology in its theory of isomorphism is just another way of evading the problem.[30]

Some of the problems that arise when we compare James' diverse statements about consciousness are easily solved when we realize that James uses the word in different meanings.

(1) One meaning is *awareness.* To illustrate: "Where in-

decision is great, as before a dangerous leap, consciousness is agonizingly intense" (I, 142) . The term signifies being conscious of objects and of their relations and qualities. There is no great difficulty here.

(2) A second meaning is *"self-awareness"*: "A mind which has become conscious of its own cognitive function, plays what we have called 'the psychologist' upon itself" (I, 272) . Whatsoever one may think about introspection as a method, it is of no use to deny the reflective characteristics of human experience. We can be conscious of our being conscious of something, and there can be no doubt that this self-awareness is important to the psychologist when he analyzes human behavior.

(3) Awareness and self-awareness may be interpreted as being passively impressed by some object or by oneself. James gives a third meaning to the word consciousness, implying the *use* of awareness or self-awareness, as in the process of reasoning, or in any truly voluntary action. "The result . . . yielded by a true act of reasoning is apt to be a thing voluntarily *sought,* such as the means to a proposed end, the ground for an observed effect, or the effect of an assumed cause" (II, 329) . In reasoning there is conscious use of data we are conscious of. An activity like that simply cannot be described as an outward bodily action. Reflection seems to suggest some inner activity, in which no bodily process is given as a constituent. That is, in thinking we are not aware, it seems, of any bodily activity essential to thinking. We certainly have no awareness of processes going on in the brain. From an experiential point of view we cannot identify our thinking with brain processes.

(4) A fourth meaning of "consciousness," developed in theorizing about the third meaning, is that of an entity, different from the body: the mind as a *substantial consciousness.* James rejected this meaning explicitly, but the difficulty is, that it seems to be implied in some of his uses of "consciousness" in its third meaning:

> The mind's relations to other objects than the brain are *cognitive and emotional* relations exclusively, so far as we know. It *knows* them, and it inwardly *welcomes or rejects* them, but it has no other dealings with them. When it seems to *act* upon them, it

only does so through the intermediary of its own body, so that not it but the body is what acts on them (I, 216) .

We shall suppose that the suggested independence here is only a method of description that has its specific dangers.

James' functionalist interpretation of consciousness as a means of adjustment to the environment obviously tends to stress the undivided unity of mind and body as one organism. If it can be proved that consciousness is a biological function, psychophysical dualism does not make sense any more. And that is what James proposed. On the other hand, it may be useful, even in that case, to maintain dualism in a methodological way, as a convenient description of the difference between mind knowing and things known (I, 218) . We may talk about mind and body as two aspects of one organism, without implying that mind and body are different entities. The criticism of Kantor then does not seem quite justified. According to Kantor, the emphasis on biological factors did much to reinforce dualism, instead of weakening it.[31] It must be admitted that the danger is there. On the other hand, there is no reason to forsake a methodological dualism.

Apart from the inner dissension arising from his different uses of the word "consciousness," there is another major problem in Jamesian psychology which hinders the development of a unified point of view. It is the problem of the relation between the description from an experiential standpoint and its causal explanation.[32]

The description of the stream of thought is an investigation "from within" (I, 224) . Causal explanation, on the other hand, takes the stand characterized by the expression "it all goes back to . . . ," back to processes and events that are not evident from within. This second point of view may lead, for instance, to the statement that, *because* succeeding brain processes are never absolutely discontinuous, successive mental states *must* shade gradually into each other (I, 243) . There are two ways of investigating the stream of thought: "First, the way of analysis: What does it consist in? What is its inner nature? Of what sort of mind-stuff is it composed? Second, the way of history: What are its conditions of production, and its connection with other facts?" (II, 283). The "way of analysis" is the description and phenomenological investigation of experiential data in their own right. The "way of history," on the other hand, looks for the connections between things experienced and objective processes lying without the realm of direct experience. There is no continuous transition from one point of view to the other, and there cannot be such a transition. The objective processes are not given in the self-awareness of any person, whereas self-awareness has the quality of subjectivity which never appears in objective processes. Every statement about their connection must therefore sound artificial. James could not reconcile his two ways in a satisfactory manner. He was convinced that both were important and even necessary in psychology. And although many of his endeavors to reduce experience to brain processes are unconvincing, as he quite well knew them to be, he maintained both approaches.

This is not a problem of James alone. Psychology in general has to face it. Human experience, as immediately given, is the field all psychological questions primordially refer to. It must be described and analyzed in such a way that its meaningful content is not falsified. Psychology must try to find relationships between succeeding experiences, and try to understand how one comes forth from the other.[33] In this phenomenological investigation psychology tries to grasp the essence of different experiences and their relationships.

It cannot be denied, on the other hand, that there are objective relations between experiential data and specific physiological processes. Psychology studies these relations too, maintaining a set of rules generally used in the objective sciences.

James could not decide whether to give priority to either his "way of analysis" or to the "way of history." He had good grounds for his indecision, as we shall see. The price he had to pay was a lack of unity in the views he expressed.

8. The Implicit Phenomenology in Jamesian Psychology

According to Gurwitsch, "psychology thus is a positive science. Like the other positive sciences, psychology chooses a well circumscribed realm of reality, as one mundane realm among

others, and connected with these realms. It is in full conformity
with this choice, that, in its exploration and explanation of
consciousness, psychology continues and, partly, relies upon the
physical and biological sciences."[34] This definition could have
been taken from Husserl[35] or from James, a fact which shows the
compatibility between James' idea of psychology and the notion
of phenomenology, though, of course, it does not yet make Jamesian psychology a phenomenological psychology. James wanted
his psychology to be open, not closed. So we are told in the
English original of his preface to the Italian edition of the
Principles: "In sum, then, my effort has been to offer in a 'natural
science' of the mind a *modus vivendi* in which the most various
schools may meet harmoniously on the common basis of fact."[36]

But what is "a common basis of fact"? Facts are what one
observes and considers to be given in experience. They are aspects of reality. This James was ready to accept and yet made it
relative in his definition of it. He certainly wanted a factual basis
for his psychology. But he also maintained that a fact is not an
absolute and unchangeable element of reality as such. According
to James, facts are experienced and stated facts. They presuppose
the knowledge of the immediate experience they are supposed to
explain. Collecting facts, drawing conclusions from them, presuppose, at least implicitly, knowledge about the world as it is
experienced immediately, and the insight that all scientific activity
lies within the context of this prescientific, everyday world. One
could refer this problem to philosophy. But that is no solution.
James had an open eye for that which is the common basis of
fact, namely, the everyday world of human experience. He af-
firmed, as we say, that human subjectivity is at least partly responsible for the way in which the world appears to us, and he
recognized the impossibility of going back behind experience.
This means that, although James never explicitly developed a
phenomenology, he came very near to some of it's fundamental
notions.

NOTES

1. The numbers in parenthesis ( ) in our text refer to a section of
a page in *The Principles of Psychology*, 2 vol., London, 1890.

2. Cf. A. Horwicz, *Psychologische Analysen auf Physiologischer Grundlage,* vol. 2/1, (Halle, 1875), p. 7.

3. James speaks of "mind," but expressly excludes the concepts of "soul" and "spirit" that connote "substance."

4. James used the terms "thought" and "feeling" in a very broad sense.

5. Quoted by Perry, *Thought,* vol. 2, p. 75.

6. Cf. my article, "Logische en Phenomenologische Analyse van de Bewegingsverschynselen," *Tijdschrift v. Philos,* vol. 12, 1950, pp. 674 ff.; here the "psychologist's fallacy" is defined as a "logical prejudice."

7. We cannot agree with the interpretation of Gurwitsch that the *psychologist's reality* "comprises first of all the extramental fact which in the case of perception stimulates a certain section of the nervous system and provokes nerve- and brain-processes to which then corresponds the mental state to be studied"; Aron Gurwitsch, "On The Object of Thought," *Phil. phenomenol. Res.,* vol. 7, 1946-47, p. 348. The *psychologist's reality* implies before all the fact *that* the psychologist *can also* think about the experience *in that way,* the fact, in other words, that he does not simply happen upon the object but constitutes it.

8. John Locke, *An Essay Concerning Human Understanding,* (Oxford, 1928), Bk. I, ch. I, §8.

9. J. S. Mill, *A System of Logic,* vol. 1, (London, 1862), p. 54. James quotes Mill's ideas in *Principles,* vol. 1, p. 187 n.

10. James, *Pragmatism,* p. 246.

11. *Ibid.,* p. 256.

12. Cf. *Principles,* vol. 1, pp. 177, 503, and *A Pluralistic Universe,* pp. 279 ff. Cf. also Perry, *Thought,* vol. 2, p. 102, who quotes a passage from James' reply to a criticism of Marillier that defended the associationist point of view in *Rev. philos.,* vol. 34, 1892, and vol. 35, 1893, which passage reads as follows: "I cannot, however, (see) why you should object to my formulation, for even if our thoughts are compounds of 'ideas,' they are at least superficially and practically all that I say they are, namely, integral pulses of consciousness with respect to the multitude of facts of which they may take cognizance in a single passing moment of time."

13. Wilhelm Wundt, *Grundriss der Psychologie,* (Leipzig, 1922), p. 34.

14. Wilhelm Wundt, *Grundzüge der Physiologischen Psychologie,* 3 vol., (Leipzig, 1908-11).

15. James, *The Principles of Psychology,* vol. 1, p. 159.

16. Gerardus Heymans, *Inleiding tot de Speciale Psychologie,* Part I, (Haarlem, 3rd ed., 1948), p. 1. First ed., 1929.

17. *Ibid.,* p. 2.

18. Cf. also William James, "A Plea for Psychology as a 'Natural Science'," *Philos. Rev.,* vol. 1, 1892, pp. 146-153.

19. W. S. Verplanck, "A Glossary of Some Terms Used in the Objective Science of Behavior," *Psychol. Rev. Suppl.*, vol. 64, 1957, No. 6; Part 2, p. 6.

20. Cf. Wundt, *Grundzüge*, 1st ed., vol. 1, (Leipzig, 1887), vol. 2, pp. 221 ff. In the third edition, 2 vol. (Leipzig, 1887), vol. 2, p. 266, Wundt retracts his explanations regarding what is hereby described as "psycho-physical processess," and he speaks of brain-reflexes on the basis of exercise. Cf. also 6th ed., 3 vol., (Leipzig, 1908-1911), vol. 3, pp. 446 ff.

21. The text speaks of "adjustment of inner to outer relations."

22. James, *Talks to Teachers*, p. 25.

23. *Ibid.*, p. 26.

24. "The Sentiment of Rationality (1879)," in *The Will to Believe*, p. 84. Also in *Principles*, vol. 2, p. 313.

25. John Dewey, "The New Psychology," *Andover Rev.*, vol. 2, 1884. Quoted by Roback, *loc. cit.*, p. 213.

26. J. R. Angell, "The Province of Functional Psychology," *Psychol. Rev.*, vol. 14, 1907.

27. G. T. Ladd, "Psychology—a so-called 'Natural Science'," *Philos. Rev.*, vol. 1, 1892, p. 37.

28. Cf. F. H. Allport, *Theories of Perception and the Concept of Structure*, (New York, 1955). Chapter 19 deals with "the unsolved problem of meaning."

29. William McDougall, *Body and Mind*, (London, 1920), p. 311.

30. Hans Lindschoten, *Strukturanalyse der Binokularen Tiefenwahrnehmung*, (Groningen, 1956), pp. 472 ff.

31. J. R. Kantor, "Jamesian Psychology and The Stream of Psychological Thought," p. 149.

32. Cf. Lindschoten, *Strukturanalyse der Binokularen Tiefenwahrnehmung*, pp. 16 ff.

33. Karl Jaspers, *Allgemeine Psychopathologie*, (Berlin, 1948), p. 250: "Verstehen . . . wie Seelisches aus Seelischem hervorgeht."

34. Gurwitsch, *The Field of Consciousness*, p. 158.

35. Edmund Husserl, *Ideen zu einer Reinen Phänomenologie und Phänomenologischen Philosophie*, vol. 1, 1913, (The Hague, 1952), pp. 4 ff. Passages from *Ideen* are quoted according to the pages of the original edition, the numbers of which are given in the margin in the 1952 edition. Cf. also *Ideen*, vol. 3, (The Hague, 1952), p. 40.

36. So did he write in the English original of his preface to the Italian edition of his work, *Principii di Psicologia*, (Milano, 1901). Quoted by Perry, *Thought*, vol. 2, p. 54.

III THE STREAM OF EXPERIENCE AND THE THEORY OF SENSATION

1. The Stream of Experience

The first datum in psychology is that *"thinking of some sort goes on"* (I, 224). Experience *flows* in a continuous stream. Consciousness does not appear to itself chopped up in bits; it feels, on the contrary, its own integrity. Words like "chain" or "train" do not adequately describe the character of ongoing consciousness; "river" or "stream" are better metaphors (I, 239).

The notion that the succession of mental states must be described as a stream is the most fundamental notion of James' psychology. When James introduced this notion, it certainly was not in fashion to talk about consciousness as a stream. On the contrary, the elementarist point of view of association psychology was predominant at that time. Associationism considered mental life as a sequence of more or less independent, finite mental states. The discontinuity of this series was suggested strongly by the terms in use to describe consciousness. Hobbes already spoke of "trains of thought," Locke spoke about "habitual trains," and such expressions have been commonly used in the psychology of subsequent centuries.[1] Now a "chain" or a "train" is a sequence of units that may be coupled in different ways. But whether coupled or not, the units or links keep their own independent and individual character. A train of thought is a series of succeeding units. Even when Hume mentioned the "course of our thinking", suggesting thereby some inner continuity, he explains this course as a succession of independent ideas.[2] Bain, using the term "stream of thought" before James, stated unequivocally that "the stream of thought is not a continuous current, but a series of distinct ideas."[3]

James, on the other hand, strongly emphasized the continuity of succeeding mental states. The streaming character of subjective life was the most important quality of consciousness in his opinion. James mentioned this point for the first time in 1884 in an article "On some omissions of introspective psychology,"[4] five years before Henri Bergson's essay on the immediate data of consciousness appeared. Many a chapter from the *Principles* shows the great similarity in the thought of James and Bergson. They shared some of their fundamental notions. A comparison of their works shows similarity even in some salient details. We shall have an opportunity to mention some of these points in a later chapter.

James was not originally influenced by Bergson. He learned about Bergson's views many years after he wrote his *Principles*. But having read Bergson, he said: "Reading his works is what has made me bold."[5] Bergson, in his turn, mentions that he knew only James' article on "The feeling of effort" at the time he worked on his famous *Essay*.[6] The similarity in the views of these thinkers is not due to any influence of one upon the other.

A real and important influence in the development of the concept of a stream of consciousness in James stems from Brentano. James referred to Brentano's principal work in the *Principles,* especially mentioning Brentano's chapter on the unity of consciousness, which James thought "as good as anything with which I am acquainted" (I, 240n) . James must have had an even higher opinion of it, for James' and Brentano's expositions of the unity of the Self are parallel and in some places almost identical in wording.[7] Some of the fundamental properties James ascribed to the stream of thought can be found in Brentano's text, which appeared in 1874.[8] Notwithstanding this fact, Perry was right when he said that "James's doctrine of the stream of thought was essentially his own."[9] The influence of Brentano is evident but the way James further developed the concept, his way of incorporating and applying it, are his own. What happened is probably that James, already thinking in a certain direction, found in Brentano's text exactly the notion he was already developing implicitly in his own mind.

The relationship between Brentano and James is of some importance because it is one of the grounds on which we must assume an original phenomenological tendency in James' thought. It explains why Husserl felt attracted by James' psychology. Husserl was also a pupil of Brentano's and made use of both Brentano's and James' works in developing his own system. It is understandable, then, that we find the stream of consciousness as important a theme in the work of Husserl's phenomenology as it is in James, for it originated, at least in part, from a common source. Here then we have immediately a reason for the conformity between James' psychology and phenomenology.

Is it not true then that, as Perry tells us "James' doctrine of the stream of thought was essentially his own"? The indications are too clear to permit us to deny Brentano's influence. But we may admit that James incorporated that influence in such a way that he no longer saw them as influences. This interpretation is reinforced by the fact that James seems to have always been ready to mention the sources from which he drew his inspiration.

2. The Five Characteristics in the Stream of Experience

But let us now follow James' analysis of the "stream of thought" or, as it is also called, the "stream of consciousness."[10] Thinking[11] goes on constantly. "If we could say in English 'it thinks' as we say 'it rains' or 'it blows,' we should be stating the fact most simply and with the minimum of assumption. As we cannot, we must simply say that *thought goes on*" (I, 224 ff.). In this context, "thought" means the thought-thinking-something, not the thing-thought-of. James complained that this distinction does not exist in English usage, as it does in several other languages (I, 195 n). A good number of his psychological notions, however, presuppose exactly this distinction. This has to be clear from the beginning. The stream of experience or stream of consciousness, is not a series of mental contents, but the activity in which certain objects are being experienced. The lack of distinctive terms in English, however, sometimes confused even James, since in some places he uses the term "thought" for conscious content, instead of confining it to the act. This is the case, for instance, in his determination of the first of five characteristics of experience:

(1) Experience tends to personal form, that is, every experience tends to be an integral part of a personal consciousness.

> In this room—this lecture-room, say—there are a multitude of 'thoughts,' or experiences, yours and mine, some of which cohere mutually, and some not. They are as little each-for-itself and reciprocally independent as they are all-belonging-together. They are neither: no one of them is separate, but each belongs with certain others and with none beside (s) (I, 225 ff.) .

Thoughts, in this context clearly conceived as contents of consciousness, are grouped with reference to the person having them. But the thoughts or experiences belonging to one person are not together like cows in a herd, they are not a collection of independent entities, they permeate each other. Their continuity makes them be parts of the larger whole of personal consciousness. We cannot enter directly into another stream of thought than our own. "It seems as if the elementary psychic fact were not *thought* or *this thought* or *that thought,* but *my thought,* every thought being *owned*" (I, 226) . Maybe there are in this room mere thoughts, being nobody's thoughts. But then, a supposition like this makes no sense, because we have no means of ascertaining whether this is the case. The supposition brings out clearly, however, that we must think of *thoughts as personal experiences.* They belong to a Self. And so we might say as well that the personal Self is the immediate datum in psychology. Nobody can deny the existence of personal Selves without denying the possibility of psychology.

The way in which James explained this first characteristic of the stream of consciousness reminds us of the beginnings of modern psychology in the Cartesian system. To Descartes, the primordial datum was the "cogito, sum," the evidence a thinking mind has of itself. But James did not think of this mind as a spirit, essentially independent of matter. To James the Self was a property of a body, although it can, and sometimes even must, be described as something different from the body.

But then the question arises: what *is* this Self, or Ego, that binds experiences together and owns them? The answers to this question vary. All of them, however, presuppose the givenness of the first character of experience, the immediate experience of myself in my thoughts. For the time being we must be satisfied with this fact. In a later chapter, "The consciousness of Self," James gave a more complete explanation of the concept of Self. These ideas we shall review in Chapter IX.

One detail, however, calls for immediate attention. Why did James say that experience *tends* to be part of a personal consciousness? For he clearly holds that experience *is* a part of it. This refers us to the problem of multiple personality that sometimes has even a memory of its own. In such pathological cases the secondary Self can be cut off completely from the primary Self. Then both of them "form conscious unities, have continuous memories, speak, write, invent distinct names for themselves, . . . in short, are entirely worthy of that title of secondary personalities which is now commonly given them" (I, 227) .

So, even in abnormal cases when one stream of consciousness is split into two personalities, both have their own personal organization, and every thought belongs to either of them. There is no reason to deny that experience, even in its most uncommon organization, tends to constitute a personal form. Hence this must be kept in mind while studying experience. It would not be right to abstract completely from the Self while speaking about experience. Psychology then cannot accept the position of some associationists who consider experience without any reference to the Self that binds them together.

The other four characteristics of the stream of experience cannot be discussed in a summary way. Their explication will be the task of the main part of this book, but for the sake of completeness we make mention of them here:

(2) Within each personal consciousness experience is constantly changing. Under this heading James took his stand against the elementarism of associationist psychology. This problem is the subject of the rest of the present chapter.

(3) Each personal consciousness experiences itself as a continuous stream. This character will be discussed in Chapter V.

(4) Consciousness seems to deal always with objects that are independent of itself. Our thought is directed to objects that appear as independent things. And yet, it can be shown that at least part of their constitution derives from personal consciousness. James gave much attention to the problem of knowledge, the problem of the relation between mind and things. We will come to this in Chapter VI.

(5) Consciousness is interested in some parts of its objects to the exclusion of others; it *chooses* from among them. To the extent that this notion still needs discussion after a review of the other characteristics, it will be treated in Chapter VII.

3. Experience Changes Continuously

When James stated that experience is in constant change he did not mean that no single experience is without duration. Continuous change here means that no single experience ever returns as it was before: it occupies the mind for some time—but not in the shape of a fixed mental content replacing the one that went before. There is continuity and change at the same time; continuity in the activity of the Self, and change in the shading of interests into one another.

Speaking about constant change, James particularly had in mind the fact that *"no state once gone can recur and be identical with what it was before"* (I, 230). No state, thought of as a composite, nor the supposed components can ever recur. Psychologists in the tradition of associationism conceived of diverse mental states as different compositions of the same fundamental, ever recurring mental elements, finally identified with sensations and ideas. But, according to James, even a particular sensation does not occur twice in exactly the same form. What is obtained twice is the same *object*. We may hear presently the same sound we heard yesterday, see the same green, have the same toothache. But, in fact, they are not the same sensations we had before. The realities, concrete and abstract, physical and ideal, whose permanent existence we believe in, seem to be constantly coming up again before our consciousness, and lead us, in our carelessness, to suppose that our 'experiences' of them are the same (I, 231). In fact, they are always different.[12] It is not very surprising that the history of sensation is a constant commentary on our inability to decide whether two sensations received apart are exactly alike or not (I, 231). We never have absolute sensations, but experience things in relation to each other. Things appear in a context that influences their appearance. James' opinions on this topic came close to a theory developed much later: the Gestalt theory of perceptual constancy.[13]

Experience changes and accordingly, things are felt differently. And yet these things appear as the same, unchanged objects. "We never doubt that our feelings reveal the same world, with the same sensible qualities and the same sensible things occupying it" (I, 232). And yet our perception of them changes with our moods and attention, with being sleepy or awake, with age, with all the experiences that from moment to moment add to our past history. We never sense the same things in the same way. This introduces the problem of the identical, unchanging thing that appears through the ever changing stream of experience.

There can be no doubt then, in James' opinion, that the recurrence of identical sensations is an impossibility. The constitution of the stream of experience is narrowly linked with the events in the brain. The hypothesis that one and the same sensation can occur twice presupposes an unchanged brain. But a brain, not modified constantly by the processes happening within it, is a physiological impossibility. On this ground already, the assumption of the immutability of simple sensations is baseless. *A fortiori,* there can be no immutability in the larger wholes of our experience. "Experience is remoulding us every moment, and our mental reaction on every given thing is really a resultant of our experience of the whole world up to that date" (I, 234). But then, this is the experience of one and the same Self experiencing identical things. If this were not so, we would get lost in what James called "one unanalyzed bloom of confusion" (I, 496), a kaleidoscope of impressions and feelings that vary constantly. It is important to have a clear notion of the relation between Self and things. We must understand what is meant by "the permanency of things and of the Self." They seem to be correlated. In a way, the permanency of the Self appears in the identity of the things.

4. Experience and Life History

But wherein resides the identity of things? Things can be changed, destroyed, or have a non-permanent character. When talking about the identity of things, James did not necessarily refer to the qualities of physical things. What he meant is things as units of meaning, as constant objects of action and thought. A table is a *table* whatever material it is made of. Experiencing identical things pertains more to their essence than to the concrete object. For the latter certainly is not necessarily stable, physically or psychologically.

> Experience, from the very first, presents us with concrete objects, vaguely continuous with the rest of the world which envelops them in space and time, and potentially divisible into inward elements and parts. These objects we break asunder and reunite (I, 487).

The things, identical through experience, are the correlates of that experience. To be experienced means having a history of experiences that changes one's way of perception and thought. On the other hand, changes in perception and thought mean changes in the things experienced. Ordinary people see grass; a specialist perceives "grasses." To him the green stuff growing in gardens has differentiated itself into more than one kind. His expertness is reflected in the distinction of "grasses" that look the same to the non-expert. Past experience in this sense is not just an inner quality of the mind, it is a quality of the world as it appears to the experienced person. When James tells us that experience is remoulding us every moment, this also means that experience remoulds our world every moment. It is, in fact, not easy to distinguish between one and the other.

Things also change their *meaning*. They look different according to our way of approach. This meaning could be described as something within the mind, but direct experience gives us meanings as qualities belonging to the perceived things themselves. A painter whom I accompany through a town does not see houses and picturesque corners as I do. His evaluation of them is not only different from mine, the scene itself must be described by him in a different way. We agree that we are seeing the same scenery, but we may earnestly disagree about its qualities. Where I can see nothing but a slum, he sees picturesqueness, artistic value. To end the debate on this question, science decided to distinguish between objective facts and subjective impressions, referring the disagreement between painters and ordinary people to the realm of the subjective. But then, the way a scientist looks at things defines his own subjective way of perceiving it. His decision does not secure him from the fact that all our impressions are personally colored and depend upon our life history. On the contrary, one must also learn the scientific outlook, and this certainly changes greatly the appearance of our human world. Whatever may be the way we prefer to think about things, we cannot deny the fact that their appearance in immediate experience is a function of our personal history. It is important to psychology, then, to acknowledge this fact and to investigate it. This implies that psychology, as James taught, must give its attention to immediate experience, to the so-called subjectivity of the world of human experience, and to the relation it has with life history.[14]

James does not give us a theory about this. He mentions the facts repeatedly, but when it comes to an explanation of the relation between experience as personal activity and the appearance of our world, he turns to physiological processes for guidance. Every brain-state is partly determined by the foregoing states of the brain. Alter the past, and the present must change. "Each present brain-state is a record in which the eye of Omniscience might read all the foregone history of its owner" (I, 234). But then, there is no such eye relevant to the psychologist. This is just the approach for which James blamed the associationists.

Supposing that the total past history of an individual is reflected in the present state of his brain, it does not help to explain the knowledge this person has of his past. The brain is not a register that keeps a record of past changes; if it did, the entries would change too. If they do not change, these entries are exactly the immutable ideas of association psychology; and, moreover, somebody would have to view them. Who is this inner person? Is there a secretary in the brain, recording the data of the past?[15] The concept of history implies a continuity; life history implies a continuity in the personal Self that changes and yet remains the same, developing and still keeping its identity.

The lack of an explicit theory of life history is one of the reasons why James did not develop a phenomenological psychology in the strict sense of the word.

5. *The Permanency of Things: The Jack of Spades*

James tried to find explanations for qualities of experience in the functions of the brain. No brain-state recurs unmodified; no experience therefore, can recur unmodified. The elementarist position then is unacceptable. It relies too much on a certain model of the mind, taking the model for the reality.

> No doubt it is often *convenient* to formulate the mental facts in an atomistic sort of way, and to treat the higher states of consciousness as if they were all built out of unchanging simple ideas. It is convenient often to treat curves as if they were composed of small straight lines, and electricity and nerve-force as if they were fluids. But in the one case as in the other we must never forget that we are talking symbolically, and that there is nothing in nature to answer to our words (I, 236).

It is not difficult to imagine that a whole is composed of little parts. But such a model has its disadvantages too. It does not explain the experienced unity of consciousness and its contents. It easily evokes an excessive confidence in its applicability. We have met somebody, spoken to him, heard his voice and noticed his peculiarities. We have an image of his personality. Do we then store this image in the form of a representation in our memory? Do we collect representations as we collect photographs in an album? And when we want to remember how this person we met looks, do we then turn over the pages of this album until we find his image? Up to a certain degree a description of this kind is not inadequate.[16] Psychologists use it regularly, or at least imply it, when they talk about the functions of memory and imagination. It immediately becomes inadequate, however, when we use it to explain the formation of the image of a centaur. We can hardly suppose that some mental agency cuts the needed parts from several pictures and pastes them together. And yet, the possibility of this procedure is implied in the original model, because it describes representations as if they were real pictures.

No such images exist. James stated: *"A permanently existing 'idea' or 'Vorstellung' which makes its appearance before the footlights of consciousness at periodical intervals, is as mythological an entity as the Jack of Spades"* (I, 236).

This is an interesting statement, not only because it flatly denies the existence of immutable ideas, but also because of the figure of speech. If we turn our attention to James' concept of "thing," the object that remains itself in ever changing thoughts, to the "realities, concrete and abstract, physical and ideal, whose permanent existence we believe in" (I, 231), are these not Jacks of Spades too? Is not the Jack of Spades, or the Queen of Hearts for that matter, a permanent ideal reality, although not existing in the way of hard, physical things? We recognize the Jack of Spades in all his different editions. When somebody talks about him, we never doubt that this talk has a very real referent.

The fact that the Jack of Spades is a reality seems even much more certain than that such things as "images" or "ideas" exist. The identity of the Jack of Spades is the identical meaning of an infinite collection of physical things called by that name. It is an identity that pervades all his different shapes and sizes and colors, his different functions in card games, and his varied historical manifestations. It seems then, that the Jack of Spades *is* a thing in the sense of James. Or, the other way around, things are Jacks of Spades, constant units of meaning. We shall see later on that James' concept of "thing" indeed comes close to this interpretation.

6. The Reason Behind Elementarist Mythology

It is usually interesting to look for the reasons for the development of a certain theory or model we reject. Philosophers and psychologists, like scientists in general, very seldom sit down to invent some weird picture of reality with the intention of confusing the issues. Theories and notions are developed to express some aspect of man's experience of reality. The analysis of a rejected theoretical doctrine may lead us back to the original fact of experience that it tried to describe. James used this method when, instead of ridiculing the atomist position, he tried to find the reasons behind it.

> What makes it convenient to use the mythological formulas is the whole organization of speech, which . . . was not made by psychologists, but by men who were as a rule only interested in the facts their mental states revealed. They only spoke of their states as *ideas of this or of that thing.* What wonder, then, that the thought is most easily conceived under the law of the thing whose name it bears! (I, 236).

It is not only the organization of speech which leads us to the belief that mental states are like the things they are directed to; the mind itself is interested in things and their qualities and not primarily in its own function. Our own experience is not, normally, the object of our experience. That is the reason why it is so difficult to grasp sensations introspectively and give an adequate report on them. When we are asked to describe the sensations occurring when we touch a pencil and turn it between our fingers, it seems that we just cannot avoid telling that we feel a *pencil,* a thing. We feel its sensible qualities, the smoothness of the surface, its temperature, the roundness, as qualities of this object, not as affections of our own skin and muscles. And yet, sensations strictly cannot be felt anywhere else than in our sensory organs, because that is where they are. In life and action, however, in the normal orientation of our mind, we are interested in the thing, not in sensations. Our interest is in their meaning. We do not say that a sensation of roughness is evoked in our finger, we say that we feel sandpaper. A lot of training is needed before anybody is able to report the sensations classical psychologists supposed us to have all the time. Experience is directed toward things.

But then, when we turn back towards our own experience, when we start analyzing the "inner life of the mind," we do not lose this orientation toward things—and so we find things within the mind too:

> If the thing is composed of parts, then we suppose that the thought of the thing must be composed of the thoughts of the parts. If one part of the thing has appeared in the same thing or in other things on former occasions, then we must be having even now the very same 'idea' of that part which was there on those occasions. If the thing is simple, its thought is simple. If it is multitudinous, it must require a multitude of thoughts to think it. If a succession, only a succession of thoughts can know it. If permanent, its thought is permanent. And so on *ad libitum* (I, 236).

Language and habit mislead us, and the psychologist is not protected from this. James Mill held the view that the idea of an army is "precisely the ideas of an indefinite number of men formed into one idea."[17] If this is too antiquated an example, Wundt's more recent discussion of intensive ideas is another one.[18]

Elementarist mythology stems from a naive approach to the problem of inner experience. And the moral in this story is that the mental laws investigated in psychology are functioning also in the process of investigation. The psychologist is not an indifferent observer, but a human being with all the peculiarities of attitude that belong to human beings.[19]

7. Sensation According to Wundt

It is difficult to overestimate the importance of James' endeavors to renew the psychological approach to human experience. To develop a just evaluation, we must get a clear notion of the atomistic position taken by associationist psychology. The best way is to study the concept of sensation.

As we saw before, Wundt considered sensations as one fundamental category of mental elements. The second category consists of elementary feelings.[20] But what is a sensation? Are they conceptual constructions, or real moments of experience? In the latter case, is there something like a *pure* sensation? There is, Wundt stated, and it makes sense to speak about it, but to get pure sensation we have to make a double abstraction.

In the first place we have to consider a sensation as a constitutive elementary (and hence irreducible) part of a perception.

From the perception of an object, we abstract for instance blue, this very blue which plays a constitutive role in the perception of that object. We consider nothing but this blue, and we may find that *the same* blue can occur in quite different objects. We have a simple constitutive moment of perception. When we are certain that this blue cannot be reduced to still more simple impressions, then we know it to be an elementary and pure sensation. Sensation$_1$ in this sense is an elementary and irreducible, abstract moment of a perception.

In the second place, we must abstract from feelings that are evoked by these elementary impressions. To have a pure sensation, any esthetic or emotional evaluation of the sensory content must be left out. Whether this specific blueness affects me as nice or ugly, warm or cold, has nothing to do with the sensation as such. Sensation$_1$ is an abstract *moment* of a perception, free of all components of feeling.

This specific blue has a relationship with other shades of blue, with red, yellow, etc. They are sensations of color; they are visual sensations. We distinguish them from other categories, from sensations of touch, taste, smell and hearing. All these different categories, however, have one important thing in common: they result from sensory stimulation. Sensations occur only when some stimulus excites the organism in one of its sensory organs. The quality of the sensation depends upon the quantitative characteristics of the stimulus. When the wavelength of the light striking the retina is changed, the sensation of color changes; when the intensity of a pressure applied to the skin changes, the sensation of touch changes. There is, then, a second meaning of the term "sensation." Sensation$_2$ is the abstract *moment* of a perception, caused by and varying with the excitation of a sensory organ. Or more briefly, sensation$_2$ is the result of sensory excitation.

But we must be more precise. Sensations are only the elementary impressions caused by elementary excitations. Moreover, the stimulus is something physical, whereas the sensation is a mental datum. But then we have already a third meaning of the term: sensation$_3$ is a content of consciousness, it is the mental experience caused by sensory excitation. In the tradition of association psychology, sensations were interpreted as things *in* the mind. It is useful to review what this means.

8. *Consciousness as a "Cabinet" According to John Locke*

"The word idea . . ." Locke tells us, "serves best to stand for whatsoever is the object of the understanding when a man thinks."[21] As in the case of James, "thinking" here means consciousness in general. Now consciousness has an object: we perceive *something*, imagine *something*, think *something*. But what is this something? When we imagine an elephant, the object of my imagination might be *the living animal itself* I think of, or it might be the *image* I have of it. Locke used to term "idea" in the latter meaning: "Whatsoever the mind perceives *in itself*, or is the immediate object of perception, thought, or understanding, that I call *idea*."[22] The real animal is the mediate object, the image I have of it in my mind is the immediate object. These mediating ideas are necessary, "for since the things the mind contemplates are none of them, besides itself, present to the understanding, it is necessary that something else, as a sign or representation of the thing it considers, should be present to it: and these are *ideas*."[23] This theory of representative knowledge implies Cartesian dualism of mind and matter: the mind, being spiritual, can know the material things only indirectly, by means of something spiritual.[24] Consequently, all things we know, must exist *twice:* first, there are the material things we know, and secondly, there are the *ideas* by means of which we know them. James, and behaviorism afterwards, rejected this reduplication of the world, but nevertheless this reduplication had a decisive role in the development of psychology.

The early philosophical psychologists sought to know what ideas are in themselves, and in what way they originated. According to Locke, ideas are *contents* of the mind. He stated that we must admit that there are ideas in the minds of men; everybody is aware of that.[25] But did Locke imply a kind of mind-space, *containing* ideas? Descartes, before him, did not think along this line. Precisely what notions Locke had in this matter, we do not know. But there can be no doubt that there is a strong suggestion in some of his statements and descriptions. And he certainly originated the tendency to speak about contents of consciousness, or mental contents.

The mind, Locke taught, is a *tabula rasa* (a clean slate) when a human being comes into the world; there are no ideas in it as yet. How then, do ideas enter the mind? "The senses at first let in particular ideas, and furnish the yet empty cabinet: and the mind by degrees growing familiar with some of them, they are lodged in the memory, and names got to them."[26] The only passages of knowledge to the mind are external and internal sensation: "These alone, as far as I can discover, are the windows by which light is let into this *dark room*. For methinks the understanding is not much unlike a closet wholly shut from light, with only some little opening left, to let in external visible resemblances, or ideas of things without."[27] And this is the "true *history of the first beginnings of human knowledge*."[28]

In our everyday language we too use such terms as "to comprehend" or "to grasp," to designate mental activities. These terms refer clearly to bodily activities; it is the hand that, literally, comprehends things when it encloses them. So comprehension seems to imply a spatial relation between the comprehending organ and the comprehended thing. But we do not mean this literally when we use the terms in everyday life, although the suggestion is there. In the philosophy of Locke it seems to be more than a simple suggestion. Ideas become contents, the mind a container, a sort of space the ideas are *in*.[29]

Locke distinguished two kinds of mental contents: *sensations* and *reflections*. Reflections originate in the activity of the understanding; they are not original contents as sensations are. Sensations are the ideas of the qualities of things taken in by the senses. They give us the sensible qualities like yellow, white, hot, cold, soft, hard, bitter, sweet.

And so sensation$_3$ is an elementary mental *content,* an idea, taken in by the senses. This really implies more than the definition of sensations as mental states. A state could be a modification of consciousness as such. A content, however, must be something within the mind. But then, a fourth notion has already been suggested: the elementary contents like sensations must combine into more complex ideas.

The qualities of things in the outer world that excite our senses, the colors, shapes, smells, sounds, etc., are, in the things themselves, so combined and mixed, that there is no separation between them. The real things are not aggregates of qualities, but they do affect us in different ways. In perception, the unity of things is broken up according to the different senses, and what enters the mind are simple elementary sensations.[30] The senses act like filters, only certain qualities of the things pass them, others do not, or pass other filters. The senses break things up into a collection of simple ideas, and the mind has to rebuild the things, using these simple ideas as component parts. Sensation$_4$ is an elementary and irreducible part of mental composites; it is a mental element. And this again implies a fifth notion: sensation$_5$ is the basic element in mental genesis.

9. Mental Genesis and Association

In British empiricism, the mind of the newborn baby is a *tabula rasa,* a blank paper without any writing on it as yet. Sensations are the first letters that experience writes on this paper. *Letters,* not words or sentences. The elements have to be reunited to get meaning. The mind develops its complex ideas, its composite picture of the outer world, only in the course of time. Sensations are the basic elements, the building bricks provided by the senses; some mortar is needed to compose wholes from them. Hence, empiricism tries to trace back the history of the mind. It does so by means of analytical introspection, or, as Locke called it, by the "plain historical method." Writing about Locke's *Essay,* Sterne stated that "it is a history-book . . . of what passes in a man's own mind."[31]

How then do the elements come to be united in the course of mental history? A newborn child learns to recognize its mother, because certain sensations, evoked by the mother's presence, always occur together. When the child hears this voice (these elementary sound sensations), sees this pattern of colored patches, is handled in this way, it learns to expect all these sensations to occur together. Repetition and togetherness take care of the integration of sensation complexes. The elementary sensations associate themselves.

In a theory of this type, the logical and the psychogenetic order are identified. Logical analysis leads to the distinction between elementary and more complex impressions. The elementary impressions must have come first, the more complex impressions therefore, develop later, as integrative forms of mental elements. Of course, it is possible to discriminate between all those abstract moments of a perception, that are called sensations. This does not necessarily mean that one is able to *have* such "pure sensations"; it does not even mean that they are ever given in experience, and it certainly does not mean that the first impressions of a newborn human being are of the sensation type. To affirm that the first impressions are pure, elementary, unconnected sensations, is to translate a logical conclusion into a psychogenetic argument. Locke's reasoning went this way: Every simple constitutive moment of perception (sensation$_1$) must be one of the basic elements in psychogenesis (sensation$_5$). Because these elements were conceived as contents of the mind, as thing-like entities or substantive mental units, the theory of association had to maintain an atomistic view of mental genesis. Designed in early British empiricism, the theory of mental association held its position for centuries. Even in the twentieth century, Ebbinghaus still stated that "when any mental formations have once been in the consciousness simultaneously or in contiguous succession, the return afterwards, of some parts of the previous experience also evokes ideas of the other parts, without a necessary recurrence of the original causes."[32]

At first, the concept of association was used only to explain the linkage between successive ideas. It explained the tendency of some ideas to follow other ideas. Indications of this theory can be found as early as Aristotle's works. British empiricism introduced association as an explanation for *synchronous* linkage of mental elements. It had to, because this was the only way to explain how the separate and independent sensations can be coupled or fused into the more complex ideas. Berkeley, for example, tells us:

"Thus, for example, a certain colour, taste, smell, figure, and consistency having been observed to go together, are accounted one distinct thing, signified by the name apple."[33] The perception of a thing then is equal to having a certain amount of associated sensations simultaneously. This complex of sensations evokes traces of past sensations in the mind; these traces, added to the actual complex, make it possible to recognize the complex as one we had before and to call it the usual name.

It is evident that it is impossible in this view to speak about a *stream* of consciousness, as there can only be a *"train* of thought." James wanted to break away from this view because it did not seem adequate. In direct experience, nothing like these mental mosaics are given. James wanted no confusion between the logical and the psychogenetic order. On the other hand, association theory in its classical form had some strong arguments in its favor. One of these was developed in the nineteenth century by Johannes Müller.

10. The Doctrine of Specific Energies

Association theory developed originally as a purely mental philosophy. Hartley was the first to complement it by a theory of physiological association that had some consistency. But the physiology of the nervous system had to wait for the nineteenth century for a significant development. The theory of mental association had become so self-evident a solution for problems of psychology at its beginning, that any more specifically physiological theory had to fall in line with it. Johannes Müller's doctrine of specific energies took mental association and its implications for granted.

Ideas represent things and their qualities. The basic ideas gotten through sensations are caused by the excitation of the sensory organs. The senses have their own way of translating the qualities of the things that affect them into mental states, but there is no good reason to suppose that the senses give true images of the things that affect them. Sensations really are mental reactions to sensory excitation, and do not necessarily have much resemblance to the things that cause them. As Locke stated, real things in the world around us have the *power* to produce certain ideas in the mind by means of the senses. These powers he called the *qualities* of things.[34] A snowball has the power to evoke the ideas of whiteness, coldness and roundness in the mind. Or, in other words, a snowball has the qualities of whiteness, coldness and roundness.

There are, however, two kinds of sensible qualities: primary qualities and secondary qualities. The *primary qualities* are the essential qualities of material things: solidity, extension, shape, motion and number. According to Locke, these primary qualities are truly represented in their ideas; they produce a valid picture of the world in our minds. They supply us with adequate knowledge about the properties of the material world.

Secondary qualities, on the contrary, do not represent things as they are in themselves. What they represent is the power of these things to cause certain specific sensations. For example, sound and color refer to some action of real things upon us, but they give no pictures or true images of them. Things, as they are in themselves, are colorless, soundless, tasteless, they have no smell or temperature. They have only the power to cause these sensations. The secondary qualities exist only for our consciousness. They exist in the mind, not in the real world.

This doctrine was developed as a part of Locke's theory of knowledge, in which he investigated the validity of knowledge. Locke supposed the real existence of both the material world and mind. His problem was, to what extent our mind knows the material world as it really is in itself.

But this philosophy easily leads to the ontological problem of whether there is any real material world at all. Berkeley, seeing no good reasons for Locke's realism, denied the existence of a material world. His pithy declaration is well known: *Esse est percipi,* to be consists in being perceived.[35] The sensations *are* the thing itself, and this holds also for primary qualities. Solidity, extension, etc., are no more true images of the outer world than sound and color are. The only substance that really exists is the mind.

Now we are not interested here in the intricacies of an idealistic ontology like that of Berkeley. But we must not forget that in this early phase philosophy and psychology were intimately linked together. In fact, psychology was part of philosophy, and only slowly became independent. By that time, philosophical traditions had set the stage for the further development of psychological doctrines. This is what happened to the doctrine of Johannes Müller. Although he supposed that there is a real material world, his theory of sensation is the physiological counterpart of Berkeley's idealism.

Müller's theory found its first expression in his work on the physiology of vision in man and animals, *Zur vergleichenden Physiologie des Gesichtssinnes des Menschen und der Thiere,* written in 1826. We shall follow here his later formulation of the theory in ten theses.[36] For our purpose a summary of the more important theses is sufficient.

(I) Every sensation, caused by external stimulation, can also be caused by internal stimulation. Sensations, seemingly referring to an outside world, may be the result of an event within the organism. Sensations of light and color, for instance, can occur when the eyes are closed, and even in complete darkness. (II) One and the same internal cause may cause different sensations according to the sense that is affected. High blood pressure causes sensations of light in the eye, a buzzing sensation in the ear. (III) Also, one and the same external cause may result in quite different sensations, according to the sense affected. A blow on the ear results in a ringing sensation. Applied to the eye, the same blow causes us to see stars. (V) An important conclusion must be drawn from the stated facts: Sensations do not represent outside qualities or events, they represent the excitatory state of a sensory nerve. The quality of the sensation depends upon the specific energy of this nerve. A sensation of sight means that the optic nerves are excited; hearing a sound means that the auditory nerve is excited. All sensory nerves cause only those sensations in the mind that agree with their specific capacity of reaction, called specific energy. (VIII) Sensation then, is primarily the mental reflection of the excitory state of a nerve. Events and states in the outer world are not perceived or sensed immediately, but only mediately, namely, in so far as sensation is the indication of something happening. But there is no possibility of determining by the sensation itself, whether the event happens in the outside world or within the organism. The mind can learn to distinguish between these two cases only by experience.

Sensation is merely the awareness of changes in the excitatory state of the nervous system. This is the sixth and last definition of sensation, implying all of the other five. In fact, our six definitions are parts of one closed system, having its origin in Cartesian dualism, (that) completely isolates the mind from an (eventual) material world. The mind is a thing in itself, an island explored for its own sake. It remained so in the psychology of the nineteenth century, notwithstanding all the research done about psychophysical relations, and notwithstanding the fact that the extreme formulation came from an outstanding physiological investigation. Müller himself pointed the way when he said that for him "the soul was only a particular form of life among the manifold forms of life that are the object of physiological examination, and on that account he was convinced that physiological research must, in its ultimate results, be itself psychological."[37]

The theory of specific energies is the logical conclusion of the trend beginning in British empiricism. Sensations, abstract irreducible moments of perceptual contents, resulting from sensory excitation, are the original contents of the mind, combined into more complex ideas by association. One of the reasonings behind this notion, and indeed a formidable argument, is, that since we have separate senses, we must have also separate, unmixed sensations before we can have more complex mental states. This reasoning was attacked by James, as it has been by many others in the anti-atomistic trend of the newer psychological systems.

11. Sensation According to Heinz Werner

In our own century there have been many reactions against analytical atomism. The general assumption of British associationism, stating that discrete sensations precede the experience of wholes, has been rejected on many grounds. One line of attack was the renewal of the analysis of direct experience. People in everyday life, and even trained psychologists, find it very hard to believe that the integration of simple mental elements is at the base of their conscious experience, because nothing of the sort is given in actual experience. When we ask what is given first, the answer must be: perception, not sensation; things, not simple impressions; wholes, not their elements. Experience consists of integral totalities, not of disconnected sensations. In experience, wholes precede their parts.

Actually we must go even further. It is a reasonable assumption that the impressions of a newborn baby are of a more simple structure than those of the adult, that there is less differentiation in their experiential field. But this does not necessarily imply that early experience consists of incoherent sensations. Even though the baby's experience is simpler, it *is experience,* and the things experienced must be already an awareness of *wholes* and *gestalts,* and hence there is no place in psychogenesis for Locke's mental elements. Pure sensations are abstractions, logical constructs, and not real moments of experience. Experience certainly develops from childhood to adulthood, but not in the way that is assumed by empiricism.

A view of this kind is set forth in Werner's developmental psychology.[38] Rejecting a mechanical and summative interpretation of psychogenesis, Werner proceeds from the principle that development proceeds from a state of relative globality and lack of differentiation to a state of increased differentiation, articulation, and hierarchical integration.

Like the basic assumption of associationism, this principle cannot be verified empirically and directly; it is the guiding principle in a theoretical interpretation of development, and it leads to experimental investigations that can demonstrate only the usefulness of the principle, but neither prove nor disprove it.

According to Werner, man's earliest experiences have the character of wholeness and unity. The different sense modalities are not yet distinguished as the person does not yet distinguish between himself and his environment, between subject and object. To take an example, the experience of sound and color are not recognized as different kinds of sensation in this stage of global experience. They are part of a total experience and only can be slowly differentiated from this totality in the course of development. The concept of sensation must then have a completely new meaning. To Werner, sensation is not related to the elementary perceptions of the different senses, it designates a state of feeling in which the body as a whole resounds to the totality of its impressions and affections. A clear distinction between things heard, seen, tasted, or smelled, is then impossible. "Feeling" here means consciousness of both, and at the same time, cognitive and affective character. It is a *pathic* consciousness that is found in the early stages of psychogenesis. From this a more differentiating and articulated, discriminating *gnostic* mentality develops. For mature Western man, a gnostic mentality is predominant, but the possibility of a more pathic way of experiencing is not excluded. The latter requires a certain passive attitude, the preparedness to be a reverberating instrument, to loosen the distinction of subject-object split and to deliver oneself to one's impressions. These impressions will then approximate the state called sensation by Werner.

When we try to examine and test this in an experimental situation, we find that a kind of experience as predicted by Werner actually occurs. Sensory impressions may lose their distinct characteristics; sound and color become, as it were, more similar, until finally their difference seems to be only that of different accents in the same global impression. The clear distinction between seeing and hearing has disappeared. They are part of one pathic affection. There finally is only the experience of being a resonant body ("das Erlebnis körperlicher Empfindungszuständlichkeit").

In order to attain this experience, the subject must have an attitude that differs completely from that demanded of a subject in classical perception experiments. The description of sensory experience in classical psychology presupposes a scrupulous and accurate gnostic observation. In a Werner type of situation, however, one is asked to relax, to refrain from sharp distinctions, to deliver oneself to bodily affections. It then appears, for example, that it is hard to say whether tones of lower pitch are heard or felt. They seem to boom within the body, and the distinction between hearing and feeling makes no sense. In such an attitude colors may harmonize completely with sounds, whereas sound and color in normal everyday attitude fall into quite different sensory categories. In the gnostic attitude, it is inconceivable that anybody could ever confuse color and sound.

This short outline of some of the more important points in Werner's view is sufficient for our purpose. There is a clear difference from the classical approach to perceptual problems in the rejection of the atomistic point of view. There are, on the other hand, some basic similarities that are worth mentioning.

There can be no doubt about the possibility of having an experience that approximates the sensations of classical psychology. Imagine a psychologist from the nineteenth century who is at a party and is bored by the common sense talk. His mind will then return to its habitual problems. Looking distractedly at a teacup, he may suddenly become quite aware of the fact that its rim appears to be round, and again, does not. It *is* round, and yet a more accurate observation shows that the rim has a more elliptic form. While observing this shape, it actually seems to become more elliptical.

This psychologist knows that his senses play *tricks on him* all the time. So he begins to do away with the sources of confusion. He immobilizes himself as much as possible, looks for a head rest so that slight motions of his head do not distort the accuracy of his observation. He closes one eye, because the doubleness of his visual organ probably adds to the confusion. He is on the look-out for pure sensation, for an instantaneous sense impression, uncomplicated by any influencing factors like motion, context, or memory traces. He uses a reduction screen, because looking through a little hole takes away contextual effects. Then the rim of his teacup is an ellipse and remains so, whether he looks at it for one minute or for all eternity.

The perception of roundness in teacups, he concludes, is an illusion, or may be an unconscious judgment; it certainly is not a primordial fact of sensation. This psychologist never thinks about a possible relation between his elementary sensations and the high degree of artificiality of his experimental situation. He never considers sensation as a possible *result* from this kind of situation, because a *logical* reasoning had convinced him that such meaningless, simple, unrelated, instantaneous sensory moments like sensations must have been at the origin of experience.

Empiricism, stating that all knowledge proceeds from experience, never bothered to prove that experience in its original form really has an atomistic structure. Empiricism presupposed atomism simply on rational grounds—and there certainly are some traces of contradiction in this position.

Werner rejected atomistic empiricism. Mental development to him meant not an ongoing integration beginning with discrete mental elements, but on the contrary, the ongoing differentiation beginning from global wholes of experience.[39] In original pathic experience, perception is predominantly physiognomic; things affect us affectively and cognitively all at once. Feeling and perceiving become differentiated only later. In the wholes, parts are articulated, details are distinguished and sharply distinct sense modalities appear.

It is a fact that Werner explicitly mentions the heuristic character of his general principle. It cannot be proved that the course of mental development in humans proceeds from globality to differentiation, although a lot of facts and observations can be related by assuming that the principle holds. And there is the evidence from experimental investigations with adults. But then, must we not say that when sensations, in the sense of Werner, occur in adults of our culture, they are also *results* of an experimental situation? When Werner in a description of his early experiments tells us that the experience of being a resonant body is the *final* stage of experience in this situation, the plausible inference is that it is a result of the attitude developed during the experiment. Werner's assumption is, that this final stage is a reactualization of the original stage of our consciousness, or at least an approximation to it. But there can be no doubt that the normal adult can have no such extreme pathic experiences *without* voluntarily adopting the necessary attitude. Here too, is some contradiction, unless one is willing to accept Werner's general

principle not only for its heuristic value, but as a general statement of fact. It seems safer to consider both the elementary
sensations of empiricism and the global sensations of Werner as
artifacts, resulting from artificial situations.

The concrete outline of mental development presupposes, in
both systems, a general rational principle that could be true, and
again might not be. There is no way to decide this from experience. There is experience however. We are now in a better
position to understand what James meant when he blamed empiricism for abandoning the empirical method of investigation:
"Most books start with sensations, as the simplest mental facts,
and proceed synthetically, constructing each higher stage from
those below it" (I, 224) . That is, most systems do not really try to
describe direct experience without presuppositions; they only
start descriptions after first making general statements about the
nature of things as it rationally must be. Our only guide, however,
is the presuppositionless analysis of direct experience.[40]

12. Sensation and Perception in Jamesian Psychology

In direct experience, consciousness appears to be an ongoing
stream, not a sequence of distinct mental states. There cannot be
such a sequence considering the fact that brain processes do not
allow for the existence of recurring distinct ideas. So James
rejected associationism, and was one of the earliest psychologists
to do so. But then, the theory of sensation and associationism had
been linked together for a long time. Together, they had greatly
influenced the general state of psychological theory. The rejection of associationism left James in a difficult position in so far as
it opened many problems that had already been solved. One of
these problems concerns sensation in its relation to perception;
another one is the problem of relating sensation to the functioning of the senses. Since the traditional approaches all presuppose
associationistic theory, James developed a tendency to avoid
those problems. Boring rightly stated that James neglected the
problem of sensation as much as possible, notwithstanding the
fact that the whole of the "new psychology" concentrated on it.[41]
He could not avoid it completely, however. So he treated it in his

own way, making it difficult for us to extract from it a systematic view.

> Within a few years what one may call a microscopic psychology has arisen in Germany, carried on by experimental methods, asking of course every moment for introspective data, but eliminating their uncertainty by operating on a large scale and taking statistical means. This method taxes patience to the utmost, and could hardly have arisen in a country whose natives could be *bored*. Such Germans as Weber. Fechner, Vierordt, and Wundt obviously cannot (I, 192).

Obviously, James could. He found "little of the grand style about these new prism, pendulum, and chronograph-philosophers" (I, 193).

> Fechner himself indeed was a German *Gelehrter* of the ideal type, at once simple and shrewd, a mystic and an experimentalist, homely and daring, and as loyal to his facts as to his theories. But it would be terrible if even such a dear old man as this could saddle our Science forever with his patient whimsies, and, in a world so full of more nutritious objects of attention, compel all future students to plough through the difficulties, not only of his own works, but of the still drier ones written in his refutation. Those who desire this dreadful literature can find it; it has a 'disciplinary value'; but I will not even enumerate it in a footnote (I, 549).

It is clear that such an attitude is not conducive to a thorough discussion of the problems involved.

In the same way James avoided a discussion of Johannes Müller's theory of specific energies. James simply did not mention Müller in this context, although he, with his broad knowledge, cannot have been ignorant of him.[42] According to the index, the name J. Müller occurs only twice in the *Principles*,[43] but not in relation with the theory of specific energies. Rothschuh, in his *History of Physiology,* mentions fourteen pupils of Müller. They all were more or less famous in the last century. James quotes only three of them.[44] When discussing the theory of specific energies briefly, he still did not mention Müller.[45]

James did discuss the "eccentric projection" of sensations, however. Berkeley had introduced the view that three dimensional spatiality cannot be perceived by the eye, because the retina is only two dimensional. If we do have impressions of visual space, this must be because the "flat" optical perceptions are associated with sensations of touch. The "visual" image of space would then in fact be an inner image, projected outwards. In Müller's theory this doctrine of projection plays an important role. In Müller's view, optical perception is the awareness of the excitatory state of the optical nerve, with spatial qualities in only two dimensions, because the retina is two dimensional.[46] The sensation of space too, is localized within the body. In thesis IX it is even stated that it is not in the nature of the nerves themselves to project their sensations outside of the body; this projection results from habitual images, and is justified by past experience.[47] From that time on, the theory of eccentric projection of "spatial" images has been linked with the doctrine of Müller.

But James had his own ideas in this matter. In the five pages he devoted to the notion of projection, Müller is not mentioned (II, 31–35). The doctrine is rejected. Consciousness cannot be said properly to inhabit any place, and certainly it does not make any sense to suppose that a sensation feels either itself or its object to be in the same place with the brain. Sensations do have dynamic relations with the brain but they have cognitive relations with everything and anything (II, 34). "I am *cognitively* present to Orion whenever I perceive that constellation, but I am not *dynamically* present there, I work no effects" (I, 214).

The difficulty seems to be that the projection theory supposes sensations to be in one place, the brain, and then, as it were, transfers them to another place, to the outside world. In James' view, sensations are not *things,* and therefore cannot be projected. His ideas in this matter merit our attention.

> Certainly a child newly born in Boston, who gets a sensation from the candle-flame which lights the bedroom, or from his diaper-pin, does not feel either of these objects to be situated in longitude 72° W. and latitude 41° N. He does not feel them to be in the third story of the house. He does not even feel them in any distinct manner to be to the right or the left of any of the other sensations which he may be getting from other objects in the room at the same time. He does not, in short, know anything *about* their space-relations to anything else in the world. The

flame fills its own place, the pain fills it own place; but as yet these places are neither identified with, nor discriminated from, any other places. That comes later. For the places thus first sensibly known are elements of the child's space-world which remain with him all his life; and by memory and later experience he learns a vast number of things *about* those places which at first he did not know. But to the end of time certain places of the world remain defined for him as the places *where those sensations were;* and his only possible answer to the question *where anything is* will be to say *there,* and to name some sensation or other like those first ones, which shall identify the spot. Space *means* but the aggregate of all our possible sensations. There is no duplicate space known *aliunde,* or created by an 'epoch-making achievement'[48] into which our sensations, originally spaceless, are dropped. They *bring* space and all its places to our intellect, and do not derive it thence (II, 34 ff.) .

The problem of sensation (or perception) in its relation to an experienced outside world is not a problem of *location,* but one of *meaning.* In our experience, space is not an empty place that we fill by projecting our sensations into it. Sensations *are* spatial experiences, and the general term "space" refers to actual and possible sensations *as* spatial. It is not even correct, for instance, to say that visual sensations are *in* space, they are spatial *themselves.* The "outsideness" of visual sensations belongs to them in much the same way as the "insideness" of bodily sensations belong to the latter. The body too, is not something given *before* the sensational experience of it, it is given *in* and *as* sensations of a certain kind. "Body" and "outside world" then, primarily are not empty locations to be filled by sensation, but meanings inherent to sensations.

By his body, then, the child later means simply *that place where* the pain from the pin, and a lot of other sensations like it, were or are felt. It is no more true to say that he locates that pain in his body, than to say that he locates his body in that pain. Both are true; that pain is part of what he *means by the word body.* Just so by the outer world the child means nothing more than *that place where* the candle-flame and a lot of other sensations like it are felt. He no more locates the candle in the outer world than he locates the outer world in the candle. Once again, he does both; for the candle is part of what he *means* by 'outer world' (II, 35).

Here is a new beginning, an endeavor to devise a descriptive theory of the relation between body, space, and sensation. These concepts cannot be defined independently. Sensation is the primitive way in which body and space are experienced. Thus to James sensations cannot be *re*presentations of things and their qualities; sensations are presentations of them. Experience makes it possible to find relations between sensations and to acquire knowledge about them, but sensation is and remains the original presentation of a world.

> In his dumb awakening to the consciousness of *something there,* a mere *this* as yet (or something for which even the term *this* would perhaps be too discriminative, and the intellectual acknowledgement of which would be better expressed by the bare interjection 'lo!'), the infant encounters an object in which (though it be given in a pure sensation) all the 'categories of the understanding' are contained. *It has objectivity, unity, substantiality, causality, in the full sense in which any later object or system of objects has these things* (II, 8).

Or, the first sensation which an infant gets *is* for him the universe (II, 8).

> And though our sensations cannot then so analyze and talk of themselves, yet at their very first appearance quite as much as at any later date are they cognizant of all those qualities which we end by extracting and conceiving under the names of *objectivity, exteriority,* and *extent.* It is surely subjectivity and interiority which are the notions *latest* acquired by the human mind (II, 43).

Sensation presents reality, not a duplicate of it. The theory of representative knowledge, that is characteristic of empiricism, must be rejected radically (I, 196 ff.).

To sum up, James' approach to the problem of sensation differs completely from the classical approach. Although it is difficult because of the changed meaning of the term, we must try to compare these two approaches.

In the empiricist tradition, sensations are (1) abstract moments of perception, (2) resulting from sensory excitation, (3) they appear in consciousness as mental contents, (4) as elementary parts of more complex mental compositions, (5) of which they are the basic components, (6) being primarily nothing but the reflections of the excitatory state of sensory nerves.

To James too, sensations are:

(1) Abstractions (II, 3), although not abstract moments of a perception; abstractions they are, because, as a rule, adults do not have them any more. Adult experience is invaded by knowledge about the sensed things and qualities, whereas sensation is the first awareness of "the *bare immediate natures* by which our several objects are distinguished" (II, 3). Sensation is already experience of real things.

(2) There is no disagreement about the fact that sensation is caused by sensory excitation: "*nerve-currents coming in from the periphery are involved in their production*" (II, 3).

(3) Sensations, however, cannot be described as mental contents; they do not represent things, they present them. They are not *within* the mind, for sensation is a way in which the mind *knows* real things.

(4) Therefore, they cannot be mental elements.

(5) Nor does it make sense to suppose that the more complex thoughts are composed from them. If there are different senses involved, the integration takes place on the level of brain-processes;

(6) in consciousness only integral experiences are given. Even the very first sensation of a newborn is not an elementary thing, but the way in which the universe first appears. "The physiological condition of this first sensible experience is probably nerve-currents coming in from many peripheral organs at once" (II, 8). From this point of view, the problem Müller was concerned with cannot even arise.

It must be noticed, however, that James did not completely free himself from the classical notion of sensation. This appears in a statement like the following: "The nearer the object cognized comes to being a simple quality like 'hot,' 'cold,' 'red,' 'noise,' 'pain,' apprehended irrelatively to other things, the more the state of mind approaches pure sensation" (II, 1). It is especially with the concept of "unrelatedness" that James presupposes the whole context of classical sensation theory. As we said before, James' ideas cannot be systematized completely.

This leads us to James' views on the distinction between sensation and perception. Sensation and perception are names for different cognitive functions, *not* for different types of psychic reality. Both functions provide knowledge of the world. However, the more the relations of an object are experienced, that is, the more the object becomes classified, localized, measured and compared; the more the experience approaches that which we call perception. Speaking analytically, the difference between sensation and perception according to James lies exclusively in the extreme simplicity of sensation.

What is the source of that difference? The difference between simplicity and complexity in that regard is related to the number of brain cells that are evoked by a particular experience. Sensation and perception on the one side differ from thought (taking the term in the narrow sense) because in the case of sensation and perception, the neural impulses playing a role in cerebral activity stem from the sense organs themselves. On the other hand, perception differs from sensation because in the case of perception, the neural currents arouse a great number of processes of association by means of which the individual "sensation," namely the object that is being experienced, is viewed in every possible relation. It is these reproductive processes in the cortex, memorial traces awakened by actual sensations, that determine the difference between perception and sensation.

The descriptive difference between sensation and perception is based upon the varying degree of complexity of the processes in the brain. Hence the theory of Johannes Müller must have seemed like a logical consequence to James who had such strong leanings toward physiology. He escapes from this only by declaring that he will deal exclusively with general questions regarding sensation in the chapter concerned, leaving to other textbooks the study of particular, individual sensations.

When we grown-ups speak of "sensations" we mean either definite *objects,* namely simple qualities or attributes of things, such as hard, hot, painful; or experiences in which the acquaintance with those objects is scarcely or not at all connected with a knowledge concerning their relations with other things. Since we are now thinking or speaking about things which we *have known all along* we feel obliged to *postulate* an experience which gave us our first awareness of the naked immediate data by means of which we distinguish between various things. This experience is the sensation. And these sensations are the first modes of experience.

A pure sensation can take place only in the first days of life, because the newborn child—like a clean sheet of paper—does not yet have the means for making associative relations in the cortex. The infant *cannot* have anything but sensations, for there are no traces in its brain that can cooperate with them. The infant has nothing through which a perception can arise. But it is also only in the first days of life that "pure" sensations can take place. But these then are certainly not what can be called *contents* of consciousness. Sensation is an experience, namely, the primitive experience of the world and of the things themselves. Our earliest experience is pretty much exclusively an experience of *this* and *that* (II, 3), which are, however, full of meaning.

The first sensation a child has is for him the universe. We are even permitted to say that his whole world will spring from that first germ by the enlargement and differentiation of that first germinal experience which *implicitly* contains all that the child will ever be able to experience afterwards. Discrimination, verbal expression and abstraction will in a little while draw from sensation even all the "categories of the mind." Objectivity, unity, substantiality, causality are all included and grasped in the first sensation (II, 8).

Sensation is already experiencing the world, it is reality itself as it *begins* to appear. Sensation is a way the Self knows the world. Sensation is *not* a (quasi)-substantive intermediary thing *between* the Self and the world. Are we going too far when we imagine that James saw already a cognitive *act* in sensation? It is certain that he never uses this term in the sense of an act-psychology.[49] But is this not implicitly contained in his view? The psychologist, he tells us, is fundamentally a dualist: he presupposes a "mind knowing and a thing known," and those two cannot be reduced to one another (I, 218).

Knowing is for him an ultimate relation which must be recognized, whether explained or not, precisely as difference or agreement, which no one attempts to explain (I, 216). Now this knowing, whether it be perception or thought, James certainly does not look upon as the passive reception of an impression. He does not imagine the mind to be like a paper that automatically receives writing; it is not a sensitive film that fixes impressions in a photo-mechanical way. The stream of experience is a succession of experiences, to which sensation also belongs as a way of experience, as a "way of consciousness." The character of an *act* is at least implicitly contained in that way of thinking.

There is at least one good reason why James does not explicitly accept the act-theory: he is fascinated by what is taking place in the brain. A thing that is perceived must send one or another signal that reaches the brain and *does* something there (I, 218). Why then not group all the problems presented to us by psychology into one great mystery, the mystery that processes of the brain lead to knowledge? (I, 689).[50] But the "activity" of the cortex is a *passivity* in respect to *the person,* it is something that happens, that takes place there. Hence sensations in James' opinion cannot be *acts,* because they have their foundation in bodily processes. The descriptive starting-point of James that proved so fruitful, is constantly overshadowed by his mythological faith in the brain.

13. The Integrity of the Stream of Experience

Experience is characteristically a stream and has unity. It is impossible to represent consciousness as an aggregate of "little rounded and finished off . . . separate entities" (I, 499). It possesses integrity in content, form and duration. This is the conclusion which James comes to from his psychological standpoint.

But when we think that he should admit discontinuity on the physiological level, that there are separate, that is, isolated processes of sensation, we find that James denies this also. The processes that are taking place in the brain are not something that is cloistered and isolated and that can be repeated identically; they are rather constantly changing resultants of incoming impulses. We can differentiate these stimuli just as we distinguish objects, qualities and events in our experiences. But to be able to distinguish things does not imply that they are originally separate.

On the contrary, the prerequisite for the *possibility* of distinguishing between two things is that they be contained and grasped in a unity of experience. Hence we are not justified in adopting the criticism of Stumpf who accuses James of maintaining that visual perceptions originally should be wholly simple, inarticulate and undifferentiated.[51]

According to James their unity does not consist in the fact that colors and forms, spaces and distances flow completely into one another. Their unity is determined as an integrity of experience. There is *one* perception in which an indefinite number of things are seen simultaneously. And if James was inclined at one time to extend and apply the simplicity of experience even to the content, we must remember that he corrected that view a long time before Stumpf published his study: fields of experience *can* be constructed from more simple "parts" although this is not generally the case.[52] It is even necessary to say that fields of experience are, in regard to content, always complex.[53] And yet experiences are integral phenomena in spite of their being *unstable* integrals.

And James notes with approval that Wundt comes to the same conclusion when he says, for instance, that he has come to understand an image as something that is no less changing and perishable than a feeling or act of the will and that therefore the classical doctrine of associationism is no longer tenable.[54] But then James, for the sake of convenience, pays no attention to what Wundt says directly afterwards, namely that the theory of association "should be replaced by the acceptance of processes of connection between the elements of experience,"[55] that is, by a theory of association! This theory happens to have greater vitality than James thought it had. And in the end he himself was unable to get rid of it. But it is to his credit that he has forcefully argued that the description of experience cannot and should not have recourse to that theory.

How then does one come to the idea that consciousness is constructed out of discrete elements? This is done, says James, by a naive use of language which makes experiences pass for things because we give names to experienced things. It is necessary therefore to examine language more closely in order to rediscover the integrity and continuity of experience that lies beyond the discontinuity of *trans*-lations. It is not enough to transfer the blame to language. It is also necessary to ask *why* language so readily and naturally understands integral experience as having discontinuity.

NOTES

1. Cf. Thomas Hobbes, *Leviathan*, (London, 1886), ch. 3; John Locke, *Essay*, Bk. II, ch. 33, §6.
2. David Hume, *A Treatise on Human Nature*, vol. 1, (London, 1909), pp. 319 ff.
3. Alexander Bain, *The Emotions and The Will*, (London, 1859), p. 29.
4. William James, "On Some Omissions of Introspective Psychology," *Mind*, vol. 9, 1884. Perry speaks of "James' most important insight," and dates its first development from 1882; Perry, *Thought*, vol. 2, p. 77.
5. James, *A Pluralistic Universe*, p. 214.
6. Bergson, in a letter to James of 1–6–1903. In *Écrits et Paroles*, p. 192. Cf. W. James, "The Feeling of Effort," *Anniv. Mem. Boston Soc. nat. History*, 1880. Parts also in *Scribners Mag.*, 1880. The article was developed in the chapter on the "Will" in *Principles*, vol. 2, pp. 486 ff. Bergson became acquainted with the French translation: "Le Sentiment de l'Effort," *Critique philos.*, vol. 2. Cf. Bergson, *Essai sur les Données Immédiates de la Conscience* (1889), (Paris, 1946), pp. 16 ff. Perry, in *Thought*, vol. 2, pp. 599 ff., made a comparison between the testimonies of the two thinkers which showed that they developed their fundamental ideas independently.
7. Franz Brentano, *Psychologie vom Empirischen Standpunkte*, (Leipzig, 1874), p. 221. Cf. also A. Horwicz, *Psychologische Analysen auf Physiologischer Grundlage* vol. 2/2, (Magdeburg, 1878), p. 2.
8. Cf. Husserl, *Ideen*, vol. 1, particularly pages 61, 69, 85, 163 ff., 168, 245 ff. according to the pages given in the margin in the first edition.
9. Perry, *Thought*, vol. 2, p. 78. Perry discusses neither the ideas of Brentano and Horwicz, nor those of Husserl in connection with the theories of James. This, considering the great similarity and James' quotations, is incomprehensible. Once more, because according to Perry, James' doctrine of experientialism and his radical empiricism, are philosophical applications of his doctrine concerning the stream of consciousness; Perry, *Thought*, vol. 2, p. 77 n.

10. William James, *Psychology, Briefer Course,* (New York, 1893), pp. 150 ff. This, as the author tells us was a shortened edition of *Principles,* accomplished principally by means of scissors and paste. It is noteworthy, however, that the scissors removed one of the five characteristics that the *Principles* attribute to the stream of consciousness. Cf. p. 64 in the present work and also *Talks to Teachers,* pp. 15 ff. about the stream of consciousness.

11. There is difficulty with the translation of this term because of a fundamental ambiguity in James of the precise meaning of the term. According to Linschoten, the term may mean *thinking* in the narrow sense, *consciousness* in general, or even *experience* as a whole. In the Dutch text, Linschoten adopted the word *experience* almost exclusively, but when he began translating the Dutch into English, he felt more obliged to use James' quotes precisely as they were given in the original English, and consequently he left the term *thinking* in English, where in the Dutch he used *experience.* However, this made the sense of many of Linschoten's own points more ambiguous, consequently as a rule, I re-inserted the term *experience* into those quotes and paraphrasings where I thought it was necessary to convey Linschoten's own meaning more clearly. *Thinking* was left only where the context seemed to imply that it was intended in the narrow sense. The author himself refers to this difficulty in Ch. 6, vol. 1, p. 209, and Ch. 6, vol. 2, p. 236.—A.G.

12. Cf. in *A Pluralistic Universe,* pp. 395 ff. the complementary considerations concerning "the notion of reality as changing."

13. Cf. B. J. Kouwer and Hans Linschoten, *Inleiding tot de Psychologie,* 4th ed., (Assen, 1958), pp. 57 ff. for a short survey. Fundamental and unsurpassed is W. Metzger, *Psychologie,* 2nd ed., (Darmstadt, 1954).

14. Cf. J. H. van den Berg, "Het Gesprek," in J. H. van den Berg and Hans Linschoten, *Persoon en Wereld,* (Utrecht, 1953), p. 145.

15. Cf. Erwin Straus, *Der Archimedische Punkt,* (Utrecht, 1957), particularly pp. 485 ff.

16. It is indeed useful to make thought-models as plastic as possible. This precisely is the advantage of a model. But this procedure shows clearly at the same time the danger contained in every model namely that the model is taken for reality, and that reality is no longer spoken about.

17. James Mill, *Analysis of The Phenomena of The Human Mind,* vol. 1, (London, 1869), p. 264.

18. Wundt, *Grundriss der Psychologie,* pp. 110 ff.

19. Cf. above, p. 33.

20. Cf. Wundt, *Grundriss,* pp. 45 ff.; *Grundzüge,* 6th ed., vol. 1, pp. 398 ff.

21. Locke, *Essay,* Bk. I, ch. I, §8.

22. *Ibid.,* Bk. II, ch. 8, §8.

23. *Ibid.*, Bk. IV, ch. 21, §4.

24. Cf. in George Berkeley, *Three Dialogues between Hylas and Philonous*, (London, 1910), the last part of the first dialogue for an interesting and instructive dialogue about that point.

25. Locke, *Essay*, Bk. I, ch. 1, §8.

26. *Ibid.*, Bk. I, ch. 2, §15.

27. *Ibid.*, Bk. II, ch. 11, §17.

28. *Ibid.*, Bk. II, ch. 11, §15.

29. *Ibid.*, Bk. II, ch. 1, §3.

30. *Ibid.*, Bk. II, ch. 2, §1.

31. Lawrence Sterne, *Tristram Shandy*, vol. 1, (London, 1900), p. 76.

32. Herman Ebbinghaus, *Grundzüge der Psychologie*, Bd. 1, ed. by K. Bühler, 4th ed., (Leipzig, 1919), p. 678: "Wenn beliebige seelische Gebilde einmal gleichzeitig oder in näher Aufeinanderfolge das Bewusstsein erfüllt haben, so ruft hinterher die Wiederkehr einiger Glieder ds frühren Erlebnisses Vorstellungen auch der übrigen Glieder hervor, ohne dass für sie die ursprünglichen Ursachen gegeben zu sein brauchen." Cf. also my inaugural address: *A Gentle Force*, (Groningen, 1957).

33. Cf. George Berkeley, *A Treatise Concerning The Principles of Human Knowledge*, (London, 1910), Part I, 1.

34. Locke, *Essay*, Bk. II, ch. 8, §8.

35. Berkeley, *A Treatise Concerning the Principles of Human Knowledge*, Part I, p. 6.

36. Johannes Müller, *Handbuch der Physiologie des Menschen*, Bd. 2/2, (Koblenz, 1838). One can find the theory in the "nothwendige Vorbegriffe" (necessary pre-concepts) for the physiology of the senses, pp. 249–275. In fact Charles Bell had proposed that theory earlier, in his *Idea of A New Anatomy of The Brain*, privately published in 100 copies in 1811. However, as we shall show, that theory had been prepared for a long time and it was first disseminated in an explicit form by Müller. Hence it should continue to bear his name. Cf. for its history R. Weinmann, *Die Lehre von den Spezifischen Sinnes Energien*, (Hamburg, 1895).

37. Quoted by K. E. Rothschuh, *Geschichte der Physiologie*, (Berlin, 1953), p. 115: "Dem Verfasser ist die Seele nur eine besondere Form des Lebens unter den mannigfachen Lebensformen, welche Gegenstand der physiologischen Untersuchung sind, er hegt daher die Überzeugung, dass die physiologische Untersuchung in ihren letzten Resultaten selbst psychologisch sein müsse."

38. Cf. Heinz Werner, *Einführung in die Entwicklungspsychologie*, (Leipzig, 1926), or the English edition: *Comparative Psychology of Mental Development*, (New York, 1948). In relation to the present

problem, cf. particularly: "Untersuchungen über Empfindung und Empfinden," *Z. Psychol.*, vol. 114, 1930, pp. 152–166.

39. Cf. the excellent survey of K. Koffka, *Principles of Gestalt Psychology*, (London, 1935), pp. 211 ff.

40. Regarding the *phenomena of constancy* which were also pointed out by gestalt psychology, cf. Hans Linschoten, "Anthropologische Eragen zur Raumproblematik," *Stud. generale*, vol. 2, 1958, pp. 86 ff.

41. Boring, "Human Nature *vs.* Sensation," p. 310.

42. Cf. *Principles*, II, p. 33 n. in which he quotes Helmholtz, *Tonempfindungen* I: "Sensations are what we call the impression on our senses, in so far as they come to our consciousness as states of our own body; especially of our nervous apparatus."

43. Namely in Part II, pp. 68 and 640. The Index wrongly mentions the first as I, p. 68.

44. Rothschuh, *Geschichte der Physiologie*, p. 124: Bidder, Bischoff, Du Bois Reymond, E. Brucke, J. L. R. Claparede, E. Haeckel, Helmholtz, Henle, Reichert, Remak, Schultze, Schwann, von Vierordt, Virchow. According to the Index, Helmholtz is quoted 25 times, Henle and Vierordt each three times. With the exception of the quotation of Helmholtz in Note 41, only *one* of Vierordt's quoted passages stands in a distant connection with the essential content of Müller's theory (*Principles*, II, p. 154).

45. James, *Psychology, Briefer Course*, pp. 11 ff.

46. Johannes Müller, *Zur Vergleichenden Physiologie des Gesichtssinnes des Menschen und der Thiere*, (Leipzig, 1826), p. 55.

47. Müller, *Handbuch der Physiologie des Menschen*, Bd. II/2, p. 268.

48. James here repeats the term he quoted from Ladd: *Physiological Psychology*. Cf. the quotation in *Principles*, II, p. 31.

49. James, *Psychology, Briefer Course*, p. 12.

50. Cf. *Principles*, I, p. 689: ". . . of 'images reproduced,' and 'claiming to represent,' and 'put together by a unifying actus,' I have been silent, because such expressions . . . signify nothing."

51. Carl Stumpf, *Erscheinungen und Psychische Funktionen*, (Berlin, 1907), pp. 16 ff.

52. William James, "The Knowing of Things Together," *Psychol. Rev.*, vol. 2, 1895, pp. 119 ff.

53. James, *Talks to Teachers*, p. 17.

54. *Ibid.*, pp. 20 ff.

55. Wilhelm Wundt, "Über Psychische Causalitat und das Princip des Psychologischen Parallelismus," *Philos. Stud.*, vol. 10, 1894, p. 123: "durch die Annahme von Verbindungsprocessen zwischen den Empfindungselementen ersetzt werden müsse."

IV LANGUAGE, EXPERIENCE, REALITY

1. The Problem

We have noted more than once that the function of language is an important object of James' psychological study. On the one hand, he saw that language can seriously seduce us, that a psychologist might be led by it to mistake for true realities the mental (psychic) realities *as expressed in words by language*. On the other hand, as we have seen, James considered language as a creative moment in the constitution of reality itself, of reality in general. We are thus in the presence of an extraordinary problem.

To let wordless reality speak by expressing it in words—at the risk of "falsifying it"—is one thing. But it is another thing to note that reality is enriched and developed by the process of expressing it in words, that it is, literally, first by expression in words that reality can be *named* and discerned as such. For this makes the question about the "falsification" through the expression in words particularly urgent.

But there is a third difficulty. It is proper to man to express thoughts in words, and verbal expression is connected with experience, with the reality man experiences. Human reality is not only a verbalized reality, it is a reality of things that "speak" and signify; it is a world in virtue of a meaningful interconnection.

These questions James does not treat systematically, but only in a fragmentary way. We shall try to bring them together by asking ourselves: how are language, experience and reality inter-related according to James?

2. *The Seduction of Language as a Semantic Problem*

Is it not natural for us to accept, says James, that a thing that we designate by *one* word is also known to us by means of *one* single phenomenon of consciousness? (I, 236). But he asks the question in order to give a *negative* answer to it. Here we notice the misleading influence of language. When we describe what appears in consciousness we do it usually by naming the phenomenon involved. And at the same time we incorrectly assume that the phenomenon of consciousness is like the object (I, 194 ff.). If a thing is round its perception must be round too; if the object is divisible its perception must be divisible. This is because we fall prey to the seduction of language.

We then develop a mythology that is based upon the organization and structure of language. Language is "made" not by psychologists nor for psychologists, but by and for people who generally are interested only in the things that are around them (I, 236). And people not only created language for practical purposes but they forgot the original creativity of language.

Listeners and readers usually understand vocal sounds and written signs in an improper way; that is, they understand them passively because those sounds and signs are spoken to us within a familiar field and horizon. The meaning is taken for granted; it is self-evident and "natural." But afterwards the original contribution that is contained in word and sign is not actively re-enacted. The later contribution is lower and sedimented. Such was Husserl's reasoning, and he adds: "It is easy for us to observe that it is with this twofold problem that James is concerned."[1]

The phenomenon of consciousness, that which is found "in our inner being," is not a *thing:* conscious phenomena do not have the structure of things. They belong to a person; they are constantly changing and are taken up in a continuous stream. They are *involved* in things and precisely on that account are *not things*.

Between the things found in reality there exist numerous external relations. Between an experience and a thing there exists an inner relation, namely, that the thing becomes known through experience. James here anticipates the concept of intentional relation. It may be true that James expressed his dissatisfaction with that concept as first expressed and recorded by Brentano,[2] but it is not unreasonable to hold that he was personally of that opinion.[3] We shall return to this later.[4]

According to James experience and "conscious phenomena" are of a totally different nature than things. They are of a different kind but not in the way Descartes conceived it. James considers the soul to be a useless concept, at least for the psychologist (I, 350). And he can speak only ironically about *"actus purus* of Thought, Intellect, or Reason, all written with capitals and considered to mean something unutterably superior to any fact of sensibility whatever" (I, 245). Suffice it to mention four things here:

(1) James considers experience to be something different than things;

(2) but experience is not a mode of some spiritual *substance;*

(3) we falsify experience when we describe it by naming it according to the *things* we experience;

(4) language, however, misleadingly prompts us to do this.

The mutual relation between experience, language and things is a central problem throughout the *Principles.* And rightly so. James puts his finger on a fundamental problem of psychology. We are justified in speaking of a *fundamental semantic problem.*

Semantics is the science that studies the relations between signs and what they signify; in our case it is concerned with the relation between word and thing. It is evident that one can use any arbitrary word to signify an arbitrary thing, provided its use is determined in a definition, and the word can function within syntactical rules. We call language a system of words that is governed by semantic and syntactical rules. We make use of a language not only in daily life but also in the sciences, and we must make a *formal* distinction between a "scientific" language and our common daily language, even though the two might be *materially* identical. Thus the proposition "there was a great tension" has two totally different meanings in those two languages. More rigid semantics are required in a scientific language than in daily conversation. The meaning of a word must be determined so as to avoid all ambiguity and it must convey that meaning as simply as possible. The latter is particularly easy when the word can be "exemplified" by pointing the finger at it: *"this* is a chair, *that* is round, *this* is running, *that* is a voltmeter." Here the semantic relation is made clear by *pointing to* something. But it is evident that this is not enough. In most cases it is not enough to know that this is a voltmeter, but we must also be able to explain *what* it is, *how* it operates, etc.

We then give a *definition,* that is, in order to define the meaning of a word we make use of other words, for example "a voltmeter is an instrument for measuring." But this has meaning only when it is clear to us what an "instrument for measuring" is, as in "an instrument to determine the size"; and this definition in turn brings up new demands.

As soon as we begin to define, we make use of a syntax of terms which also need to be defined. Now it is the ideal of a scientific language that all definitions could, as far as possible, be traced back to "pointing to" things. This means only that a science tries to base its language on phenomena that can be *pointed out,* on phenomena that, literally, require no *explanation,* on phenomena that are so close at hand that it is sufficient to point them out. Hence it desires to have phenomena that are perceptible, that we can see, hear, touch, taste or smell.

This suffices for our present tentative orientation. But it is clear that psychology must be constantly in a state of timidity in so far as it is occupied with experiences. For the only things it can define by pointing to things are precisely the "contents" of experience and particularly those of perception. And so one is prompted to engage in "content psychology" while an "act-psychology" or an "experience-psychology" are faced with major difficulties. For the "things" with which it deals cannot readily be pointed to, because they *are not* things, qualities nor properties of things. Soul, spirit, intellect, feeling, joy, experience, can be used verbally only when they are, *literally,* trans-lated. Here phenomena acquire a certain consistency only by being defined in words, by receiving a certain delimitation which they do not possess in their natural condition. Psychology speaks about things which have already been "verbalized." It is then a language of the second order and it is constantly facing the task of first tracing back to direct experience any verbalized experience it desires to examine.

3. Psychology as Metalanguage

When we speak about a syntactical or semantic system this implies that we are using a language of a "higher order," a *metalanguage.* "The student is going home" is a sentence in English, a language of the first order. But the previous sentence in which we said *something about* "the student is going home" is a sentence that belongs to a metalanguage. Similarly the language of a grammar that teaches the rules for good English is a metalanguage. This goes to show that a language *is* not once and for all a metalanguage, but that it functions as such only when we speak about an (other) language. Hence a metalanguage is one whose terms are connected with "objects" by semantic rules, which objects are themselves terms in another language and are therefore connected to their proper objects by their own semantic rules.

The problem raised by James can then be formulated in these terms. Psychology speaks of phenomena, and to that extent is a (scientific) language. But the phenomena of which it speaks are already themselves phenomena that are contained in a language, but these phenomena do not have to exist in the way that they are contained in the language. James defends the thesis that the mental (psychic) phenomena do not really exist in the way they are called in language, because language is directed toward things.

The psychologist is thus exposed to the danger of neglecting the phenomena that should occupy his attention and of speaking about a purely fictitious reality. This is what happened with the representations and contents in association psychology. And the same mistake could be made in modern, strongly "substantizing" (substantiverende) schools such as psychoanalysis. In such a system one handles verbal constructions that transform mental reality into a *pattern* that falsifies the original; a pattern that works with psychic "things" and with "energies" that things exercise upon one another. It would certainly be worthwhile investigating to what extent various psychological systems have become entangled and caught in their own patterns and confine themselves to the study of the possibilities contained in the pattern; possibilities which they themselves have put into it and that are no longer directly connected with the original phenomena.

But we are not now concerned with examining the inadequacy of particular systems of psychology. James suggests, in a more general way, that psychology is, *of necessity*, a metalanguage. This is so because the phenomena of the stream of experience (at least in some measure) cannot *be* expressed in words, and yet they are already verbalized before psychology speaks later on about the phenomena of the second order. In this way a psychology that wishes to start from direct experience is already interfered with in its very foundations. For it is not merely a question whether particular phenomena have been improperly formulated but if they can be formulated at all.

4. Language as a Naming of Facticity

According to James, if experiences, wholly or in part, cannot be expressed in words, things can. I can give names to things. Things are, as we call them, discrete units that have a defined closed-in character. They also justify a language. More than that: they point to the origin of a language. Here James' thought is rather positivistic. At least it seems that way. Let us begin by examining what is considered "self-evident" from the standpoint of a positivistic opinion, regarding the origin and function of language.

A world exists; the world in which we find ourselves, which we see, in which we have developed as individuals and as a species. The world had been in existence for a long time before men or animals appeared and before there was any sort of life on this planet. The world is a reality. It is to this reality existing in history that language also belongs. Animals appear, and finally man, who makes special kinds of sounds, *language*-sounds, that is, those that have an abstract meaning. But this too is a reality. If a Martian of superior intelligence were to visit this earth for the purpose of studying man, he would be justified in writing home that he had discovered a species of beings that makes use of language.

Language then has come with man. However, animals that preceded man on earth do react to meanings. For we notice that particular events produce changes in animal behavior. When a chick runs around looking for food and a vulture suddenly appears above, it hastily and chirpingly seeks shelter under its mother's wing. Whatever the way we try to explain it, one thing is certain: a definite, specific event results in a specific change in the animal's behavior. We can also say that the troublesome event has *meaning* in the life of the chick; it has meaning for its behavior. Behavior is attuned to such meanings. We can leave out of consideration whether the animal itself has knowledge of it.

At this stage let us listen to a passage from the work of H. J. Pos.

> When highly developed vertebrates began to walk upright, the larynx developed into an organ which modulates outgoing breath transforming it into sounds of language. A new branch in the life of meanings had thus arisen: from then on sounds would be able to take the place of what until then had been the object of speechless memory, recognition and reaction. Much had thus been gained although the dangers were not insignificant. Much later would come linguists who would objectivate language and fix it by means of signs. And philosophers would teach that speech and words are fundamental in regard to reality, that, in fact, they call the silent world into being. Are these not, clearly, the illusions of those who let themselves be captured by 'meaning' as if no meaning or significance existed before the existence of language?[5]

Language is a reality and it must be understood on the basis of the reality of the world and the reality of man who produces vocal language sounds and also does something with them. Man makes use of them in order to handle something without having to use his hands. This he does by attaching a meaning to speech-sounds. He gives names to things enabling himself to deal with them in a new way. He can handle them in the absence of the things. Now he can ask his slave or his wife: "bring me the axe." He no longer has to run and get it himself.

Now man can designate things, point to them by means of signs. He does not thereby create a new dimension in the world. Everything remains as of old but what was already there he now can handle with greater ease. This is somewhat the way James describes it, too. Words are directed to things for the simple reason that men who fashioned the words are interested in things (II, 356 ff.). In this James concurs with Stuart Mill according to whom names express a faith in regard to things. Words are names of the *things themselves.*[6] Reality is "named" in language. What we find in the world, or produce, is given a name so that we can henceforth represent the thing by a name.

5. Facticity as Experienced Facticity

But how can James adhere to such a view? For the reality that is "named" is an experienced reality. What is given is experienced as given and hence refers to experience. More over, we shall see that, according to James, reality too *is* experience; a "substantive" experience, it is true, but experience all the same. Things as directly given to us must not be mistaken for objects that are absolutely independent from man. Objectivity, exteriority and extension James called qualities of experienced things. His quasi-positivism once more refers us to experience.

When Stuart Mill says that words are names of the things themselves, he thereby puts a period and finis after a way of conceiving things that was predominant for a long time in empiricism. This view we find already in Hobbes when he declares:

A name is a word taken at pleasure to serve for a mark which may raise in our mind a thought like to some thought we had before, and which being pronounced to others, may be to them a sign of what thought the speaker had, or had not before in his mind.[7]

In this way of thinking the word does not refer to a thing that is *outside* us but to a phenomenon of consciousness that is *within* us; it refers not to the object but to the "thought." The word is clearly an expression of something that takes place in the mind. Hence we read also in Locke:

> The use of words is to be sensible marks of ideas, and the ideas they stand for are their proper and immediate signification . . . But though words, as they are used by men, can properly and immediately signify nothing but the ideas that are in the mind of the speaker, yet they in their thoughts give them a secret reference to two other things. First, also of other men with whom they communicate.

Secondly,

> because men would not be thought to talk barely of their own imaginations, but of things as they really are, therefore they often suppose their words to stand also for the reality of things.[8]

We have then to reconcile two views. On the one hand that of Pos and Stuart Mill whom we have quoted as two examples of a widely ramified way of thinking: words indicate (real) things; and they borrow their meaning from things. On the other hand there is the opinion of Hobbes and Locke: Words indicate phenomena of consciousness; they derive their meaning from experience. But is experience not an experience of things? Surely we experience things; but not everything we experience is a thing in the sense of Pos and Stuart Mill!

If we draw experience into the relation of word and thing we are forced to admit that this relation is one of words to *experienced* things. Our language, our daily speech, does not speak of a reality that is divorced from and independent of all human view of it, but it speaks of the meaningful world-for-us, the experienced world. And this world is full of human subjectivity. This too is accepted by James: the world is truly malleable and it is waiting for us to put the finishing touches to it.[9] James himself thus suggests a widening of the original problem.

We must, therefore, ask ourselves to what extent the world as we experience it, is not also the "product" of experience itself, of an experience that, among other things, uses words for the purpose of producing this world. In this case speech and language perhaps are not fundamental (primary) in regard to reality, but they are nevertheless more important than Pos thought them to be.

By means of words we explain and make clear our experiences to ourselves, to others and with others. At the same time, words bind the experiences together in things, figures and forms (gestalts), and open our world as something actually given in our experience. Did not James himself point out the pragmatic character of language? Evidently, this characteristic that leads to "falsification" in psychology, also has a meaningful role in pre-psychological life.

6. Bergson's Views About Social Life and Reality

In this respect there is a fundamental agreement between James and Bergson. In all probability, says Bergson,[10] an animal does not, as is the case with us human beings, know an outside world that is distinct from itself nor one that is the same for all conscious beings, as we picture it to ourselves. There is a world around me and I am sure of it, and I am convinced that I have this world in common with other men. Why is this so? The inclination to think of things as existing outside us is the same inclination that prompts us to live in society and converse in it. To the extent that social life becomes more fully developed there is also greater emphasis on the "objectivation" of our phenomena of consciousness as being phenomena of an outer world.

Conscious phenomena are gradually transformed into objects or things; they not only become separate from one another but also from us. And the means by which that objectivation (making objective) of the subjectivity is accomplished is language. It is language that created the possibility of "objectivating" the "données immédiates de la conscience" (the immediate data of consciousness) into things that, for all of us as members of society, have an individual existence.

But here language does not mean a mere expression of what one has experienced; it means *primarily*, to express *together*, to speak together. Language is then not only a result of social human life but it constitutes the foundation of that social life to the extent that the social milieu in which we live together, the world of life, is put into shape by and in language.

In this way does Bergson defend the view which Pos discarded in the passage we have recalled. He maintains that language and words are "primary" with respect to reality, at least with respect to the reality that is *ours,* in which we live *before* every notional construction of a completely independent *physical* reality. This Pos denies; there is first, he maintains, a reality; in this reality a man comes into being; a man makes sounds and uses them to designate things. And this again is a reality. If sounds signify things it is because there are things. This Bergson refuses to admit; the things that are "already there" are things as people speaking together see them. That they see them that way comes precisely from the fact that they are *speaking* men.

Here are two views that are perhaps not totally opposed to each other but they are at least juxtaposed. Words merely translate what already exists, this is the first view. The other says that the word, as social word, has beforehand first established that reality. When we now ask ourselves which view James adopted, we apparently have to say that he accepted both. On the one hand he chooses the view of Pos which is that of "natural science"; on the other he accepts the way of thinking of Bergson which is fundamentally identical with his own. And this is so fundamental for him that it is only on the basis of the latter way of thinking that James develops his ideas regarding "real things." These ideas constitute an important element of James' psychological system.[11]

7. Naïveté as Partisanship

The question we must now put to ourselves is whether the impression we have in our daily lives of our relation to the world is a correct one. For we know already that our daily concepts of our relation to the world are in many respects not in harmony with what the sciences tell us about it. We know that much of what is given us in perception does not exist that way in "reality." Not only the secondary qualities, but the particular emphases in certain situations, and the way the meanings of things speak to us in perception cannot simply be attributed to reality as a reality that exists in itself.

We know on the other hand that the motivation of our behavior is not always "objective" and "rational"; on the contrary, we start rather from prejudices and uncritical opinions; we react to a situation as seen from our own actual standpoint. There is partiality in our naïve view of the world. Partiality or partisanship here does not mean that we knowingly and on purpose act from a definite standpoint we have chosen, but it means being party to what is taking place, to be involved in what is happening. Is it not characteristic of what we call an impartial, factual and objective attitude that we are in a certain sense standing aside and keeping at a distance from the problem? And don't we say about those who thus stand aside that they are insensible and show a lack of feeling in the presence of an actual human situation? And yet we expect of them a calm and sober-minded judgment.

But both the naive partiality and the deliberate aloofness we show in our daily lives are contained within a broader species of naiveté in a natural partiality. We are "party" not only individually but socially. Reality about which we speak in our daily lives is a social reality. When I tell someone that he thinks unrealistically, that he indulges in fantasies, I am not referring to a metaphysical or physical reality in itself, but to the daily social and human reality. After all, we can diagnose a case as "hallucination" only because we who consider ourselves sound in mind, do not see what is seen by the patient. Perhaps there is something when the patient sees something which does not exist for us. In any case that something exists *really* for him to the extent that he must take account of it in his conduct, although it does not exist in our social world.

When we say about somebody that he has hallucinations, we express thereby a social, but partial, communality of men among themselves; we then uphold a social idea and image of the world that is not necessarily in accord with what we can think of as an absolute reality. Objectivity, a term frequently heard nowadays, means in the first place nothing more than we do not wish to be wrong, we *all together;* or, in reverse, we call objective that about which we agree and that is valid for everybody.

In the passage of Bergson quoted above it was said that it is precisely society that establishes that partiality or partisanship. It is our common, social interest that forces us to live in a social and objective world and we could also say that forces us to uphold the social naiveté. For naiveté means only that one takes things as they present themselves in the first uncritical experience, whatever the meaning may be in ordinary life. Naiveté is upholding the ordinary, the customary, as self-evident, as "natural," as that which "is as it is." When we say that the world consists of things which we handle and with which we deal, this is naiveté. It is also naiveté when we declare: "there are things; those things are named by us; language is an achievement; language makes it possible for us to grasp a thing that is not there, but that thing, has to be somehow already there." Naturally! Imagine for a moment that everybody who speaks thereby creates new things . . . likewise when we think or make poetry, ideas and images precede the words that give expression to them.[12]

Phenomenology begins where that social partiality, the naiveté which Husserl called "a natural attitude" is broken through. It begins as a suspension of what is a matter of course. It begins with a *crisis,* a judgment and distinction, that is completed in a *reflection,* bent, as it were, back upon our own partiality.

Of this partiality we shall speak later as of a "doxical confidence," the ever necessary "faith" in the reality of the things amidst which we live. To "doxical confidence" belongs also the fact that we possess an "interiority" and that we can speak about this interiority as though it were an inner space. So long as we are all doing this but remain aware of the fact that it is a manner of speaking, there should be no occasion for misunderstanding. But it is a different matter when the science of experience dogmatically confirms the doxical language, when critical thought takes over the habit of trite commonness as representing self-evident reality. This is the reproach James addresses to the psychologist. The psychologist, he tells us, incorrectly makes a thing of inner happenings. Or more precisely, the psychologist assumes naive use of language to his own detriment.

We are more or less justified in making such assumptions in daily life. We say for example, "there is something in the way, something is blocking me." Such expressions describe quasi-things. It needs little thought to realize that there is here no real thing, no rock or piece of wood blocking my way. But when talking in this manner we do not pay attention to that; we say things through habit and do not ask ourselves what is the original and true meaning of those expressions with respect to the proper nature of an experience that is translated in such words as "something is blocking the way."

Expressions like that are crystallized meanings, *sediments* that have acquired *doxical value* in their state of sedimentation so as to mean: not only is there something wrong in my mind or my will but there is some*thing* there that is in the way; not only do we feel a constriction in our throat but there is some*thing* sticking in here; anger *wells up in me; passion overwhelms me;* a certain *thought* irresistibly oppresses me . . . It is only one step from that doxical self-evidence to the dogmatic self-evidence of content-psychology that sees consciousness as a container to be filled with forms and shapes, with *things* that follow one another, repress and push aside one another . . . *the* feelings, *the* ideas, *the* memories, *the* representations, *the* sensations, etc., thus arise. It is this dogmatizing of doxical self-evidences that constitutes a threat to psychology:

> Every hour of human life could contribute to the picture gallery; and this is the only fault that one can find with such descriptive industry—where is it going to stop? Ought we to listen forever to verbal pictures of what we have already in concrete form in our own breasts?[13]

Is it then not necessary for us to speak of the *impotence* of language, of its inability to express experience? Let us understand well what is meant when this question is brought up once more. That daily life "falsifies" experience for practical reasons does not matter much. It happens to be one of the ways in which a social world develops. So argue James and Bergson. But, they add, it is a falsification all the same, and one in which the psychologist, in his study of experience, should not lend a hand.

8. The Impotence of Language

Language gives form and shape where a form is inadequate. Language clothes interior events with a structure and form that these interior happenings do not have in themselves. James and Bergson are in agreement regarding this point.

According to Bergson,[14] perceptions, sensations, emotions and thoughts have a twofold aspect. At one time they are clearly defined, precise, but impersonal. At another they are confused, infinitely changeable and inexpressible, because language cannot master them without fixing their mobility; nor can it adjust them to its daily structure without allowing them to degenerate into something that is socially common. But social life, after all, is more meaningful to us than our own inner life. And so we are instinctively inclined to give fixity to our impressions so that they can be expressed in language.

By this, however, we confuse the emotion itself which is in a constant process of becoming, with its outward and permanent object, and above all, we confuse it with the word that designates that object. Experiences appear to me as things as soon as I isolate and name them, and yet there is in the human soul nothing but movement and progress, nothing but change. If I do not notice that every repeated sensation is also a change, it is because I grasp that sensation by means of the object, by means of the word that translates that object.

This view is truly in accord with James who describes the stream of experience as "one unanalysed bloom of confusion" (I, 496). But mankind as a whole is agreed to a great extent as to what will be observed and named and what will not (I, 289). But it is senseless to express the stream itself in words. We try in vain to describe in concepts and words what at the same time transcends both concepts and words. We cannot turn back and return to life by means of speech.[15] Language is impotent.

When I ask someone to describe precisely what is taking place in him, he remains silent. What he would have to say is: I can no longer grasp anything, or: how can I express that? Everything is running together in utter confusion. The Wurzburg school has discovered or re-discovered or, in any case, described a whole series of mental experiences that possess that remarkable ambiguous character of mobility, of non-fixedness.[16] Bühler, for instance, speaks of "Zwischenerlebnisbeziehungen" (between-experience-relations). These can only be described as implications, or more literally, side reflections.

There is for example the *knowledge* that we have had this or that thought before; there is the *feeling* that this or that sentence is incorrectly constructed. These are ideas we have when we express—or even do not express—something, but they actually co-determine the meaning of the spoken word. They are, sometimes, ideas that intermingle with what we hear expressed by another, but this way of stating the fact is already incorrect, for it is not an idea that joins another idea; it is a sudden invasion of a complex of different interrelated meanings that is imbued with emotion.

Messer speaks somewhat in the same sense saying that those particular ideas are surrounded by a "Sphärenbewusstsein" (sphere of awareness). Ach introduced the term "Bewusstheit" (being aware) but it is a term hard to define. We could say: an implicit awareness of meaning. We hear something, someone unfolds an argument and we say: yes, there is something to that. But what? Try to describe it! We then realize how difficult it is. How *empty* in general are the notes we have taken! What we have heard is not in them. What we wanted to record has flown away. There was something in the whole argumentation, or even in one way of formulating it, even in an intonation. A little later we realize that what we wanted to fix and retain in words has disappeared.

This constitutes a great difficulty for psychology. For this science would like to know more about these modes of experience. But even if it learns more about them it is faced with the difficulty of giving proper expression to them. This applies particularly to phenomena that are not attached to objects but belong to situations and personal relations such as: joy, sorrow, excitement, etc. But *what kind* of sorrow? The sorrow of someone who did not win the great prize in a competition? That of a mother who has lost her child?

One by one experiences come to us that have a common keynote, otherwise we could not call them all by the same name, and yet we know that one sorrow is not the same as another. When we compare the sorrow of a mother who has lost her child with that of a child that has lost a piece of candy, how great the difference between those two sorrows though they have some note in common. And this note we call sorrow. And so we can speak about them and refer to them. We can say: look, Johnny cries, he has sorrow. But when it is a question of describing or expressing our experiences, we repeat over and over again that we cannot find any words, that we are speechless with joy or sorrow.

What does this mean? Does it mean that we are filled, are so overwhelmed by a feeling or emotion that we can no longer say even one word? This is partly true. But being speechless also means that we realize that there are no words to express *this*. Hence we have always to tell one another: you don't understand what I feel. The other replies: I understand you very well, you have sorrow. Both sayings are true. It is true, on the one hand, that what I intend to express, that experience itself, cannot be expressed, cannot be put fully into words. On the other hand, the meaning of the experience in our relation from man to man is completely exhausted in the words "I have sorrow." Has language then anything to do with strictly individual, personal experience? This question can be raised not only in respect to feelings; we can ask ourselves whether anything can ever be totally rendered and expressed in a word so that its concrete meaning, its full experiential content is completely exhausted.

It is then a matter of what is strictly personal, of which the poet Kloos spoke when he said he was seeking for the most individual expression of a most individual emotion. But words are social, general, schematic. Words do not take in what is particular and individual. Stirner said similarly: "We say about God: 'Names do not name you.' This is true also of myself: no concept (*Begriff*) expresses me, nothing that is proposed as ex-

pressing my being exhaustively says what I am; those expressions
are mere names."[17] This is true not only for Stirner personally; it
is true for every individual, for anything one might fancy. The
whole rich content of experience is unutterable; and Rilke in his
Ninth Elegy has expressed this experience that is well-known by
all:

Alas, but the other relation—
what can be taken across? Not the art of seeing, learnt here
so slowly, and nothing that's happened here. Nothing at all.
Sufferings, then. Above all, the hardness of life,
the long experience of love; in fact
purely untellable things.[18]

This inability of language to express the unutterable is not
limited to the field of the individual-concrete, to flitting thoughts
or fading emotions, but it is a fact much more general and, as a
consequence, language divides and breaks unity. All this is manifest in Fink's endeavor to make Parmenides' philosophy accessible from within.

Whatever has a name is already particularized, is isolated, is cut
off from the whole, appears in a delimited singularity. To be
named is equivalent to being particularized. What is one, whole and
sound and has in itself no division or dismemberment is downright
unnameable, unutterable—and when we nevertheless try to express
it, through the transparency of a name, it loses the firmness and
hardness of enduring exactitude. . . .[19]

It is clear then that we must speak of the impotence of
language, of its inability to express experience. All experience
is characterized by fluidity, has the flowing, personal and changing character that James attributed to it. All experience also has
an integral character which led James to reject association theory.
What we have found up to now in the field of language is a
confirmation of the opinion of James.

9. Subjective Experience and the Tendency to Objectify

There is no conjunction or preposition, and scarcely any
subordinate clause, syntactical form, or vocal inflection in human
speech that does not express some nuance of a relation we experi-

ence between the more important objects of our consciousness. So says James (I, 245), and he continues: when we speak objectively, we are concerned with real relations of things outside of us. When we speak subjectively, the stream of our experience then follows the nuances of relations of meanings that are always innumerable. No language is capable of doing justice to all nuances: "We ought to say a feeling of *and,* a feeling of *blue* or a feeling of *cold.*" The expressions "perhaps," "it could freeze," or "it could thaw," do not express the uncertainty as something experienced, but they designate or point to an experience that still has a fluid indefiniteness, which totally disappears in the assertion: "a fifty percent chance." Here language no doubt manifests its impotence. Language manifests a tendency to objectification and hence is inadequate when it is a question of expressing the subjective element of experience.

How could we possibly seize and express in language what is constantly changing and flowing in our inner happenings? But is that inner activity really as flowing as is suggested? On this point Bergson goes farther than James.

Here, says Bergson,[20] we encounter the shadow of ourselves. We imagine that we have analyzed our feelings; in fact we have replaced reality by motionless situations that exist side by side and that are translatable into words. When, however, an audacious novelist tears apart the easily woven veil of our conventional logic, when he reveals to us underneath the juxtaposed situations an endless interaction of thousands of diverse impressions that no longer exist at the moment we name them, we are grateful to him because he knows us better than we know ourselves.

These are daring writers that Bergson has in mind, for instance a Proust, an Amiel, or a Dostoyevsky; writers who pierce the logical veneer of our conduct and give us a glimpse of all that is irrational, flowing and scarcely definable in our motives.

We can also think of one who, like Sigmund Freud, has systematized such a daring view. For the latter, the orderly life of the mind is a blanketing superstructure which hides from view what is really taking place underneath. He who confines himself to what belongs to the surface of experience, limits himself to a superficial study; only depth psychology penetrates to what lies beneath the mirror, to where the water is full of fishes and even of monsters that cannot bear the clear light of the mind. Let us have a look at a passage from Amiel, in which he tries to express the true nature of what happens inside a person:

> I feel as if I were a chameleon, a kaleidoscope, protean, variable and polarizing in all sorts of ways, fluid, virtual and hence latent, even in my manifestations, absent, even in my representation. I exist, as it were, at the molecular whirlwind that is called individual life. I perceive and am conscious of that constant metamorphosis, that irresistible moulding of existence that takes place in me. I feel the flight, the renewal, the change of all the particles of my being, of all the drops of my river, of all the radiations of my unitary energy.[21]

Is there still anything in this inner swiveling that has a form? Is there something in the fixed form that manages to bring experience into the field of thought, that still brings up the memory of the original fluidity?

According to Bergson even a description like that of Amiel remains totally inadequate. For the writer also makes use of *words*. Perhaps he does make us suspect something by means of his turns of phrase; he invites us to reflect, for through his choice of words and expressions he lays bare the contradictions that are contained in what takes place in us. But they remain words. Even the description of what is irrational must falter because of the fundamental inadequacy of words.

Are experiences then so foreign to the reality of things and words? Does this conclusion not bring us much greater difficulties than those that led to it? From the idea that what is mental (psychic) cannot really be expressed, it is only one step to spiritualism that looks upon the mind as a guest who is on a visit in an unreal world; or to irrationalism that speaks of "the mind as the adversary of the soul" (*Geist als Widersacher der Seele*).[22]

James does not go so far as that. Although it is impossible to express in words any experience as it is in itself, the word is not *simply* a falsification. If there is a word it is because it has a function. And words are there *precisely because* experience itself has no word structure but *needs* to be translated into words in the society in which men live. Words are signs of a human community and thus, in a certain sense, make man a man. And we can emphasize even more James' appreciation of the value of the word, although he himself shows hesitation: human experience itself is at the same time characterized by that which is achieved in the process of expressing it in words. Language itself is a constitutive element of experience.

10. Experience Prompts Formulation

We must not generalize immediately, but we are permitted to declare at this time that James, at least in some cases, ascribes to language a constitutive function in experience. He thus mentions, for instance, the reality which an inner experience can acquire through the word:

> The opinion so stoutly professed by many, that language is essential to thought, seems to have this much of truth in it, that all our inward images tend invincibly to attach themselves to something sensible, so as to gain in corporeity and life. Words serve this purpose, gestures serve it, stones, straws, chalk marks, anything will do. As soon as anyone of these things stands for the idea, the latter seems to be more real (II, 305).

We know that when we want to come to a decision we often experience the presence of an inner struggle of motives in our hesitation, and we settle the matter best of all by putting into words *what is* what, what we actually want, even if it were only to see in our formulation that we do not really want what we have expressed in words. Meanings we have lived through, however vaguely defined or flowing into one another, seemingly need a *"form"* nevertheless, and prefer a substrate in which they become materialized. Experience then can prompt formulation.

James himself makes use here of the terms *corporeity* and *life,* and he thus implicitly holds that a meaning exists first by means of one or other incorporation, by acquiring a shape in something that can be seen or observed. That which is "pure" meaning or a "pure" experience, cannot be well represented. A feeling, which I say I cannot describe in words, is also, as feeling, involved in a situation.

Perhaps in history we have conceived the mental (psychic), the world of experience, too much as an immanent sphere, as something that exists in itself and within man. Perhaps we have too often left out of consideration the fact that all that man experiences is concerned with objects, with the world. We are then less astonished to find that inner experience needs something that will enable it to become materialized. A pure experience is, however "pure" it might be, the experience of *something;* it is, in this sense, the "animation" of a substrate. Meanings do not exist independently of their incorporation, as purely spiritual entities.

Husserl, in one of his later writings, developed a view regarding the so-called "ideal objects" (ideale Gegenstände) that can shed some light on this subject.[23] The mathematician works with abstract "things" such as *the* triangle, *the* number four, etc. We can ask ourselves what those "things," those "universal objects" (*Allgemeingegenstände*) are. But we are here principally interested in how they continue to exist. And this is evidently by their being incorporated in writing and signs. They were "thought out" once. By contemplating, and thinking about concrete triangles, we have arrived at *the* triangle; about this "universal triangle" we can say the things that are true of all concrete, actual triangles. But can we say that such a "general object" (Allgemeingegenstand), that I obtained from experience, and that expresses its essence when I behold any concrete triangle, also *exists?* It certainly has a certain kind of being, as something general, about which I can say something. But I do not admit that *the* triangle floats around somewhere like a mathematical ghost that has its own independent existence. If it does "exist" and continues to exist, it is because of the sign that fixes it. By this it is placed into time and space and it can be found again, even when Euclid is gone and can no longer speak to us.

Husserl tells us:

> It is the important function of writing that it makes possible the lasting objectification of ideal 'objects' (Gegenstande) in the form of a 'virtuality' (Virtualität). Being documented in writing, the 'object' is virtually 'in the world,' it *exists* in the sense that it can be observed, seen, over and over again by means of the sign.[24]

Must we not repeat the same reasoning with respect to the example James gave us a moment ago? What is interiorly experienced gets its reality by the word; it is objectified by this word, and thus at least, to a certain extent, becomes accessible to others. My experience receives an existence by the fact that I communicate, or can communicate it to others. For it is now expressed, materialized in the "matter" of a vocal sound. It needs to be *formed,* even when it is *not* spoken out, when I do not in fact express what I experience, but merely have the experience. Our experience, though unexpressed, can thus anticipate the possibility of being expressed and thereby acquire an inner structure and articulation which, according to James, neither belongs to nor is due to "pure experience."

But we are faced here with one of the ambiguities of James' system for which he has given no solution. Language, he tells us, is a system of signs that differ from the things signified but are capable of evoking these things (II, 356). The word "apple" has nothing to do with the fruit we pluck from the tree, but it is able to represent it. But he also says: man is well aware of his inclination to attach a sign to everything, hence to give a name to everything. By that "everything" he means "everything that actually is there." After all, is it not true that the world exists? Surely it was fully in existence when men with their inclination to give names appeared on the scene. Nevertheless, in order to *be able* to do this, in order to be able to confer a sign on all things, it is necessary that the concept of the "sign as such" should come into being (II, 357). But "the sign as such" does not *exist*. It is a *universal* that I do not find in concrete reality as I find apples, pears, chairs and men.

By the fact that someone has opened his eyes and said: look, an apple, a basketball, the moon, a globe, they are all *round;* *roundness* came into being for him. Roundness does not exist in the world as an independent thing, but it is a characteristic that I discover in things and fix by means of a word. Does James himself not teach that so-called "simple ideas" do not *of themselves* evoke similar "ideas"? The experience of a particular shade of blue does not make us think of another shade of blue, *unless* we have some particular intention in mind such as calling that particular tint by name (I, 579).

What we have noticed in one thing and then again in another, such as roundness, we take away from both things; it becomes the object of an abstract view (I, 506). But this can take place only when we see things *in this way,* if the possibility of abstraction is visible to us men; hence when we *experience* things already in a way that can be expressed in words. Similarities are not existing, pre-given, so-called things, but ways in which we order concrete things. And so we can say not only that we see the world by means of language, through the transparency of language,[25] but we can also say that we behold language in the world —or at least the world's capacity to be named. And it is precisely in that capacity of being named which belongs to things and their properties, a characteristic of our human experience, that something that is really part of our experience is expressed. When we express things in words we do not falsify experience, but we express what has been experienced in its experienced "expressibility." Would not James have agreed with the words of Gusdorf? For they say what James also believed, that the name creates the object; the name alone reaches the object transcending the lack of firmness (un-substantiality) of phenomena.[26] But it is not because words themselves have that magic effect. They translate what exists (for us): human reality.

Now is this reality always experienced reality? James rarely has a misunderstanding about this. Is then all that is taking place "in the interior" really an experience of reality? James has stepped down from the immanence of the mental. "What takes place in my interior" does not at all happen "in me." When it cannot be expressed in words, this means that the *reality* which we experience is not always capable of being expressed in words. But then the incapacity of language that is directed to things, is not based on the opposition between our interiority and the outside world, but on the structure of experienced reality. And James agreed with Bergson that it is precisely through language that the socially experienced reality comes into being. Language concretizes the fluid reality of the first experience into fixed things that can be handled. But does this say anything more than that experience seeks formulation, that it seeks to be expressed in words?

11. Language Formulates What is Formless

If experience strives for formulation, this implies that it is already disposed for being expressed in words—although perhaps not everything can be expressed in words. Let us examine whether the constitutive function of language now becomes clearer. Let us, for instance, look at the description James gives of the effort to recall a name we have forgotten:

> When I vainly try to recall the name of Spalding, my consciousness is far removed from what it is when I vainly try to recall the name of Bowles. Here some ingenious persons will say: 'How *can* the two consciousnesses be different when the terms which might make them different are not there? . . .' We can only designate the difference by borrowing the names of objects not yet in the mind (I, 251).[27]

Does James then argue against himself? How *can* the two situations of consciousness be different, when the contents by which they differ are not given? All that is given to us so long as we are fruitlessly searching is merely the pure effort itself. It is true that this seems to be different when I am seeking now for one word and then for another, but it is so only because I presume that the hiatus is determined by the word I have not yet been able to find.

This seems more complicated than it is. I am, for example, looking for the name Spalding, and at first am unable to find it, but finally find it nevertheless. I then say: I always suspected that it had to be something like this. But if we confine ourselves to the effort itself of recalling at the moment when we are seeking for something that has escaped us, then we are not capable of indicating any point in which this effort differs from the effort we made in seeking for another word.

But this shows precisely that our psychological vocabulary is absolutely insufficient and hence such pronounced differences in "hiatus-feeling" cannot even be designated. "But namelessness is compatible with existence," objects that have no name can nevertheless exist. There are, after all, numerous experiences of "hiatuses" and of emptiness that have no proper names and yet differ from one another. We usually accept that they all come down to an emptiness of consciousness and are therefore identical. But "the feeling of an absence" is totally different from an "absence of feeling." The feeling that something is not there that ought to be there, is a very intense feeling (I, 252). In the case that was described it is clearly a "word-feeling," a feeling that only a definite word is capable of solving the remarkable situation of the experience of an hiatus.

James himself, in this example, calls our attention to the fact that experience can seek for a formulation; it strives for a form, and it is "complete" only when it has attained that form. Let us compare this with some ideas of Freud.

Freud, in his theory about the unconscious, has given attention to the relation between the unconscious and the word. In one of his earliest works he distinguishes the *conscious* idea as an idea of fact (Sach) or object *including* the idea of a word that belongs to it, from the *unconscious* idea, the idea of the object alone.[28] An idea that is conscious, that I *know* about, is always the idea of something, of an object, together with the word that is connected with it and names it. According to Freud, unconscious ideas which I can*not* name and of which I have no *knowledge,* are the same object—ideas (Sachvorstellungen) but minus the ideas of the words that belong to them.

The conscious sphere, according to Freud, is the field of the person who entertains relations with the outside world, knows about himself, chooses, decides, etc. The unconscious sphere is by definition the one about which I know nothing, it is that which remains hidden underneath, the field in which the true driving forces of conduct are found. These are forces that do not appear in consciousness but that can be represented there by particular ideas.

The unconscious is the wilderness of the person; the conscious is the small piece of cultivated ground that is cleared and made free. The wild beasts that live in the wilderness simply cannot be admitted to the civilized culture-land. This is approximately the way Freud develops his mythology and it is one he has tenaciously worked out. No wonder that James remarked about Freud's ideas: "They can't fail to throw light on human nature; but I confess that he made on me personally the impression of a man obsessed with fixed ideas."[29]

When the wild beasts of the unconscious appear at the frontiers of the "culture-land," they are held up by the frontierguard and sent back. This frontierguard is the "censor." It is he who represses, prevents the contents of the unconscious from penetrating into the field of consciousness. How does this take place? Freud answers: by the fact that the censor *refuses that a translation be made* in words of the object—ideas that try to enter from the unconscious into the conscious field. We believe that Freud characterizes the passage from the unconscious to the conscious as a formulation of the formless, and the connection of this view with the reasoning of James is evident.

Elsewhere Freud gives an account of his treatment of a young woman.[30] He records the following dialogue. Freud tells his patient: "You are afraid that others will notice something about your desire and you are afraid that they will ridicule you on that account."

"Yes, I think this is so." (Her desire was that she would be able to marry her boss).

"But if you know that you loved your Director, why didn't you tell me?"

"Because I didn't know it, or rather, I did not want to know, I wanted to put it out of my mind."

Freud adds in a footnote: this is now what we must understand by repression. To know something without knowing it; to

know that one does not know something because one does not
want to know it, and yet not to have this knowledge at one's disposal so that one could express it in words. Is this now to know,
or is it not to know; is it conscious or unconscious?

Under treatment this lady recovers what remained hidden for
years, even to herself. Afterwards, when it has been expressed in
words, she knows that she has known it all along, and yet she did
not know it in the sense that it could be expressed in words.
According to Lacan, "the unconscious is that part of a concrete
discourse between men, that is not at the disposal of the person
for reestablishing the continuity of his conscious conversation."[31]

We are not concerned here with the general theory of the
unconscious but with language. In this connection the "unconsciousness" of that which one is unable to say, of what is repressed, or sought again, can be understood in two ways:

(1) The "repressed unconscious" is what cannot be formulated, cannot be translated into words because I turn away from it.
The simile of the frontierguard is, after all, only a figure. Freud is
even of the opinion that repression is a constant activity, not an
occasional checking of things of which we wish to get rid.[32]
Repression then, according to Freud, is a situation in which one
holds to be unnameable that which of itself strives for formulation and expression. This unnameable something strives for formulation, for a form in conversation and in our relations and
dealings with others. When this repressed thing "influences my
behavior without my being aware of it," and another notices the
discrepancy between my expressed knowledge of my behavior
and the meaning—for me hidden—of my behavior, he says that I
am repressing something. It remains unnameable only so long as,
it strives for expression in words, but I, abstain from expressing it.

(2) The "forgotten unconscious" is unformulated, it is not expressed in words because it is not "actual." It is impossible for me
to have simultaneously present to me all that I know, experience,
or have experienced. If, for example, my total knowledge consisted of nothing more than the multiplication table, even then it
would be impossible for me to have all its contents simultaneously present to my mind. No, they are "stored in my mem-

ory." They are, in principle, at my disposal and in such a way that they can be formulated anew every time I have need of them. Sometimes there is something amiss, for instance on account of an interference. I look for a name; the form "Exner" thrusts itself upon me but I know it isn't that; I discover that it must be "Flexner." The affinity of the forms occasions interference. Sometimes no form is obtained and I experience only what James described as a "hiatus." I try to chain and fix, and allow to solidify a meaning that is fluid and fading. I know it all right but cannot say it, at least not now. I try to think of something somebody gave me, and of which I can no longer remember what it was.

This can be painful. How shall I rediscover that object? I rediscover it with and in the word, at least in a form that can be expressed in words. The denomination of objects, says Merleau-Ponty, does not come after the *re*cognition, but the denomination (act of naming) is the re-cognition itself. I cannot re-cognize anything unless I name it, if not aloud, at least interiorly; I re-cognize things in a *"word-form."* A word, then, does not translate something that before was present in us as a complete psychic piece, as an image might be present to us. A word does not translate any idea that is already fully formed in me, but a word fulfills, "accomplishes" the idea.[33]

But we find the same thoughts in James already half a century before Merleau-Ponty devoted a brilliant exposition to that problem. Have we ever stopped to ask ourselves what sort of psychic datum the *intention of saying something* is, before it is expressed in words? It is a totally definite intention, that differs from all other intentions, hence it is a perfectly distinct conscious situation. But how much of it consists in clearly defined sensory images, be they representations of words or of things? Scarcely anything. When the words arrive, they are greeted by that intention and accepted as right or rejected as wrong.

This intention then has a very positive definiteness, but what can we say about it without using words that come to us only afterwards? The only name we can give to that intention is that it is one *to-say-this-and-that* (I, 253). I know what I want to say, but I don't know it in words. At the moment I am going to say something, I have nothing in me that has content, that is formulated. It is only when I am hesitating, says James, that words and objects come to my mind; but at the same moment the intention disappears and I no longer know what to say.

No doubt I am able to *evoke* visual or auditory images, and to see and hear interiorly; I can equally well form a "motor image" of them. But I do not *possess* them in that form. I do not have to represent the word to myself in order to know and express it. It suffices that I have at my disposal an *"articulate* and sonorous essence" (*une essence articulaire et sonore*), as one of the ways in which I can use my body.[34]

These considerations give us another aspect of the question concerning the relation between experience and language. What should we think now about the views of James and Bergson that we have rather amply described? For they maintained that theories and words falsify what has been experienced. We have even defended that idea to some extent. But we have seen also that our experience tends to an expression in words and that it is only through those words that it can be communicated to others and becomes knowable to ourselves.

Of course, one can maintain that the deepest feelings and impressions are so personal, and exist so exclusively as experience that no words can do justice to them. Pure experience, we say, slips from all words that might try to get hold of them. It is the nameless world of a "pure experience." But, as Straus already declared, that nameless world of pure experience is never fully attained by us, and even then only by turning away from the real world of men.[35]

Is the stream of experience then only a changing, flowing and formless, watery consciousness? No, James has already told us repeatedly; the stream is a "structured" and differentiated stream. But differentiated means: to be divided in organs, in parts, although the frontiers between them may not be clearly defined or divisive. And in this consists the principle of "nameability" (of a capacity to be expressed in words). Moreover, naming things, expressing them in words, is the way forms arise in experience and become fixed. Otherwise we should not even be capable of saying: I am down-hearted. For pure water has no parts nor joints.

Let us listen once more to James.

> An immediate experience, as yet unnamed or classed, is a mere *that* that we undergo, a thing that asks, *What* am I? When we name and class it, we say for the first time what it is, and all these whats are abstract names or concepts.[36]

Hence we do not "name" an individual, and yet it becomes *this* thing for the first time by the "naming" of it, a "nomination" which it grasps under a general concept. And the "that" *asks for* it. We experience it, all the same, as a "that," that asks for a "naming" that does not do justice to its individuality, concreteness and uniqueness, but raises it to a universality, and thereby to objectivity. For here "universal" certainly does not mean merely "abstract" but it means also *communicable* and hence accessibility to others. *And this abstraction is given in the observation or vision;* not the mere possibility of abstraction, but *abstraction* itself. Properties, similarities, partial identities, which we "separate and free through abstraction," are first *seen.*[37] To put it in other words, human experience has already a reflective structure.

12. Experience and Reflection

"Each concept means a particular *kind* of thing, and as things seem once for all to have been created in kinds, a far more efficient handling of a given bit of experience begins as soon as we have classed the various parts of it."[38] And so we have to say nevertheless that the *formulation* of, and the *theory* concerning experience—which, according to James falsifies the pure nature of experience—on the other hand so fixes and formulates experience that it becomes communicable and can be handled scientifically. This is made possible by the reflection that is already pre-given in pure experience.

Take the problem that was enunciated by James himself, namely that of trying to find again a name that was forgotten. I have lost it and yet know that I know it, and I know that I have lost it. I know that I forget many things, although I do not know *how much* (*what*) altogether. Even if it is true that experience is characterized by constant changes and fluidity, it is nevertheless "structured" in itself to the extent that my backward reflection can *at least* say about it *that* it changes and slips away.

Here is the chasm between man and beast that cannot be bridged, as Nietzsche expressed it in his story about the man who said to the animal: "Why don't you speak to me about happiness and not only look at me?" The animal wishes to reply and say: "This is because I am always immediately forgetting what I want to say," and the animal forgot also this answer, and was silent, so that the man was astonished.[39]

We human beings know that we forget, or we know at least that we forget things without knowing which things. There is a reflective reversion to our knowledge, understanding and experience. This reflection also enables us to exaggerate and to say that the unformed and unnameable experience is the true experience. But he who proclaims this theory does it with words and hence does harm to his own theory. It would be better for him to remain silent and no longer to make use of words.

What constitutes our reality is not the unspeakable, the inexpressible, but it is that which is said, what is spoken, what can be said, what can be named. And the unspeakable too, when we call it unspeakable, is understood and defined in its relation to what can be said, not vice versa. In this sense we can say that language is a transformer; more than that, that language fashions the changeable stream of experience into expressed, pregnant, articulated forms and figures.

Human reality is an expressed reality. The psychologist, like any other scientist, expresses once more what was already expressed, with his own accent, in his own idiom and his own grammar. It was this that James meant when he spoke of the "psychologist's reality." The psychologist is a reporter who has his own outlook upon things. I am even permitted to say: with his own particular things. Another man does not see them as the psychologist sees them. The psychologist even creates situations, concepts, figures that play no role in every-day reality, unless he introduces them there. Intelligence, complex, mother-fixation, etc., owe their existence to the psychologist who presents by words what he has observed in human behavior, thereby giving it a structure, yes even an almost tangible solidity, from which the "layman" often shrinks away.

Human experience is already language-minded. That does not mean that experience has already a rational, reflective structure from the beginning; this James has rightly opposed. But it does mean that the reflective return to what has been experienced discerns in it a structure that suffices to make one realize that it is accessible to reflection.

13. Language, Experience, Reality

Language is not only the use of ready-made words that indicate, bit by bit and univocally, phenomena of reality. Reality is not an unchangeable datum given once and for all *before* every language. The reality that is expressed in language is a human reality, an experienced reality, in which the language was already active. Language is a means by which categories of things, similarities and meanings become visible in that reality.

And so it seems to us now that the relation between language, experience and reality is much more intimate than was formerly believed. It was naive to think that language repeats in words what already exists in reality, just as it is naive to believe that experience is truly and actually a stream of strictly inner, inexpressible events. Experience is experience of something and this "something" is primarily what concerns *us;* neither is it, as language and reality, a strictly individual concern that only occasionally is brought more or less into agreement with the experience of others.

Our life is primarily a corporeal life; the reality in which we live is primarily a corporeal world; our language is above all a communication attuned to this sort of world. Only when seen from this standpoint do the questions we have successively examined in this chapter manifest their fundamental connection and affinity. But we have reached this point of view only to the extent that it is implicitly present in James' biological orientation, and in the view that language has something to do with the fundamental social structure of the life of all of us. Hence it is better not to go more deeply into the question for the present but to wait until we have more fully explored the meaning of corporeity in James' psychology.

Only then also shall we be able to understand better the meaning of reflection. And it is precisely reflection which, to some extent, and in any case in an important way, had to lead to the thesis concerning the impotence of language. For it is reflection that, looking back and returning to experience, sees this experience as an original stream that wells up from our interior, which as regards structure and origin would seem to be radically different from reality.

But at the same time that reality, the experienced reality, is the substantial core of experience. And if reality can be expressed in words this implies that experience cannot be so foreign to words as it seemed. This means that experience itself, in its own structure, not only makes language possible but already conjures it up. This gave us the insight that experience strives for formulation. In other words there occurs a *translation* of reality: when we try to understand language, experience and reality, in their interdependence, the one constantly refers to the other.

Hence we cannot simply say that language falsifies experience. Language is "impotent" to the extent that it does not completely duplicate experienced reality. But this, after all, is not the purpose of language. Language primarily expresses the *core* of experience. And when we divide experience according to core and periphery, to what is substantive and transitive, this is already fundamentally present in experienced reality.

We saw already in Chapter III that the integrity of experience does not imply a perfect homogeneity of experience. On the contrary, the continuity and integrity of experience presuppose a certain inner *structure,* a differentiation of what is experienced. It is to this that we must now give particular attention.

NOTES

1. "Es ist leicht zu bemerken, dass in menschlichen Leben das ursprünglich anschauliche Erkennen und Denken und anschaungsge-

bundene Aussagen, das in Activitäten auf dem Grunde der sinnlichen Erfahrung seine ursprünglich evidenten Gebilde schafft, sehr schnell und in wachsendem Masse der Verführung der Sprache verfällt, eben der Verführung zu einem teils mit 'sedimentierten' Sinnen operieren-den, teils von Associationen bestimmten Reden und Lesen anheim-fällt." Edmund Husserl, "Die Frage nach dem Ursprung der Geometrie als Intentional-Historisches Problem," *Rev. int. Phil.*, vol. 1, 1939, pp. 212 ff.

2. Cf. Brentano, *Psychologie*, pp. 115 ff.

3. James, "The Knowing of Things Together," p. 108: "The scholastic philosophy, which is only common sense grown pedantic, would explain it as a peculiar kind of existence, called *intentional inexistence.*" In the reprint of this article which James sent to Husserl and that is presently in the Husserl archives in Louvain, those sentences are underlined, as one might expect.

4. Cf. below pp. 153, 181, 186 of the book.

5. H. J. Pos, "Betekenis als Taalkindig en als Wijsgerig Pheno-meen," in *Taal, Mens, en Cultuur*, (Assen, 1957), p. 185.

6. J. S. Mill, *A System of Logic*, vol. 1, p. 24.

7. *Ibid.*, p. 14.

8. Locke, *Essay*, Bk. III, ch. II, pp. 1–5.

9. James, *Pragmatism*, p. 257.

10. Henri Bergson, *Essai sur les Données Immédiates de la Con-science* (1889), (Paris, 1946), p. 103.

11. Cf. below, ch. 6.

12. That a naive prejudice lurks also in this sentence we shall see further on.

13. James, *A Pluralistic Universe*, p. 375.

14. Bergson, *Essai sur les Données Immédiates de la Conscience*, pp. 96 ff.

15. James, *A Pluralistic Universe*, p. 290.

16. Cf. the survey and commentary by Albert Burloud, *La Pensée d'après les Recherches Expérimentales de H. J. Watt, de Messer et de Bühler*, (Paris, 1927).

17. M. Stirner, *Der Einzige und Sein Eigentum*, (Berlin, 1924), p. 357.

18. Cf. Romano Guardini, *Rilkes Deutung des Daseins*, (Munich, 1953), p. 339:
"Ach, in den andern Bezug,
wehe, was nimmt man hinüber? Nicht das Anschaun, das hier langsam erlernte, und kein Ereignetes. Keins.
Also die Schmerzen. Also vor allem das Schwersein,
also der Liebe lange Erfahrung,—also
lauter Unsägliches."

19. "Was einen Namen hat, ist schon besondert, ist vereinzelt, ist abgestückt aus dem Ganzen, tritt in einer abgegrenzten Besonderheit hervor. Namenhaft-sein und Vereizeltsein entspricht sich. Das Eine, Ganze und Heile, das Keine Zerstückung und Zerreissung an sich hat, ist das schlechthin Namenlose und Unsägliche,—und wenn es dennoch ausgesprochen werden soll, so doch nur durch Namen hindurch, die die Festigkeit und Härte einer stehenden Bestimmtheit verlieren . . ." Eugen Fink, *Zur Ontologischen Frühgeschichte von Raum—Zeit— Bewegung*, (The Hague, 1957), pp. 68 ff.

20. Bergson, *Essai*, pp. 99 ff.

21. H. F. Amiel, *Fragments d'un Journal Intime*, vol. 1, (13th ed., Geneva, 1919), pp. 245 ff.

22. This is the title of the principal work of Ludwig Klages.

23. Husserl, "Die Frage nach dem Ursprung der Geometric als Intentional-Historisches Problem," pp. 210 ff.

24. *Ibid.*: "Es ist die wichtige Funktion der Schrift, die ständige *Objectiviertheit* der idealen Sinngebilde zu ermöglichen in der eigentumlichen Form der *Virtualität*. Schriftlich documentiert ist der ideale Gegenstand virtuall 'in der Welt,' jederzeit aktuell erringbar."

25. "Wir sehen die Welt vonmittels der Sprache." Erwin Straus, *Vom Sinn der Sinne*, (Berlin, 1935), p. 34.

26. Georges Gusdorf, *La Parole*, (Paris, 1953), p. 35: "Le nom crée l'objet; seul il l'atteint par delà l'inconsistance des apparences."

27. Cf. regarding this "hiatus-feeling" also *Principles*, vol. 1, pp. 584 ff. and 589. On this last-named page James seems to have borrowed this pregnant figure from his friend Hodgson.

28. Sigmund Freud, "Das Unbewusste," *Gesammelte Werke*, vol. 10, (London, 1946), p. 300: "Was wir die bewusste Objektvorstellung heissen durften, zerlegt sich uns jetzt in die Wortvorstellung und in die Sachvorstellung . . . die bewusste Vorstellung umfasst die Sachvorstellung plus der zugehörigen Wortvorstellung, die unbewusste ist die Sachvorstellung allein."

Ibid.: "Wir konnen jetzt auch präzise ausdrucken, was die Verdrängung bei den Übertragungsneurosen der zurückgewiesenen Vorstellung verweigert: die Übersetzung in Worte, welch mit dem objekt verknüpft bleiben sollen. Die nicht in Worte gefasste Vorstellung . . . bleibt dan im Unbewussten als verdrängt zuruck."

29. James, *Letters*, II, p. 328.

30. Sigmund Freud, "Studien über Hysterie," *Gesammelte Werke*, Bd. I, (London, 1952), p. 175: "Ja, ich glaube, es ist so.—Wenn Sie aber wussten, das Sie den Direktor lieben, warum haben es sie mir nicht gesagt?—Ich wusste es ja nicht oder besser, Ich wollte es nicht wissen, wollte es ist mir aus dem Kopfe schlagen, nie mehr daran denken, ich glaube, es ist mir auch in der letzten Zeit gelungen."

Footnote: "Eine andere und bessere Schilderung des eigentumlichen Zustandes, in dem man etwas weiss und gleichzeitig nicht weiss, konnte Ich nie erzielen."

31. Jacques Lacan, "Fonction et Champ de la Parole et du Langage en Psychanalyse," in *La Psychanalyse,* vol. 1, (Paris, 1956), p. 104: "L'inconscient est cette partie du discours concret en tant que transindividuel, qui fait défaut à la disposition du sujet pour rétablir la continuité de son discours conscient."

32. Sigmund Freud, "Die Verdrängung," in *Gesammelte Werke,* vol. 10, (London, 1946), p. 253: "Man darf sich den Verdrängungsvorgang nicht wie ein einmaliges Geschehen mit Dauererfolg vorstellen, etwa wie man etwas Lebendes erschlagen hat, was von da an tot ist; sonder die Verdrängung erfordert einen anhaltenden Kraftaufwand, mit dessen Unterlassung ihr Erfolg in Frage gestellt ware, so dass ein neuerlicher Verdrängungsakt notwendig würde."

33. Maurice Merleau-Ponty, *Phénoménologie de la Perception,* (Paris, 1945), p. 207: "La dénomination est la reconnaissance même. La parole ne traduit pas, mais elle accomplit."

34. *Ibid.,* p. 210.

35. Straus, *Vom Sinn der Sinne,* p. 123: "Wir erreichen die sprachlose Welt nicht vollständig und nur in einer Abkehr von der eigentlichen Menschenwelt."

36. James, *A Pluralistic Universe,* p. 217.

37. Fink, *Zur Ontologischen Frühgeschichte von Raum-Zeit-Bewegung,* p. 5: "Sprache ist wesentlich die Eröffnetheit des Seins, ist die Weise, wie dieses sich uns zustellt, sich uns gesellt. Die Sprache, in der wir wohnen, ist die ursprünglichste 'Ontologie.' Der Logos ist immer Logos des On."

38. James, *A Pluralistic Universe,* p. 217.

39. "Der Mensch fragt einmal das Tier, warum redest du mir nicht von deinem Glück und siehst mich nur an? Das Tier will auch antworten und sagen: 'das kommt daher, dass ich immer gleich vergesse, was Ich sagen wollte,' da vergass es auch schon diese Antwort und schweig; so dass der Mensch sich darob verwunderte." Quoted by F. J. J. Buytendijk, *Wege zum Verstandnis der Tiere,* (Zurich, no year), pp. 253 ff.

V THE CONTINUITY OF EXPERIENCE

1. What Is the Meaning of Continuity of Experience?

Continuity, says James, can be defined only as that which is without a break, crack or division (I, 237). Consciousness is not an aggregate of contents, it is a unity; but this does not imply that we cannot discern parts in it. However, we cannot separate them without changing their nature so that something else arises other than the part as it was originally. The "smallest" conscious situation "overflows its own definition."[1]

The stream of experience shows continuity. We must understand well what this means, because, after all, we can think of a break in our conscious life. Two things are possible here. I can imagine a total interruption of consciousness during which consciousness "goes out," just as light goes out when I turn the switch. Or secondly, I can imagine that there occur such abrupt changes in quality and content in the stream of consciousness that the previous segment has no longer any connection with what follows.

James sheds light on this problem by making two considerations:

(1) Suppose that there is a total interruption, we *feel* that our consciousness after the interruption is nevertheless solidary with the consciousness we had before, as another part of the same Self.

(2) Changes in the quality of experience from one moment to another, are never completely abrupt. Hence that experience is a continuous flux does not exclude at all that there can be interruptions. But we do not *feel* them.

James also defends continuity in another respect. Experience also manifests an inner articulation in which we distinguish between a centre and the periphery. My momentary field of consciousness consists of a centre, that is surrounded by a margin that imperceptibly fades into subconsciousness. The terms are arbitrary; we use three, but we could make use of three hundred: "for the fact is all shades and no boundaries."[2] And yet we feel obliged to speak about a structure, about another organization of the field of consciousness into a centre and a periphery. Here then we have a view that is most important and James deals with it extensively in the *Principles.* We shall now examine these problems in the order in which they are given in that work.

2. *I Experience Myself in an Uninterrupted Progress*

Are we ever wholly unconscious? Experience tells us that interruptions of consciousness are rather common occurrences; there is sleep, there are fainting spells, coma, epileptic fits; these take up much of what, in spite of it all, we consider the history of *one* individual man (I, 199 ff.). If sleep is not evidently an interruption of consciousness, we feel certain that during a coma, an anaesthesia or the unconsciousness that follows a severe blow on the head, there is a real interruption: we passed out and were "out" for a certain time. Is it even not possible that such interruptions are constantly taking place without our being aware of them? This is a possibility we are not allowed to exclude.

However, one thing is certain. After such an interruption, the beginning of the "new" consciousness is nicely joined to the end of the "old" consciousness. In anaesthesia the two ends are smoothly united. Do we really notice that we have been "out"? Surely we do not notice the "being out" itself. We wake up with the unpleasant taste which ether leaves behind; we recall the fearful experience of fading out, and those two ends interlock. What happened between them has disappeared. There are other situations in which we do feel that we "know" something about the interruption. When we are caught resting in our chair with our eyes closed, we say: I wasn't sleeping, I was merely dosing; rarely, after our sleep, do we have no impression at all of the time that has elapsed. But whether we have an impression of an "empty time" and void or not, all these examples bring before us the possibility that consciousness is truly discontinuous, and only *felt* as continuous. Who can answer this question?

Descartes held the opinion that thinking constitutes the nature of the soul, and hence that there could never be interruptions without causing the disappearance of the soul itself. Descartes' spirit *cannot* sleep without thereby losing its existence. But no ordinary mortal has ever looked upon this as a frightening problem. Whoever does not accept an *a priori* theory like that of Descartes readily admits that the spirit as well as the body sleeps from time to time. Locke joked about Descartes and his followers when he remarked: it seems to me that every sleepy nod shakes the foundations of that doctrine.[3] But what difference does it make if interruptions *really* occur? If consciousness knows nothing about them, it cannot experience them *as* interruptions. There is a great difference, however, between "unfelt gaps" and "felt gaps" (I, 238 ff.).

In anaesthesia, in profound unconsciousness, consciousness feels that it was interrupted. Ordinarily a couple of hours of life are gone. But after our sleep, we know not only that we have slept but we *feel* that we have slept. That the stream of experience goes on during sleep, though on a lower level, seems to be indicated by numerous phenomena that attest to a relation with what is interesting in the outside world; and also by the fact that we can to some extent judge the amount of time that has elapsed.

But now precisely what is the common whole to which belong both our consciousness before sleep and consciousness after our awakening? According to James it is our "I" or Self. If Peter and Paul sleep in the same bed, and simultaneously awake, do they wonder who is who? The idea is absurd; one sleeps *as* Peter and awakes *as* Peter. Sleep is unable to break the "I" into two (I, 239). We do not experience sleep as a "leaving off," as interrupting our history, but as withdrawing oneself with the certainty that we shall re-awake.[4]

I do experience my sleep afterwards as an "empty time," but nevertheless as one during which I was truly there, as a time that actually belongs to the history of life. I *am not being* slept. *I* sleep, *I* watch. Continuity is given to us. The experience would be totally different if it consisted in experiencing from day to day a passing away from life, a dying, a danger of never awaking again. But this is not so. We entrust ourselves to sleep with the firm feeling that tomorrow we shall take up the thread where we let it lie today. It is this thread we are concerned with.

When James speaks about a "community of self" that is not broken by sleep (I, 239), this figure might easily suggest that he accepts a substantial Self. We shall see later that he does not have such an intention.[5] Hence he expresses his mind more clearly when he speaks later of a "co-conscious transition": "What I do feel simply when a later moment of my experience succeeds an earlier one is that though they are two moments, the transition from the one to the other is *continuous*."[6] The stream of experience is characterized by an experienced continuity. We shall see later why that must be so.[7]

3. Continuity in Abrupt Transitions

"In every crescendo of sensation, in every effort to recall, in every progress towards the satisfaction of desire, this succession of an emptiness and fulness that have reference to each other and are one flesh is the essence of the phenomenon."[8]

Experienced unity spans the contrasts. But are there never any sudden changes in experience that manifest discontinuity? At first sight the hypothesis of gradualness seems to be contrary to our daily experience; for instance when there is an explosion that paralyzes me with fear and all that occupied my attention before has suddenly disappeared, and after I have recovered from the shock, I find it difficult to come back to the point I had reached at the time of the explosion. Fright is characterized precisely by abrupt change. If I had been warned beforehand about what was to happen, I should not have felt that kind of fear.

Moreover, we do not have to think only of such explosive occurrences. The sudden appearance of something new is an abrupt experience (I, 239 ff.). Generally, the unexpected, that which cannot be foreseen, gives us the feeling of discontinuity and abruptness in our experience. Whatever calls for or forces my immediate attention, a flashing neon sign, or a thought that suddenly appears before my mind, all are experienced as a break.

But let us not fall prey to so fatal a "psychologist's fallacy." For, says James, we must distinguish between experiences and things. The discrete, the discontinuous is found precisely in things, in outward changes. It cannot break up the stream of experience itself. The transition from quiet to a clap of thunder is no more a break in experience than the joint in a bamboo stem. A break occurs in the situation in which I am placed; but there is continuity in the stream of experience. Let us try to clarify this point.

The experience of the previous quiet is prolonged in the experience of the clap of thunder that suddenly bursts from a clear sky. For what we hear is not a pure clap of thunder, but thunder-which-breaks-the-quiet-and-thus-is-in-contrast-with-it (I, 240). It is precisely because there remains an echo of the quiet that went before that thunder makes such a strong impression.

Experience is the spanned unity of actuality, retention and anticipation (*protention*). Let us imagine a being for whom the "now" of experience coincides perfectly with the precise actual physical instant of time. There would be no question of memory for what now occurs has for him no connection with what went just before. Remembrance is possible only when the now-of-experience has a certain density, when there is retention, and we anticipate what will happen in a moment. But more than that. It is only under that condition that self-consciousness too is possible. This spanning (bridging) experience is also an elementary datum. We already mentioned the "co-conscious transition." The *Principles* expresses this point clearly: Our experience of what is actually given is always mixed with the past and future phases of the stream of experience, with what is close and what is distant (I, 606). When something suddenly happens in our surrounding, it is precisely in the experience of it that we notice the abruptness. This means that the abrupt does not interrupt the stream, but is taken up in it.

4. Brentano: The Unity of the Stream of Consciousness

In a footnote added to his example of the thunder-and-quiet, James asks the reader to compare his example with what Brentano says on page 219 of his *Psychologie,* and he then remarks: "This chapter of Brentano's on the Unity of Consciousness is as good as anything with which I am acquainted" (I, 204, Note). And, although James does not say so, that chapter is the foundation on which he (James) established his theory of the stream of experience, his theory of the Self, and of the perception of time.

Even after the most severe and sudden changes, says Brentano, there is a connection between the earlier and the subsequent parts of consciousness. Unity is always guaranteed.[9]

The question which Brentano asks in his chapter about the unity of consciousness is one we have already looked at from diverse standpoints: it is the question about the interrelation of the so-called contents of consciousness. When there are more complicated situations of consciousness, are we in the presence of a collection (collectivum) or does the whole of mental phenomena belong to one individual thing, both in its simplest and most complicated situations?[10]

A collection is an assemblage of objects that are put together and have no real unity. Twenty cows in a meadow are such an assemblage. I can give it a name and speak of a *herd.* But it is clear that the cows themselves remain diverse, individuals that act independently. If now we imagine consciousness as a herd of all possible sensations, memories, ideas that are grazing in the meadow of consciousness, we must then explain how it happens that one content of consciousness can show relationship with the others.

For example we *hear* a sound, we *see* a color; and, however much they differ we can make a comparison between the color and the sound; even if it be only a matter of noting the difference. But what sort of a mental content is that difference itself? Do I see the difference as a property of the color? If so, how do I know that it is connected with the sound? Or do I hear that difference *in* the sound? What then has that to do with the color?

Or is it a property that belongs separately to both contents, to color and sound? How then do I come to say: this is *the* difference? Or should I say: the consciousness of the difference between color and sound is a third content of consciousness? I then have three contents instead of two, but there is as yet no inner relation. How shall we solve that problem?

Brentano tells us: only if sound and color are represented in one and the same reality is it possible to conceive them as being compared with each other.[11] And James too says literally: "It is obvious that if things are to be thought in relation, they must be thought together, and in one *something*, be that something ego, psychosis, state of consciousness, or whatever you please. If not thought with each other, things are not thought in relation at all" (I, 277). But if they are experienced in a relation it must be that they are *"from the outset in a unity, in a single pulse of subjectivity"* (I, 278).

He who hears a melody will notice, if he pays attention to it, that, while one note is present to him, he remains conscious of the other as "past."[12] This is identical with the argumentation of James: That which is experienced as "past" must be experienced *together* with the present (sensation) in order to be experienced as "past" (I, 629). When he presently experiences ABCDEFG, the next experience will be that of BCDEFGH, and the following, CDEFGHI—"the lingerings of the past dropping successively away, and the incomings of the future making up the loss" (I, 606).

It would be impossible for me to hear a melody, as melody, if, besides hearing each note successively, I did not also have present to me the connection, the transition from note A to note B. He who notices that he sees *and* hears, notices also that he does both things together. If seeing and hearing are related to different contents, hence if the word "seeing" signifies that visual sensations are present in my consciousness, and the word "hearing" signifies that auditory sensations are present in my consciousness, with what then is the experience of simultaneity connected? For, on the other hand, we cannot claim that all mental activities that take place simultaneously are identical to one another. For if they were I would not be able to distinguish them. That is why Brentano[13] calls simultaneous mental activities *"divisiva,"* parts or joints of one mental reality:

> The unity of consciousness, as we know it from the *'innere Wahrnehmung'* (inner perception) consists in this that all mental phenomena that appear simultaneously, however different they may be, such as seeing and hearing, thinking, judging and inferring, loving and hating, desiring and shunning, etc., belong to one only true unity, as *'divisiva'* (Part phenomena).[14]

This is different from maintaining that consciousness is only one unarticulated whole.

But the aims of Brentano and James do not coincide. They agree that consciousness is an articulated unity. The systematic Brentano is interested above all in the nature of that unity; James, on the other hand, starting from the concept of unity, desires to combat association theory, and he looks for means to get a descriptive idea of the manifoldness, the inner diversity, the constantly changing variegation of experience:

> In the pulse of inner life immediately present now in each of us is a little past, a little future, a little awareness of our own body, of each other's persons, of these sublimities we are trying to talk about, of the earth's geography and the direction of history, of truth and error, of good and bad, and of who knows how much more? Feeling, however dimly and subconsciously, all these things, your pulse of inner life is continuous with them, belongs to them and they to it.[15]

5. *"It All Goes Back To . . ."*

Every experience implies a vast amount of impressions, memories, etc., that are taken up in an extensively ramified context of meanings that usually undergo only a gradual change. Neurophysiological data can give us an insight into the reasons why this is so. For no state of the brain disappears immediately. When a new situation develops, the old still re-echoes in it and modifies the new. "It all goes back to what we said . . . a few pages ago . . . as the total neurosis changes, so does the total psychosis change"

(I, 243) . And just as the processes in the central nervous system are never totally discontinuous, but flow into each other, so is the whole of experience never completely discontinuous from one moment to another.

This reveals the mind of James. He considers his descriptive data to be safe only if he can justify them in physiological terms. And hence he immediately "infers" his doctrine concerning the *substantive* and transitive parts of the stream of experience, from the brain processes—although in fact it comes down to a translation in a contrary direction. But let us follow James' way of reasoning.

The brain situations *abc* and *bcd* follow one another in such a way that during the change the continuity and the inner connection of the experiences are preserved. But then we have not yet said a word about the pace of the succession. The change can be rapid or slow.

Let us suppose that the changes proceed slowly. A plant, according to our ideas, grows very slowly. I do not *see* the "growing" of a plant. The process is too slow. Let us now imagine a slow-changing brain process. Is not this the condition under which we experience an object that appears unchangeable to us? If, on the contrary, the brain processes proceed rapidly, is this not the foundation for our experience of transitions, relations, changes, and at the same time the reason why they cannot be formulated in words?

The stream of experience is like the life of a bird; flying and alighting follow one another. The periods of rest are filled with sense images that can be kept before the mind for a long time and that have great stability. On the contrary the periods of flight are taken up by feelings of relations, for the most part relations between the stable objects of the periods of rest. But perhaps we can speak preferably of *substantive* and *transitive* parts of the stream of experience (I, 243) .

6. Substantive and Transitive Experiences

James then, on the basis of his physiological considerations regarding the speed of brain processes, wishes to distinguish two kinds of experiences. It is clear that we must not look upon that *substantivity* and *transitivity* as upon actual classes; they are rather qualities that differ in degree. For, if we adopt James' way of reasoning, we have to say that the changes of speed in the processes can vary between a certain maximum and a minimum. All experiences then are actually transitive, but in different degrees.[16] Hence there would be question here rather of a polar opposition within one dimension, in which we characterize the extremes in an ideal-typical way.

Now life happens to be concerned with substantive parts or, leaving James' mode of expression aside but preserving his intention, let us say rather that life is concerned with substantive experiences. Transitive experiences have a guiding function: they carry us from one substantive experience to another; they represent the changeable, dynamic character of experience whereas the substantive experience has a certain fixity, a static character.

Transitive experiences are hard to grasp introspectively. As soon as we stand still to look at them and fix our gaze upon them, they lose their transitivity; they are objectivized, they become substantive—if they do not vanish completely. Now it is to these transitive phenomena precisely that feelings, "feelings" of "if," "and," and all "feelings of relation" belong.

Hence we are no longer astonished that they have no name, and we cannot simply call them with one single term as we call objects, for they do not exist as things. They exist solely as transition, relation, reference to connections: as meaning-and relation-"ideas," as intuitions, that escape from any formulation in words. And if we do give them a name, we do so with the help of the substantive experiences to which they lead. We then speak of an idea about something, about this or that object, for the stream of experience is a directed, purposeful stream. It goes somewhere and appraises the end, the substantive, that is higher than the transitive or the movable, for the latter is the means to reach the substantive.

Let us for a moment recall the problems we examined in the previous chapter. We see there that James contradicted himself when he so insistently rejected every naming of experience as being inadequate. For he seemed to imply that *all* experiences are in the first place characterized by transitivity. But we are now told that "the main end of our thinking is at all times the attainment of some other substantive part than the one from which we have just been dislodged" (I, 243). But James does not mention the fact that thereby formulation in words (naming) comes to stand in a totally different light. We shall not examine this more closely for the present, because later on we shall try again to analyze the fundamental ambiguity of James' thought that is present not only here but also in other problems.[17] But there is still another point that calls for our attention in connection with the distinction between substantive and transitive experiences.

7. "Thought" and "Feeling"—"Akt" and "Erlebnis"

In experience there is question of substantive parts; the transitive parts, on the other hand, lead us from one substantive experience to another. It is evident that James gives a certain priority to perception, image, remembrance and thought as opposed to feeling. For although he introduces the distinction between substantive and transitive parts as a general distinction into all experience, it is already clear from his own terminology, that he conceives the substantive experience as that which knows, whereas he looks upon transitive experience as that of feeling.

Or must we say the reverse? Is knowing experience a knowing to the extent that it is substantive, and the feeling experience feeling so far as it is transitive? It is then not a mere matter of polar opposition that is defined by an idealization of the speed of the process, but there is present a *difference in nature,* a difference *a priori* in purposiveness (directedness). This James did not notice because of the unfortunate "inference," or conclusions he drew from the speed of brain processes.

On the other hand, are we not permitted to say that he meant that there was a difference in nature? This is at least implicitly contained in his explanations and it is my opinion that it is so. To determine this we shall once more examine the distinction between "thought" and "feeling" as these are handled by James.

He uses both terms for the phenomena of experience in general and indeed "to the convenience of the context" (I, 186). Hence it is likewise from the context we must learn the difference that is expressed by the use of these two terms.

Obviously James considers that there is a fundamental value in the classical opposition between "impression" and "idea" that was proclaimed by empiricism. The actual experience of a "toothache" *cannot* be expressed by "thought of a toothache" (I, 186) for this experience is too direct, too corporeal, too much "something that affects us." "Thought," on the contrary, "suggests the omnipresence of cognition (or reference to an object other than the mental state itself), which we shall soon see to be of the mental life's essence," (I, 186) whereas "the essence of feeling is to be felt" (I, 163).

"Thought" stands for experience in so far as experience is cognitive, is related to an object (I, 271 ff.). "Feelings" are to be specified more closely as "feelings of relation"[18] (I, 244 ff.) or "feelings of tendency" (I, 249 ff.). In other words "feeling" is what cannot-be-substantized, what cannot be formulated; it is a "feeling" or "intuitive" experience of meaningful references, of relations between contents, of purposiveness and directions in experience that, like affections, are characterized as "something that comes into me," "that befalls me," "what I suspect," as something that is given from outside my activity, outside my will and effort and speaks to me in a way that gives me no chance to repeat it again. It was thus that we could speak of a "feeling of absence" (I, 252) on the occasion of a name we had forgotten, and can speak of a "feeling of rationality" when something that is significant fits or does not fit in a certain context (I, 262). As certainly as there are relations between actual objects, there are also "feelings to which these relations are known" (I, 245; I, 258 Note).

Hence "knowing" designates not only the relationship of experience to definite objects, but also the relationship with verbal connections and directions and all that directly "affects" us must be called "knowing." But there are then also two kinds of "knowledge," two ways of experiencing things. They can be distinguished as "knowledge of acquaintance" and "knowledge-about." For James, the words *feeling* and *thought* give voice to the antithesis: "through feelings we become acquainted with things, but only by our thoughts do we know about them. Feelings are the germ and starting point of cognition, thoughts the developed tree" (I, 222). James also speaks about the same distinction in a longer passage:

> I am acquainted with many people and things, which I know very little about. . . . I know the color blue when I see it, and the flavor of a pear when I taste it; I know an inch when I move my finger through it; a second of time, when I feel it pass; an effort of attention when I make it; a difference between two things when I notice it; but *about* the inner nature of these facts or what makes them what they are, I can say nothing at all. I cannot impart acquaintance with them to any one who has not already made it himself. I cannot *describe* them, make a blind man guess what blue is like, define to a child a syllogism, or tell a philosopher in just what respect distance is just what it is, and differs from other forms of relation. At most, I can say to my friends, Go to certain places and act in certain ways, and these objects will probably come. All the elementary natures of the world, its highest genera, the simple qualities of matter and mind, together with the kinds of relation that subsist between them, must either not be known at all, or known in this dumb way of acquaintance without *knowledge-about*. In minds able to speak at all there is, it is true, *some* knowledge about everything. Things can at least be classed, and the times of their appearance told. But in general, the less we analyze a thing, and the fewer of its relations we perceive, the less we know about it and the more our familiarity with it is of the acquaintance-type (I, 221).

We shall now leave out of consideration the fact that James here identifies "to-be-acquainted-with" and "to know-about" with "feeling" and "thought" respectively, whereas he does the reverse at a later time. At this later time he maintains that "knowledge-about" is an object-knowledge of a thing-in-its-relations, of which relations we have a notion for the most part "in the penumbral nascent way of a 'fringe' of unarticulated affinities about it" (I, 259), that is, through "feeling." He is thus simply contradicting himself but this is not to be wondered at if we remember how unsystematic James is. We give the preference to the first interpretation because James evidently means by "knowing-about" that the relations of one thing to other things are known *explicitly* and not in a "penumbral nascent way."

James tried to put too many contradistinctions under the general opposition of "feeling" and "thought," and those contradistinctions are not all on the same level nor can they be reduced to a common denominator. Let us classify in good order the principal contradistinctions we have met with in our discussion. We then get the following schema.

"FEELING" as against	"THOUGHT"
A. transitive, marginal	A. substantive, central
B. relations, significance, meaning, direction	B. object
C. "feelingly," unspeakable, irreflective, acquaintance	C. (pre) reflective, known rational, nameable
D. original sensation, intuitive impression	D. inferred thought, discursive idea
E. vague, confused	E. circumscribed (defined), clear and distinct
F. implicit	F. explicit

Let us make only the following remark about this schema. The contradistinctions given under E cross the other categories. For example both the transitive and the substantive parts can be vague or circumscribed (defined), but each in its own way. There are clear "feelingful" or "intuitive" meaning-ideas and vague suspicions as there are clear and confused concepts. Both have their own manner of clarity and the possibility of clarification; a "feeling" can be made clearer and can be clarified in its own way; a "feeling" can be made clearer by going and seeing what it is; a "thought" by making it explicit and formulating it as exactly as possible. It is only when we judge "feeling" in general from the standpoint of pregnant "thought" (Descartes) that these two appear in the relation of confused against clear and distinct. James' antirationalism prompts him rather to judge the fixed "thought" on the basis of a "feeling" in flux, in order then to disqualify "thought" as the inadequate, as falsifying reality ("feeling") .[19]

If now we try to take the most general denominator from that schema (which however does not do justice to all of the contradistinctions that are classified under it) , it then agrees with Husserl's (also not completely clear) distinction between *Erlebnis* and *Akt:*

> We understand by *Erlebnisse* in the *broadest sense* not only all and everything that can be found in the stream of experiences, the actual and potential *cogitationes* (thoughts) , taking these in their full concreteness (Konkretion) ; but also all the elements of reality that can be found in that stream and its concrete parts.[20]

According to Husserl, there are "Erlebnisse" (experiences) , such things as the data of sensation (Category D) ; for example the whiteness of a piece of paper that, though truly the bearer of intentionality, is not itself consciousness-of-something (-else) : it is a simple datum. On the other hand he speaks of "intentional experience" (intentionales Erlebnis) when the experience is the "Bewusstsein *von* etwas" (awareness *of* something) , ("reference to an object other than the mental state itself characterizes thought") (I, 186) .

If we leave Husserl's "Empfindungen" (sensations) and James' "impressions" out of consideration, we must then say about James' "thoughts" *and* "feelings" that they are "intentionale Erlebnisse" (intentional experiences) . For James ascribes a cognitive function also to "feelings": for example "feelings of relation," "feelings of tendency."

But within this general character of intentionality that "feeling" and "thought" have in common—still abstracting from sensations—James nevertheless makes a distinction between the two. Husserl makes the same distinction between "intentionale Erlebnisse" (intentional experiences) in general and their particular form that is expressed by "Akt" or "cogitation."[21] "Akte" are the intentional experiences in which there is a "herausfassendes Achten auf die Bewusstseinsobjekte" (an apprehending attention to the objects of consciousness) . "Acts" are executed[22] (Cf. Category C) . They are therefore truly special moments in the stream of experience. James characterizes them by reflectivity and substantivity.

Between "feeling" (Erlebnis) on the one hand, and "thought" (Akt) on the other, there exists a real difference; but only in the sense that "thought" is a special *kind* in the category "feeling." Because of their essential relationship James at a later time abandoned that twofold division and speaks in general of "experience."

We have already noted that James introduces too many contradistinctions under his two headings. Before publishing his *Principles* he had already clearly expressed his opinion regarding the relations between "thought" and "feeling":

> The contrast is really between two *aspects,* in which all mental facts without exception may be taken; their structural aspect, as being subjective, and their functional aspect, as being cognitions. In the former aspect, the highest as well as the lowest is a feeling, a peculiarly tinged segment of the stream. This tingeing is its sensitive body, the *wie ihm zu Muthe ist,* the way it feels whilst passing. In the latter aspect, the lowest mental fact as well as the highest may grasp some bit of truth as its content, even though that truth were as relationless a matter as a bare unlocalized and undated quality of pain. From the cognitive point of view, all mental facts are intellections. From the subjective point of view all are feelings.[23] (Cf. Category C)

This distinction between a (self-) experience-aspect and an intentional aspect can be reconciled with the interpretation we have just given, but not with other parts of James' *own* theory. For now an experience should be simultaneously transitive *and* substantive, from different standpoints. How does this harmonize with the speed of brain processes that is either rapid or slow?

We have certainly not solved all the problems brought up by James' terminology. But it becomes clear once more that they are the same problems as those with which Husserl has struggled. And the arrangement which we have offered, even though it is schematic, will be useful with respect to what follows.

8. Marginal Experience

Transitive experiences are always present around substantive ones. They are a sort of mental overtone, a fringe, in which relations and objects appear in a shadowy manner. In experience there is always a margin of vague happenings that are nevertheless connected with substantive ones. In these fringes lie the relations of the object of our thought with innumerable other objects (I, 258 ff.).

I see an object. I recognize it. When someone asks me what it is, I answer: a clock. It is something that is used to measure time and it works this way. But did I *see* all this in the clock? Certainly not explicitly. It is true that this knowledge was ringing in the background of my perceptive experience, and when someone asks me: what is that? I dig up this knowledge from the margin and make it explicit.

However, it is usually impossible for me to bring everything that lies in that shadowy realm into the clear light of conceptual thought. There is much that remains shadowy, unarticulated and implicit. But that does not make it insignificant. The term "fringe" must not suggest to us that these are unimportant appendages. The fringe is not like the barb of an oyster, but it forms a part of the experienced object. Substantive qualities and things appear in a fringe of relations (I, 258), that constitute the realm of marginal experience. And this plays an essential role in respect to the *focus,* to that in which the experience is centered. James ascribes this especially to thought and language.

When I reflect I have as a focus what James calls a "topic," but we shall call it a *theme.* I think about something (somewhere) and not merely in a static sense. My thought is not dealing only with circumscribed (defined) substantives such as "my dog" or "the theory of Pythagoras"; it is also going somewhere. I am moving towards one or other conclusion, even though this is not at all in sight for me at this moment. When I am thinking, all marginal images and feelings that turn up in me are somewhat related to the theme. Hence I sift them in respect to that theme. I say, for instance: now, how is it that I am thinking of that? I then have the (marginal) feeling that the marginal happenings are diverting me from my theme, that I am not entirely governed by the proper ideas.

In other words, I respond to the fringe-like, shadowy phenomena that constantly crop up in my experience. From this also

comes my feeling that I am "hot" or "cold," that I am getting
closer (to the solution) or farther away from it. When I feel that
I am "hot," it does not mean that I know *why* I have almost
reached a solution. Experiences like: "Now I'm almost getting
it," "just a moment, I shall get it" can remain purely and solely
in the marginal sphere.

These marginal activities or happenings are then a part of the
process of thinking even when they do not become explicit.
Frequently I do not know how I came to this or that conclusion;
and when I reflect and reach a conclusion that gives me the
feeling of evidence that is (in reality) prompted by what lies in
the marginal field, and I say: "Yes, this must be so," it is impossible for me afterwards to say how I came to that conclusion.
Likewise the course of thought itself has no significance for us in
our natural behavior. We are interested in the substantive, in the
conclusion (I, 260).

Hence it is also to those "resting-places" that we cling. That is
why a forceful demonstration necessarily disappoints me when I
re-read my notes, for these contain only the substantive, the
conclusions. The margin that was spun around them while I was
listening has disappeared. And we ask ourselves now and again:
how is it possible that I found it so beautiful at that time? Was I
perhaps in a good mood? True enough, but it means among
other things that the speaker knew how to open a realm of
margins around his conclusions and I thus saw connections, and
heard overtones which slip away when I try to make them explicit. This also explains why the study or teaching of logic and
chemistry is so sterile in the life of many. It is because, in their
official course of thinking, these logicians or chemists give so
small a place to marginal experience; they try to fix every step in
a clear and substantive way.

Every argumentation that begins with A and ends in Z, leads
to the remembering of A and Z as substantial parts. Whatever lay
in between fades away. The paths by which we come from A to Z
disappear from our consciousness. In figure 1 we trace five ways
from A to Z. He who reasons, starting from A, does not have to
follow the straight road to reach the final Z; he can reach Z in

many ways, by all sorts of round about ways, and going at first in a variety of directions. Let us imagine that the five ways illustrate the thought processes of five different men who all start from A and reach Z. James maintains that the five men think all *alike,* in that they have their eyes on the conclusion Z and that the diversity of paths is irrelevant.

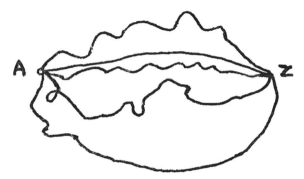

Figure 1, (according to *Principles,* vol. I, 269)

The thought expert, the logician, could say that the one who followed the shortest road is the one whose thinking was the best. This is because he has spared himself much trouble, he has always kept his eyes on the straight road; he had thus the best opportunity to know what he was doing, and also had the least chance of going astray. But the others reach the goal, too.

If we explain the course of thought logically we lose that which constituted the truly motivating, guiding and important element in the course of thinking of those men, even in the one who chose the direct way. We then introduce in thought a formalization that was not really present in the actual thinking of those men. The man who thinks in syllogisms is not yet born.

The margin also plays an essential role in the understanding of things (I, 262 ff.), just as, after all, the phenomenon of the meaningful character of expressed thought is generally most closely connected with marginal experience (I, 472). When someone wants to talk French, French words come running to him, sometimes to his astonishment. They well up from the margin of his experience, which at that time is attuned to French. Learning a foreign language—and one's own!—consists to a great extent in acquiring that margin.

In virtue of that same margin, I understand another person while often I am not able to translate adequately the foreign words into the better known words of my own language. But precisely because the marginal represents the implicit, the undefined and the complex, it can also lead me astray. When I introduce the English term "paint" pronounced into a French context, I have a good chance that the students will not detect that this word is "strange"—at least when the word, as pronounced, is not far removed from French diction.

The marginal perception that all the words we hear or read at a given moment belong to the same language or to a special treasury of words, is, according to James, "practically equivalent to an admission that what we hear is sense" (I, 262). It is precisely the marginal context that gives the character of meaningfulness to separate words (I, 281). This can be broken through only when some one puts an unusual word in his vocabulary. He who gives a solemn address may cause his hearers to hear nothing but the emotional atmosphere suggested by the speaker, until the moment he injects a vulgar word in his solemn speech. Then everybody sits up straight, for they have *heard* this word. Why is that? Because it does not fit into the margin.

A misprint can so change a word that it drops out of the context. It can also change the word so little that I do not even notice the mistake in my text. If I want to take away a meaning from words I must let something take place *in the margin,* not in the words themselves.

On the other hand, sentences that are senseless when considered substantively, can affect us meaningfully when they evoke the required marginal context. And we may ask one who knows Latin very well what this sentence means: "Lucebit inde per onus decus." In all probability it will take him sometime before he discovers that this is colloquial American: "Lucy bit in the pear; on us the cuss!"

Sometimes it is even wholly impossible to make out at the first hearing whether some one is talking sense or nonsense. James quotes a passage which runs thus:

> The flow of the efferent fluids of all these vessels from their outlets at the terminal loop of each culminate link on the surface of the nuclear organism is continuous as their respective atmospheric fruitage up to the altitudinal limit of their expansibility, whence, when atmosphered by like but coalescing essences from higher altitudes,—those sensibly expressed as the essential qualities of external forms,—they descend, and become assimilated by the afferents of the nuclear organism (I, 263).

This is an arbitrary passage from a serious-minded book entitled *Substantialism or Philosophy of Knowledge* that was published in 1879. James, who dislikes becoming too personal, remarks: "There are every year works published whose contents show them to be by real lunatics." But he immediately takes back that judgment asking himself if it is not possible that those combinations of words had, nevertheless, a real meaning for their author. The reader who wishes to see a text as meaningful must first become acquainted with the margins.[24]

Every science has its own technical language and its thematic content with its proper margins. It is only when I master them and make them my own that I shall understand a text expressed in those technical terms. This, after all, is precisely the problem of learning a particular mode of scientific thinking. It is useless to learn all the technical terms by heart; I must above all penetrate into the context, into the margin. The same applies to the understanding of poetry or any other art.

Hence marginal experience is not an incidental phenomenon but a constitutive part of experience as a whole. In fact, the marginal is in some respects more determining and more important than central experience. We must now examine them in their mutual relations.

9. The Field of Experience

For a number of centuries Western thought has tried to make reality explicit in such a way that the human aspects of the experience of reality were ignored. This is James' opinion. We are told by our tradition that scientific thinking must be determined by clear, sharply outlined images, ideas and concepts. James, in anticipation of the philosophical thinking of today, prefers a point of view that respects the play of light and shadow. It is only thus, he believes, that one truly seeks for reality. For he who takes for reality what is enacted in clearness, is mistaken. Our consciousness is not confined to that which we "know": it cannot be defined solely by its focus; it consists in a *field:*

> *We have thus fields of consciousness,*—that is the first general fact; and the second general fact is that the concrete fields are always complex. They contain sensations of our bodies and of the objects around us, memories of past experiences and thoughts of distant things, feelings of satisfaction and dissatisfaction, desires and aversions, and other emotional conditions, together with determinations of the will, in every variety of permutation and combination.[25]

All these conditions in the field of experience are organized around a focus which we call the theme.

> In the successive mutations of our fields of consciousness, the process by which one dissolves into another is often very gradual, and all sorts of inner rearrangements of contents occur. Sometimes the focus remains but little changed, while the margin alters rapidly. Sometimes the focus alters, and the margin stays. Sometimes focus and margin change places. Sometimes, again, abrupt alterations of the whole field occur. There can seldom be a sharp description.[26]

James describes this field of experience as something that can be identified with what a phenomenological psychology calls a *situation.* "When we reflect," I wrote earlier, "the problem that occupies our attention is central; but it is surrounded by a horizon of associations, relations of propositions with other problems, which sound together with our reflection." And,

> While we are busy thinking, we are not wholly confined to our thinking; we hear also the noises around us, each with its particular significance in its appeal to us. The ticking clock refers to the partition of our day, a voice in the hall signifies a possible claim to our attention. We see all sorts of things around us, the cigarettes

that are ready for the smokers, the inkwell that is ready to fill our pens, and other innumerable things that are present only implicitly. We sit on a chair that stands on the floor, that is strong and will not collapse, no more than the ceiling above our heads will fall down; this we know implicitly and are confident that these certainties will remain. All this is present in the background.

For a situation of thinking, the thought is the centre of our field of activities, thinking is the act which specifies and gives structure to the situation. We are before the problem with our 'attention' because this is what we choose. But nothing prevents us from putting the problem aside, taking a cigarette and going out for a smoke—hence changing our situation. This means then that, at the same time—correlatively—the landscape has undergone a change. The matches and the cigarette, which were already present in our reflection, will now become the centre of our field.[27]

If we go one step further and define a situation as the totality of the personal world that is "perspectively" structured by a specific "intentionality," we can question, with respect to all relationships, whether James would have accepted this. On the other hand we are justified in saying that it is implied in his explanations of the field of experience. This will be seen more clearly when, starting from James, we try to determine to what extent his views permit generalization.

10. The Context Theory and Its Generalization

Let us summarize the construction of James' theory. He introduced the transitive experiences as a fringe around the more substantive experiences. Reflection upon the significance of this fact led to the notion of a margin, of a realm of marginal experience that extends around the centre of the field of experience, but constitutes the whole field together with the centre. The margin forms the context of the "theme" and it has constitutive significance for that theme. We also saw illustrations of this in examples taken from the realm of words. This context theory can be expressed as follows: *To determine the concrete meaning of a word, or a sentence, it is not enough to know the proper logical meaning of the word or of the sentence, but it is equally necessary to know the field in which that word or sentence appears.*

This context theory we now generalize in three propositions:
(1) Generally, the concrete meaning of a phenomenon is not determined by the mere proper thematic meaning of that phenomenon, but equally by the field in which it appears. What James maintained regarding words and sentences is thus generalized.

(2) All phenomena appear in a field.

(3) The relation of theme and field is formally invariant in regard to all its concrete transformations. In other words, the relation between theme and field, taken in itself, is always the same, regardless of the subject in which this consideration of "theme-field" is introduced.

In order to prove that this generalization is justified, we would have to prove, in turn, the truth of each one of those three propositions. But this would lead us too far away from our plan and would require too much space. We shall content ourselves with a few remarks. First, we shall examine whether the context theory is applicable also outside the field of language. Secondly, we shall examine the necessity of admitting a "theme-field" division; in other words, whether we can justify the view that that structure is present everywhere. Lastly, we shall say a few words about the relation of "theme-field" as something that is unvarying.

11. The Generality of the Context Phenomenon

Taking into consideration the present situation of psychology, we are permitted to say that there is no longer any need of proving the "generality of the context phenomenon." It is especially to Gestalt psychology that the credit must be given for establishing that universality. One same human figure, when integrated in diverse backgrounds, exhibits a variety of expressions and makes us suspect a variety of intentions. In the theory of perception, the relation of figure to background is fundamental and determining. The "figure" could be called the "theme" in the field of perception; and the background could be called the "field." A few more data concerning this matter we shall discuss a little later. Suffice it to remark that we have here indeed a similar, even structurally identical relation, to which James' theory about the context is perfectly applicable. The same is true of the other modalities of perception, and the other mental functions such as thinking, remembering, feeling, etc.

We have also learned something about theme and field in our investigations in a totally different domain, namely that of psychoanalysis. The opposition between the conscious and the unconscious is not different from that which exists between the theme and its field. The conscious is that which is present to me and that I can bring forward as motivation for my conduct. But, says the depth psychologist, when I imagine that I am doing something on the basis of the reason I *name*, it is not certain that this is the actual reason. The actual motive could be unconscious and it could influence the alleged conscious motive from its unconscious location.

But if so, the relation between conscious and unconscious must be identified with the relation between theme and field: the meaning of the conscious phenomenon lies not only in that of which we are "conscious," that which we can name, but equally in the marginal field, that which as such is not "conscious," in other words, is not nameable.

We know how this principle is presently applied in advertising on the basis of "motivational research." The sales of products can be fostered by advertising material that appeals to marginal experiences. The particular product appeals to us although we do not know why.[28] Everywhere we find similar manifestations. James' context theory has a general validity.

12. Necessity of the Theme-Field Organization.

Here also we limit our considerations, and point to a topic in which many experiments have been made: the figure-ground relationship in optical perception. We are thus permitted to start from a thesis that can be verified experimentally: there is no figure without a field. This proposition should not be converted so as to read: there is no field without a figure, for we know that there are fields without figures, such as the homogenous "Ganzfeld."[29] A "Ganzfeld" is a homogenous optical field in which no single part is differentiated from any other part. The observer then sees no plane or super-plane, but a cloudy, nebulous substance of a certain thickness. The character of super-plane (surface) does not appear in a field that is not "figured." When a small difference is introduced in that "Ganzfeld," for example a small figure that brings a non-homogeneity into the field, that whole phenomenal structure of the "Ganzfeld" is changed; it becomes a surface that depends on the presence of that figure. Does not this kind of proof show precisely that a "figure"—a "theme"—is a magnitude that is totally dependent on the "field"? For we brought an (already existing) figure *into* the (already existing) "Ganzfeld," and noted that there occurred then a change of the phenomenal structure of the field. But that "bringing in" of a figure (conceived without its background) was a manner of speaking.[30] That is how it appears to us when we describe the experimental situation. It is true, to be sure, that the figure appears to us as something "substantive" that can be transposed, that can be transplanted from one field to another because it possesses its own determined form; but it is not possible to have a figure in a perception in any other way than *in* a field or *against* a background.

It is perceptible as figure, as foreground, as theme, only because it is outlined against a certain terrain that has no figurative character; that in contrast with the organization and articulateness of the figure, has a non-organized, homogeneous structure. When I transpose a figure from one field to another, that implies only a quasi dependence on the figure. A figure is always a differentiation within a field.

This we can explain with the help of the concepts of *boundary functions* and *"Zusammengefasstheit"* (comprehensivity) as developed by Kopfermann.[31] Figures arise when boundary lines appear in a field. Now it is a fact that a boundary line, in itself, does nothing more than divide one territory into two territories. A boundary line indicates where A goes over to B, or B to A, where a figure goes over to background or vice versa.

Now Gestalt psychology has taught us that a contour, "phenomenally" seen, belongs always to the figure and not to the ground. But the contour itself, as *boundary line*, does nothing more than divide, and when the contour is nothing more than a straight line that marks the boundary between two terrains, we are unable to say which one is figure and which is background. Thus we cannot say which one of the two equal terrains in Figure 2a is figure and which is background. This is the most simple reversible drawing at our disposal. At the moment that the left plane functions as figure in my perception, I see the right plane as a field that passes under the left plane. Why? Because then the boundary line belongs as contour to the left plane, and hence does not bind the right plane; or conversely, when the right plane is figure, then the left plane passes under the right plane.

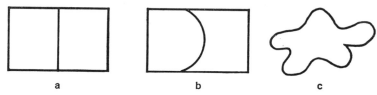

a   b   c

If we wish to make that reversible drawing less ambiguous, our contour must then not only have the function of boundary but must possess a structure that brings into being a "comprehensivity" (Zusammengefasstheit). Then the contour must not merely separate two terrains but must circumscribe one, as in Figure 2b. The common boundary line is, however, bent around the left terrain, and now it not only divides two territories but separates also an *inside* and an *outside*. Hence we see, by preference, the left terrain as figure.

We see then that it is through the "comprehending," circumscribing and encircling structure of the contour that there arises the opposition between figure and background, between theme and field. The theme is inside, the field outside. The onesidedness of the *boundary-function*, the fact that the contours, in perception, belong to the figure and not to the field, is therefore dependent upon the "closed-ness" of the contour and not—which is an essential point—on its being a boundary as such.

When someone now notes that the curved line in Figure 2b nevertheless forms a part of a closed circumscription of the right terrain, it must be said that he is right. This figure then is not unambiguous. But the curved line suggests that it delimits the left field more strongly than the right. And this is clearly connected with the fact that the curved line bends leftwards upon itself and that it envelops the left field.

In Figure 2c we have the picture of an unambiguous division of figure and ground, of inside and outside, of theme and field. This Jordan-curve, that is, one that is closed and crooked and never cuts itself, differentiates and divides the white surface of the paper into two territories. If we count the contour as being inside the territory, then each point in that territory, except the contour-points, has a "surrounding" of neighboring points that are entirely within the territory. This is not true of the contour, hence it is also here that varying interchanges with the surrounding territory take place. In psychoanalytic terms, we would say that the contour is here the censor who separates the conscious from the unconscious. And that which lies outside, is by definition (by the bounding line!) *other* than that which lies inside; it has, so it seems to us, nothing to do with what lies inside. But it is obvious that the "outside" is as much connected with (involved in) the shape of the contour as the "inside."

Whoever goes to the trouble of re-discovering the general significance of the Jordan-curve as a thought-pattern that appears in all possible psychological problems, will realize how fundamentally important is this matter that presently occupies our attention, namely the relation of theme and field.[32] A theme, even when taken in a more general sense, of itself has a "closedness." Just as, in perception, we adjudge the contour to the figure and not to the field, so is it right to say that we adjudge the boundaries to the themes and not the field. That which lies outside is that which, on the face of it, has nothing to do with the theme. That is why such a theme acquires a quasi-substantivity in respect to the field in which it is found. Now we see why it has been actually (uberhaupt) *possible* to have a content-element-psychology. For, however much we may combat such an antiquated view, we must not forget that the development of that theory has been possible on one foundation or another.

It is interesting to examine how one came to the conclusion that a "memory," for example, is a separate isolated entity that is stored up somewhere in the psyche. The obvious reason is that the one who constructed that theory did not know the distinction between boundary-function and the form of the boundary. It is true, of course, that when I remember something distinctly, there appears before my "mind's eye" a situation that possesses a certain circumscription and "enclosedness," but it is not like a photograph that is fixed once and for all and does not change. My remembrance gets sharpness and contour only *now* in virtue of my present field of experience.

If the content-psychologist replies to this that the field-hypothesis is not based on experience, we can say in reverse that *his* view, after all, is impossible if there exists no theme-field relation. Here what we called the "deception" or misleading role of language, presents itself as the deception caused by the *contour*.

No figures or themes possess individuality without a delimitation in respect of a field in which they distinguish themselves from the non-circumscribed as the "figurated," as the well-circumscribed; as closed with respect to the open; as the named with respect to the unnamed. In other words, the figure (the theme) is the expression of the *articulateness* of a field. At the moment that this articulateness is present, there is before me a polar opposition between the articulated part and the rest, namely the homogeneous part or margin. There is no question of an absolute opposition here. There exists a hierarchical relation between figure and field. They are mutually continuous though the transition may be more or less sharp.

Contours can sometimes be blurred, hazy. They can become so wide that they no longer form any sharp boundaries but create intermediate, border terrains. We have seen that James really would have preferred to deny *every* sharp contour, and thus spoke of "all shades and no boundaries."[33] In any case his exaggeration points out the continuity of theme and field. Hence it is also preferable not to look upon them as totally different categories, but as the results of polar tendencies that are mutually implicit.

Consequently we know that there are two directions of development that belong to the field. One tends toward a greater articulateness and hence to a greater individuality of parts in that field; the other tends to a lesser articulateness, lesser differentiation and a lesser "figuration." The two imply each other. Contours are places where the field energy accumulates. The more this energy is concentrated the sharper becomes the opposition between the thematic centre and the homogeneous periphery. The less it is concentrated, the more theme and field flow into each other.

Do these considerations not remind us of the development of the terminology and the contents of James' psychology? We recall, for example, the terms "Abhebung" (withdrawal) and "Einbettung" (in-bedding) of Stern. Every experience tends to an "Abhebung" *out of* the whole, or to an "Einbettung" *into* the whole. Actually both tendencies are always at work. And so does the figure (Gestalt) stand at one extreme pole of "Abgehobenheit" (withdrawal) , but the background, the field, simultaneously stands "in the sign" of "Einbettung" (in-bedding) .[34]

But also Werner's opposition between the diffuse, unarticulated, pathic experience, and the differentiated, articulated, gnostic experience means fundamentally the same opposition. We have already examined the sensation theory of Werner and recognize in it the same line of thought. What a person begins with in this world is a rather undifferentiated "unarticulated" field, although we must not say that everything in it is reduced to a homogeneous soup. For, after all, we can also distinguish waves in the homogeneous milieu of a mass of water. But there is no question of *clear* contours in original experience. So development is accomplished in the direction of a greater "Gliederung" (articulateness) . We find in Werner's theory the same thing that we saw in James: the fundamental distinction between theme and field. Hence we are permitted to conclude: theme and field are continuous; the theme is a thematizing *of* a field, and *within* a field; or more exactly: *thematization is the delimiting of the essential in respect to the accidental in a field of experience.* The differentiation of a theme within the field is a *necessary* general form of organization of the field of experience.

13. *The Theme-Field Relation as Invariant*

It already follows from what we have seen that the theme-field relation is invariant. Not only in all *realism* but on all levels of experience there is a core and an environment, a theme and a field. We meet with the same relation, because we see always that the decisive factor, the difference between theme and field lies in the boundary-function of the contour. When we now maintain that the formal relation of theme-field is invariant, we mean to say that the theme-field organization is a constitutive formal element (moment) of every experience, however it might be determined as regards to content, and whatever may be the reflective level on which it takes place.

Hence every reflective modification of an experience will show forth that same organization. In perception, the object appears within its field of perception. If, at a later time, I try to recall that perception, my remembrance is concerned with perceptual object *and* field. If I designate the two together, calling them the "object-of-remembrance," then this also has its field of remembrance. If next I represent to myself that I recall this, then my representation is concerned with the "object-of-remembrance" and a "field-of-remembrance." If I name the two together the "object-of-representation," this too has its own field of representation.

If we can speak here of an *iterative* theme-field organization, we can likewise speak of an *implicative* theme-field organization. The object of perception has its field of perception. To perceive is to have an object in a field. But now the perception itself has a thematic character within the field of experience; there is in my experience, "outside" my present perceiving, also that which I think on that occasion, the mood in which I perceive it, etc. Hence I have once again a theme-field organization. We can then say that in every one of my acts there is the marginal cooperation of the whole of possible experiences and of my experience. But if this is so, experience in general has necessarily the character of *thematizing within a field,* and it possesses not only its own inner continuity, but, because of the co-sounding of my experience, it has also its *permanent* (enduring) continuity, a closedness throughout the varieties of experience. We have seen already that James defended that view. We shall see later that when he argues in favor of it, he implicitly reduces it to the theme-field organization, although he no longer sees their direct connection.[35]

Theme-field organization then is indeed an invariant, and it was thus possible to arrive at a general declaration such as that of Gurwitsch who, continuing to build on the foundation of James, gave us the following formula: Whatever may be the object that functions as a theme, it presents itself within a definite order of existence and as a member of that order. The experience of an object is a confrontation with that order.[36] This is a declaration that is worth keeping in mind.

When I see a chair I do not see only the concrete thing; I see just as much a representative of the category of things, a particular member of the order of things; something on which one can sit and which we expect to possess certain properties. It must not collapse when we sit down on it for it is built to hold up a human being.

Do I ever realize this? No! Only when I have reason to think that someone has detached the legs from the seat, because he is trying to play a trick on me. The chair refers also to the one who made it, to the human community, to a period of culture, yes, to the whole of human experience and activity. That chair contains a world within itself. Here is the ultimate meaning of James' view regarding the continuity of experience.

14. Addendum: The Relevance Thesis of Gurwitsch

In the foregoing considerations we have made a distinction between theme and field or margin, and we declared that the marginal has a constitutive meaning for the theme. It goes without saying that it is possible and even necessary to make more precise differentiations in this matter. When we go more deeply into the study of the structure and interconnections of the field of experience we see that all that is marginal has not equal significance for the theme. If we say that the field of experience is constituted by a centre and a periphery in analogy with the field of vision, this implies also that marginal data are more or less *distant* from the theme, (although there is no question here of a space-like distance) , and that there are degrees of clarity, etc.

Gurwitsch[37] introduced here a distinction that calls for our momentary attention. It is concerned with a more precise differentiation of context and margin. When we are occupied with some scientific problem, he tells us, we are not merely aware of that theme. We have also *first of all* a more or less clear consciousness of the context within which the problem is located; and *in the second place* we are more or less aware of our actual environment, of the room in which we are, the objects in it, the time of day, etc. The *first* Gurwitsch calls the *context,* the *second* he calls the *margin.* The "contextual" is that which stands in a relation of *relevance* with the theme. It is an intrinsic relation that is based on material contents.

Contextual data have something to do with the theme; they stand in relation to it. The context embraces all the data that are present with the theme and thereby are connected with it through their material content. Other data, that are merely co-present with the theme, but have no intrinsic relation with it, are *marginal* data. Thus, with respect to our theme, namely the scientific problem that occupies our attention, it is absolutely irrelevant that we are presently in this environment or in another. The context is defined as a "realm of relevancy,"[38] the margin as the "realm of contingency."[39]

However significant the relations of relevancy and irrelevancy may be, it seems to us that Gurwitsch makes too sharp a distinction. For we also find degrees of relevance within the context (in his definition) and we do not see why there could not be a gradual transition and continuity between relevant and irrelevant data. Hence the distinction is a *logical* one which one can make afterwards with respect to particular fields of experience, on the basis of the material relation of the "contents"; it does not concern the structure of the field of experience as such, and does not belong to the same order as the distinction we have made between theme and margin according to James.

We do not deny in the least that we have here a significant

attempt at a closer determination of the ways in which relations
occur within the field of experience. But the psychologist hesitates when there is an attempt to determine the relevance by
means of (clear and vividly conscious?) material relations. Psychoanalysis, for instance, rightly starts from the supposition that
there can be a relation of relevance between data that are, materially, very little related within the field of experience. It is not
always possible to judge the degree of relevance of marginal data.
This we see also when Gurwitsch examines more closely the
measure of remoteness within the context. He argues that as a
rule the indefiniteness prevails in the 'remote' terrains of the thematic field. A given datum refers not only to the neighboring parts
of the thematic field, that is to the objects, the data, etc., which it is
immediately concerned with, but also to the distant zones that
have relatively little direct relation with the theme and, beyond
those zones, with the data which, poorly distinct among themselves, melt into an inarticulated mass.[40]

That the inarticulated mass has a relation to the theme we
can postulate but not prove; and it is no longer possible to
postulate that the inarticulated does *not* gradually pass into the
irrelevant. On the contrary, if the fields have their horizon and
finally have all their fundamental involvement in a world of life,
then the most remote, the most *irrelevant* must be considered as
something that has a certain relevance in respect to the actual
theme. Relevance and irrelevance are therefore not oppositions,
they are not "terrains" that are "inside" and "outside" with
regard to one another, but they are extreme degrees of relevance.
Relevance arises with thematization as polarization of a field of
experience. Relevance is the way a thematization still operates in
the margin, or inversely: the theme is that part of the field in
which relevance attains a certain strength. This, in other terms,
we have shown in what has gone before. Hence we shall henceforth use no longer the distinction between context and margin
in the sense given to it by Gurwitsch.

NOTES

1. James, *A Pluralistic Universe,* p. 286.
2. *Ibid.,* p. 288.
3. Locke, *Essay,* Bk. II, ch. I, §13.
4. Cf. my article: "Uber das Einschlafen," *Psychol. Beitr.,* vol. 2, 1955–56, pp. 70–97; pp. 266–298.
5. Cf. *Ibid.,* pp. 215, 220.
6. "A World of Pure Experience," in William James, *Essays in Radical Empiricism,* (London, 1912), pp. 47 ff.
7. Cf. p. 219.
8. James, *A Pluralistic Universe,* p. 283.
9. Brentano, *Psychologie vom Empirischen Standpunkte,* p. 219.
10. *Ibid.,* p. 206.
11. *Ibid.,* p. 209. "Nur wenn in ein und derselben Realitat Ton und Farbe gemeinsam vorgestellt sind, ist es denkbar, dass beide miteinander verglichen werden."
12. *Ibid.,* p. 210.
13. *Ibid.,* p. 211.
14. *Ibid.,* p. 214: "Die Einheit des Bewusstseins, so wie sei mit Evidenz aus dem, was wir innerlich wahrnehmen, zu erkennen ist, besteht darin, dass alle psychischen Phänomene, welche sich gleichzeitig in uns finden . . . sämmtlich zu einer einheitlichen Realität gehoren."
15. James, *A Pluralistic Universe,* p. 286.
16. Cf. the short commentary of Bergson in a letter of January 6, 1903, *Écrits et Paroles,* (Paris, 1957), pp. 192 ff.: "J'avais été conduit, par une analyse de l'idée de temps . . . à une certaine conception de la vie psychologique qui est tout à fait conciliable avec celle de votre psychologie (sauf toutefois que je vois dans les *restingplaces* elles-mêmes, des *places of flight* auxquelles le regard fixé de la conscience confère une immobilitè apparente)."
17. Cf. below, pp. 129 ff.
18. Hence that James once speaks about "thoughts of relations" (*Principles,* vol. 1, p. 243) we consider irrelevant.
19. Cf. James, *A Pluralistic Universe,* p. 19: "Think of German books on *Religionsphilosophie* with the Heart's battles translated into conceptual jargon. . . ."
20. Husserl, *Ideen,* 1, p. 65: "Unter *Erlebnisse im weitesten Sinne* verstehen wir alles und jedes im Erlebnisstrom Vorfindliche; also nicht nur die intentionalen Erlebnisse, die aktuellen und potentiellen cogitationes, dieselben in ihrer vollen Konkretion genommen, sondern was irgend an reellen Momenten in diesem Strom und seinen konkreten Teilen vorfindlich ist."

21. We leave out of consideration that "Akt" and "intentionales Erlebnis" are still synonymous in *Logische Untersuchungen.*

22. Husserl, *Ideen,* vol. 1, p. 63.

23. On some omissions, etc., pp. 18 ff. Also as a Note in *Principles,* vol. 1, p. 478.

24. James had, moreover, an unvarnished dislike for bombastic language. This is evident from his commentary on the following passage of Spencer: "Evolution is an integration of matter and concomitant dissipation of motion; during which the matter passes from an indefinite, incoherent homogeneity to a definite coherent heterogeneity; and during which the retained motion undergoes a parallel transformation." This, says James, we could translate by the following: "Evolution is a change from a no-howish, untalkaboutable, all-alikeness to a somehow-ish and in general talkaboutable not-all-alikeness by continuous stick-togetherations and somehint-elsifications." Quoted by Henry James in "Remarks on The Occasion of The Centenary of William James," in *In Commemoration,* p. 4.

25. James, *Talks to Teachers,* p. 17.

26. *Ibid.,* p. 19.

27. Hans Linschoten, *Postscript,* in J. H. von den Berg & Hans Linschoten, *Persoon en Wereld,* (Utrecht, 1953), p. 248.

28. Vance Packard, *The Hidden Persuaders,* (New York, 1957).

29. See my *Strukturanalyse der Binokularen Tiefenwahrnehmung,* (Groningen, 1956), pp. 21 ff.

30. Here also it is a question of deceptive substantivation, a linguistic seduction.

31. Hans Kopfermann, "Psychologische Untersuchungen über die Wirking Zweidimensionaler Darstellungen Körperlicher Gebilde," *Psychol. Forsch.,* vol. 13, 1930. Also W. Metzger, *Gesetze des Sehens,* (Frankfurt a. M., 1953), Ch. 3, 4, 5, 12, 13. Cf. also my *Strukturanalyse,* pp. 87, 96, 98, 104, 180.

32. Cf. also the application in Kurt Lewin, *Principles of Topological Psychology,* (New York, 1936).

33. James, *A Pluralistic Universe,* p. 288.

34. William Stern, *Allgemeine Psychologie,* (The Hague, 1950), p. 103.

35. Cf. below pp. 218 ff.

36. Gurwitsch, *The Field of Consciousness,* pp. 319-320.

37. *Ibid.,* pp. 340 ff.

38. *Ibid.,* p. 341.

39. *Ibid.,* p. 344.

40. *Ibid.,* p. 336: "We have repeatedly stated [that] the relationship of the pointing reference between the theme and the thematic field need not necessarily be completely articulate and distinct. It may be

dim and penumbral with little or no differentiation of structure. Relations between the theme and items of the thematic field may be more or less indiscriminate and somehow nebulous and obscure." And, p. 338: "Full determination, differentiation, and articulation may prevail only in those zones of the thematic field 'near' to the theme, whereas the more 'remote' zones are affected by vagueness and indistinctness."

VI CONSCIOUSNESS AND THINGS

1. The Ambiguity of James' Formulation

Human experience seems to deal with objects that exist independently of man's conscious existence. Experience is cognitive, it has the function of knowing (I, 271). This is for James the fourth characteristic of the stream of experience. We have seen repeatedly how important the theory of the "object" is in James' psychology. We must now try to examine that theory. I say we must *try,* for we are now entering a field that contains such great ambiguities that it is almost impossible to get a clear idea of James' conceptions. This may also be the reason why he himself has not dealt separately with this fourth characteristic in his *Briefer Course.* But this does not give a solution to the problem.

We know that James unambiguously demands that a psychologist should adopt a twofold standpoint in regard to the questions that concern knowledge: the psychologist presupposes two elements, the knowing psyche and the known thing, and the one cannot be reduced to the other (I, 218). This is a necessary postulate since the psychologist must dismiss the philosophical questions about knowledge. In any case, by accepting dualism, he joins the common way of thinking of the man in the street. But was Titchener entirely wrong when he called the *Principles* not so much a psychology, as a work regarding the principles of knowing that was written from a psychological standpoint?[1] A work therefore in which no account was taken of the fundamental problem?

Let us begin by making an inventory of the difficulties. The exact words of James with which we began run as follows: *"Human thought appears to deal with objects independent of itself; that is, it is cognitive, or possesses the function of knowing"*

(I, 271). We have translated "thought" by "experience"; perhaps it would be better now to speak about "consciousness." Or must we in this context translate it more narrowly by: *thinking?* Here the rather vague use of the term "thought" will have its revenge.

Secondly, James speaks about *objects* that seem to be independent of consciousness, particularly of thinking. When we now proceed further and examine what James subsequently deals with, we see that he looks upon the object as a reality, as something that is observed by many persons in the same way and thus demonstrates its independence from the observer. This position seems then to imply that our consciousness or thinking is involved in *things,* independently of that thinking.

But when James comes to the part that, for him, constitutes the essence of the paragraph, he speaks about something totally different, namely about the *object of consciousness* (particularly the object of thinking). In other words, he speaks about that which is being thought. And we shall see that this is definitely not something that has a thing-structure, especially not for James himself. But then we do not know exactly what James meant by his "objects." For when a thing appears as something that is independent, the object of thinking is definitely not determined independently of thinking itself. And in this way the saying that consciousness "possesses the function of knowing" has become rather indefinite as to content. We shall therefore try to give an interpretation which does the least injustice to James. It goes without saying that what we shall say is in line with the results obtained in the previous chapters.

2. The Sense of Identity

Idealism, says James, identifies thought (thinking) and things. Things *are* by the fact that we think them. The mind *is* by the fact that we think things (I, 271). In any case, this viewpoint is not manageable for the "practical mind," and the psychologist has this kind of "practical mind." We must start from men and psyches that exist really and independently of one another. That is why we must also believe that the objects of our consciousness have a twofold existence. They do not exist for my consciousness alone, but they exist also in the outside world, and for the consciousness of innumerable other human beings.

For I can talk with my neighbor about the ashcan and this implies that it exists for both of us. That which is for both of us, for us and for many others, is independent of us in its existence. It is *the same,* and hence is *itself,* for all of us. And precisely in this lies the foundation of our faith in its independent existence. It has its own identity (I, 272).[2]

But when something is discerned as substantive and independent, this presupposes that we ourselves are able to discover that identity underneath the variability of the stream of experience, that we have a *sense of sameness.* James speaks here about a "principle of constancy in the mind's meanings." I am always able, and am always aware of being able, to think about *the same* I thought of before. This means that *"the same"* is an original datum.

When I compare and distinguish various things, then the basis for this comparison must be a "sense of sameness," a sense of identity, of agreements. This "sense of sameness" is the backbone of our consciousness (I, 459). But then is that "sense" not also the basis for identity of the thing itself? James started from actually existing things that are observed by many people. This is a *philosophical* standpoint, he says later, and we must remain psychologists (I, 459 ff.). And so it is not our concern whether there exists any *real* identity *in the things themselves,* whether our experience of the identity of things has a foundation in reality or not. Whether it is so or not, we would never notice an identity if we had no sense of sameness. This is the important point from which psychological analysis must start: that there are in our experience nuclei of constancy. We choose "the point of view of the mind's structure alone" (I, 459). The sense of sameness forms, psychologically speaking, the basis of the experience of (identical) things.

It is through this sense that structure-nuclei arise in the everflowing stream of experience. "The first spaces, times, things, qualities, experienced by the child probably appear . . . as simple *beings,* neither in nor out of thought" (I, 272). They are, in the way the child experiences them, neither in his consciousness nor outside of it. The child experiences them simply as a this, as a that, which has not yet a name. "But later . . . he [the child] corroborates in himself the notion of realities, past and distant as well as present, which realities no one single thought either possesses or engenders, but which all may contemplate and know" (I, 272).

The child does not pose such questions. The child sees something, but he does not see that he sees. Only later will he see that he sees, and that other people see the same thing. The child then develops an opinion about the independent thing. He attains this opinion later because he gets experiences other than the momentary, and repeatedly judges the objects of consciousness to be alike.

If this were to occur explicitly so that the child knows what is taking place, we would then have to suppose that a child at a given moment—this could be after a week or after three years—gets the idea: I have seen this before! At the moment that identification is accomplished through that "sense of sameness," there must arise a notion of something that remains identical amidst the variation of impressions, and hence that is evidently independent of the impressions.

3. The Sense of Sameness Is Not Yet Reflection

Does identification take place in such an explicit way that it can be called a rational process? When the human psyche becomes aware of its own functions, it makes man his own psychologist; he not only knows things that appear in experience but he knows that he knows them. He develops a reflectivity that in grownups becomes habitual (I, 272 ff.).

I am not satisfied with seeing, but I develop a consciousness *of* seeing. So long as I do not in some way distinguish seeing from hearing and feeling, I am not able to say that I *see*. The child cannot yet say this about himself so long as he has not yet made that distinction, and hence is not yet able to distinguish himself from the other, from what is sensed.

But this reflectivity, this knowing that one knows, is not

necessary for the perception of things. On the contrary, the perception of objects, and hence the identification through the "sense of sameness" precedes the development of self-consciousness (I, 273). Consciousness *can,* but *does not have to,* distinguish between itself and the object that it perceives. A man can be totally absorbed in perceiving without accomplishing self-consciousness. Pure experience that precedes reflection already knows structure-nuclei, without any "knowing-about" entering into consideration. James characterizes this pure experience as follows:

> 'Pure experience' is the name which I gave to the immediate flux of life which furnishes the material to our later reflection with its conceptual categories. Only new-born babes, or men in semi-coma from sleep, drugs, illnesses, or blows, may be assumed to have an experience pure in the literal sense of a *that* which is not yet any definite *what,* tho' ready to be all sorts of whats; full both of oneness and of manyness, but in respects that don't appear; changing throughout, yet so confusedly that its phases interpenetrate and no points, either of distinction or of identity, can be caught. Pure experience in this state is but another name for feeling or sensation. But the flux of it no sooner comes than it tends to fill itself with emphases, and these salient parts become identified and fixed and abstracted; so that experience now flows as if shot through with adjectives and nouns and prepositions and conjunctions.[3]

The "articulation" of the stream of experience belongs to the pre-reflective properties of experience. Sense of sameness is not yet reflection, and does not yet presuppose reflection. But, in contrast with Bergson, whose influence is evident in this matter, James adheres firmly to the constitution of thing-experiences, or of structure-nuclei, in the stream of pure experience.[4] The "purity" of this experience is a relative term that is related to the quantity of unverbalized sensation.[5] Hence it is also true to say that unverbalized sensation contains structure-nuclei. This is a conclusion we already reached at an earlier stage of our discussion.[6]

Indeed, on this level of unverbalized experience there is already a primordial *identification, fixation* and *abstraction,* as we have learned in the text just quoted. And this is in perfect agreement with the manner in which the formation of concepts is dealt with in the *Principles:* namely as a pre-reflective event, that *afterwards* is *spoken out* once more in reflection. But it is therefore better not to translate James' term "conception" by "formation of concepts." Let us then say a word about *conception*.

4. *"Conception": James' Term for Intentionality*

Conception here is the function by which we identify a numerically distinct and permanent subject of discourse. Strictly speaking, the term applies neither to the "state of consciousness" nor to that to which the latter refers, but to the relation between the two. Conception is the function of a "state of consciousness" which means precisely that particular thing (I, 461). Conception, we could also say, is the involvement (being related to) of an experience with *something. "Conception" here is James' term for intentionality.*

Any datum, be it a thing, an event, or a quality, is sufficiently "conceived" (conceptualized) to enable us to identify it when it is in some way singled out, differentiated, or so marked out that it is distinguished from the other (I, 462). A polyp would have conception if the experience "Hello again, thingamabob!" were ever to flash through its mind (I, 463). Hence if the animal experienced something as *something,* it is because its consciousness was a consciousness *of . . .*

It is this conceptualizing-consciousness that evidently attains to the formation of things in the stream of experience. And here we must not understand "thing" in the sense of "concrete and individual, actually existing thing." For although mental life is attuned to practical realities, although all abstract concepts are convertible into perceptual experiences,[7] James nevertheless considers "round-square" and "black-white" things as completely definite conceptions; with respect to conception it is only by pure accident that these concepts have no counterpart in the world of what is perceptible (I, 463). And here we have access to a phenomenological doctrine of eidetic contemplation which James never made use of. We certainly do not do justice to James when we point solely to the pragmatism he so strongly defended. His practice is stronger than his doctrine.

We must hereafter keep in mind that such achievements as

abstraction and identification, which we usually consider as rational, reflective activities, are activities that, according to James, are already at work in pre-reflection. And this reminds us of his declaration that thought is exclusively concerned with surfaces It can name the thickness of reality, but it cannot sound its depth; and this incapacity is real and lasting, it is not temporary by nature.[8]

Reality is richer than we imagine. Much of what we consider human and hence "rational" is already taking place in that which reason thinks of most of the time as an impenetrable realm of pre-reflective experience. But this does not solve our problem regarding the way James conceives the birth of a pure experience that is genetically speaking also the oldest. Here we are evidently facing a difficulty. We can only think or speak of relations of objects that we already know. In other words, we cannot return and try to penetrate into what lies *behind* experience (II, 3 ff.) .

Of course, I can ask myself: What did a child experience before he experienced anything, but such a question is meaningless. At the moment that a child experiences something, he experiences *something*, a thing, a happening, a quality which therefore is already identified and hence has already become recognizable. We cannot return beyond that. It is impossible for us to explain how we pass from being-unconscious to being-conscious. There exists no transition between the two.

Neither can we describe how we come to a conception when we have not yet had a conception. So we simply have to *construct* that pre-conceptual experience. We are thus forced to postulate a form of experience by which we get the first notion of the pure, immediate datum. This form of experience, this most simple function of experience we call *sensation* (II, 3) .

5. Sensation and Perception

So we have come back once more to the previously fully discussed distinction between sensation and perception. Because of the problems we have studied since, it has become clear to us that James uses the term "sensation" in an ambiguous way, namely at one time for the actual gathering of information through the senses, and another time for the most primitive ideal-typical level of experience we have postulated. Now the gathering of information is taking place constantly, but it is impossible, except perhaps in early childhood, to realize a pure sensation-experience. Our original experience is practically only sensation. The first experience coincides with the universe (II, 8) .

In contrast to sensation, perception is the experience of things that are present to the senses; for example, the perception of an ashcan, of a thing, that is present to my senses, that is visible, that I can hear when I let it fall, that can be felt, tasted, smelled, etc. That which is given in this manner is "perceived." If I had only impressions of light and sound, I would have sensations. But in fact this is not possible for an adult, but we can act *as if* the first (postulated) exercise of experience were still taking place. In this theoretical supposition the adult still has sensations, although in reality this is not so.

If these primitive impressions are integrated, and signify for me *something that is there,* I then speak of "perception." Perception, therefore, differs from sensation because in it we experience other facts that are associated with the object of perception (II, 76 ff.) . When I say, I see an ashcan, I do not merely say that I have a visual impression; I see an ashcan that I can get hold of, break, or in which I can throw various things. I have it *in* that context of associations. When I say "ashcan" I name in principle the whole of my experience. This is perception: to perceive is to have an integrated whole that is open to all our (moments of) experience connected within a horizon.

This is why the psychologist who wishes to examine sensations descriptively, begins with immobilizing the subject of his experiment. He lets the subject sit still, covers one eye and says: "You must also keep the other eye still; I will plug your ears, and you must think of nothing. Now look once very hard at the immovable object; what do you see?" He is then trying to find again the pure, bare character of an impression in a situation that reduces the context to a minimum. The subject is now unable to make an adequate use of his normal vocabulary and says, for instance: "It makes me think of . . ." or "it looks indeed like . . ." and then what he sees stands once more in a relation of reference to something, it is again open to the whole of experience.

This is what James means when he says that every perception is an *acquired* perception (II, 78). And we thus conclude that every perception of an object is an acquired perception. But in what way is it acquired? James quotes with approval a definition of Sully, in which "perception" is defined as the process by which the psyche,

> supplements a sense—impression by an accompaniment or escort of revived sensations, the whole aggregate of actual and revived sensations being solidified or 'integrated' into the form of a 'percept,' that is, an apparently immediate apprehension or cognition of an object now present in a particular locality or region of space (II, 79).

But we must not imagine this integration as if it were a composition of contents of consciousness that are independent of one another. We have seen what solution James chooses in this matter. The integration does not take place on the level of experience, but lower, as an integration of brain processes. It is only with this integrated brain process that an experience of the object of perception correlates, as an experienced and connected whole. But the integration does not occur with perfect automatism, nor does it take place solely on the physiological level. The integration rests on *association* (II, 76), and in it the *experience* of impression, the conscious (perhaps pre-reflective) identification plays an important role. In other words, there is required an active process of experience before a concept arises.

6. Discrimination and Association

The things we perceive, such as trees, men, houses, microscopes, which seem to be the materials out of which the world is constructed are in fact nothing but collections of qualities that so melt together in virtue of simultaneous stimulation that when one of them arises through actual stimulation it functions as a sign by which the connected qualities are called forth in the representation (I, 555). It is the doctrine of synchronous association which James here brings back to life. But it does not exercise

its function on original isolated impressions. For these do not
exist. On the contrary, James thinks that it is an irrefutable fact
that every arbitrary number of impressions that comes from every
arbitrary number of senses fuses into one undivided object, *if the
psyche has not yet experienced these impressions separately* (I,
488). Wholes of complex origin precede in experience their differentiation in definite elements; a differentiation according to
senses or according to qualities which impressions have in
common.

In other words, *discrimination* plays as great a role in mental
(psychic) development as association. Our original sensory
wholes are, on the one hand, subdivided by discriminating attention and, on the other, are united with other wholes. Hence
concretized objects are given in experience from the beginning
and they are vaguely connected with the rest of the world that
embraces them in time and space. We thus break up objects into
parts and reunite them (I, 487).

It follows that the beginnings of distinction and differentiation must already be present in the original experience. Things
must *be* different, either in time, place or quality. No one can
prevent himself from distinguishing a black line from its white
background (I, 494). Later, distinguishing things becomes easier
by the fact that things appear successively (I,495 ff.). For what is
given simultaneously readily melts into one.

This enables us to understand why James held, on the one
hand, that "things" arise through association, and on the other
hand that he energetically defends the view that association is
always an association between *things,* and not between *ideas* (I,
554). For this he constructs a physiological model, which we shall
observe in passing.[9]

Hence what we have called "structure-nuclei," James already
calls "thing." We were therefore right in saying that experience is
always an experience of things or objects. However, James tells us
that thing (A, P, X) and thing (P, M, L, F) are broken up and
re-integrated into other things (P, X, M) and (V, F, A, L), etc.
This structural change goes on constantly during development.

Association through agreement plays an important role in this
and we should not call it automatism. One shade of blue does *not*

make us think of another shade of blue, unless we have an intention that invites such association, as when we want to give a name to a particular shade. That like calls up the like is in itself simply not true (I, 579). This is one of the gratuitous suppositions of association theory. For there can be question of agreement between two things only when they can be compared, and hence when both are already there. Hence agreement cannot produce the thing (I, 591).

James explains fully that we have here an original human property. An animal does not reason as we do. This can be explained because in man there is a more highly developed association through agreement (II, 345). And *this* difference makes us understand other characteristic differences between man and animals, such as the use of language, which presupposes association through agreement, discrimination and identification. For without that it is impossible to make use of a sign (II, 356 ff.).

But this means, as we have already shown, that the beginning of language is already present in the original human experience. Substantization, conception in the sense of James, and being directed to the *thing* are the things that characterize man. A pure experience in which the transitive has precedence over the substantive is then truly "in-human." It is an idealistic construction that can only serve to show us that what essentially characterizes human experience is precisely substantization or, let us say rather, *thematization*. And so we must conclude that the thing is an original datum that is most intimately connected with *intentionality*. True enough, James does not say this in those exact words. But when we say this, are we doing anything else than to thematize what lies marginally in his considerations? Are we not permitted to say that the concept of intentionality which did not become thematic in James was a concept that was operative in his whole system?

7. Pure Experience and Sartre's "Nausea"

In the chapter concerning language we heard James' strong defense of the originality of and the impossibility to express the proper and true "pure" experience; and so we are now in the presence of a strange affair! According to James there is so great a similarity between pure experience and sensation that one is permitted to identify them for convenience sake. We have seen how we can approach sensation: by breaking through the context in experience. James himself gives striking examples of this.

If someone is lying on the ground and looks at the mouth of another who stands behind him and is talking, he notices that the latter's underlip is animated with an extraordinary and unnatural mobility. For it has taken over the place and room of the upperlip and this change in context leads to the most strange experiences. When we were children we have probably looked with astonishment at such a head that was upside down; it may have been when a member of the family was sick and lying in bed; and we then had the grisly experience of a mouth in the arched forehead, and the nose above the eyes and underneath, that extraordinary bulbous and mouthless chin.

James suggests that the reader look for a considerable time at one isolated printed word on the page before him and repeat it with sufficient frequency. He will quickly ask himself whether this is really the word he has used throughout life with *this* meaning. It stares at him with glassy eyes and is soulless (II, 81). This has been confirmed by experiments. When a person is in a passive attitude, the meaning of a one syllable word that is repeated three times per second, is lost in from three to three and a half seconds. The same thing takes place when we look fixedly at a typed word; the word becomes empty, meaningless; it is a speechless and fortuitous figure. When we look at it in that way, we bring it back to its sensory nakedness (II, 81). It refers to nothing.[10]

Is the relation of this experience to Sartre's description of the nausea-towards-existence accidental? Sartre gives the most pithy description of that nausea after he has pictured Roquentin, the principal character of his novel, as sitting in a park and staring at the root of a tree.

   . . . This was the very paste of things, this root was kneaded in existence. Or rather, the root, the gate of the garden, the bench, the sparse grass of the lawn, all this has disappeared; the diversity of things, their individuality, was only a semblance, a varnish. This varnish had melted; there remained monstrous and soft masses, in disorder—naked, with a frightening and obscene nakedness.[11]

Things lose their individuality. Nothing remains other than masses, monstrous and soft, that flow into one another. They are divested of their meaning and lose, in their nakedness, their vast, trustworthy structure.

> The word Absurdity is presently born under my pen; a moment ago, in the garden, I did not find it, but neither did I look for it; I did not need it: I was thinking without words, *about* things, *with* things. Absurdity, this was not a thought in my head, nor a vocal breath, but a long snake at my feet, that wooden snake. Snake or claw, or root, or talon of a vulture, it does not matter.[12]

The word "absurdity" comes to me only at the time that I want to describe the experience. In reality this is impossible because in the experience I thought without words, hence I did not think at all, but "thought" *of* things, *with* things. This is, nevertheless, an attempt to express in words directness and nonreflectivity, to name the absurd by referring back to the dead snake at my feet, the wooden snake, root, claw, or whatever it was. What difference does it make what *that* is?

> That root, there was nothing with respect to which it was not absurd. Oh! How can I set this in words? Absurd: with respect to pebbles, to tufts of yellow grass, to dry mud, to the tree, the sky, the green benches. Absurd, irreducible.[13]

That which in the fullness of its *own* reality is present in itself is absurd in its unrelatedness. This "thing" that has no relation to anything else, and hence is absurd in relation to everything, is absurd now in relation to itself. Absurdity is, evidently, experience in a broken context. The unconnected "thing" is a slow, flowing, nauseating oil:

> It was useless to repeat: 'It is a root,' it didn't work. I saw well that it was impossible to pass from its function of root, to suction pump, *to this*, to this hard and compact skin of a seal, to

this oily, horny, stubborn aspect. Function explained nothing; it helped to understand roughly what a root is but not at all *this one*. This root, with its color, its form, its fixed movement, was . . . below all explanation.[14]

We have already seen that one word refers to another, but, for Roquentin, the whole of words no longer refers to things, and certainly not to this which is incapable of formulation: words talk about it, hovering above, for it is "below all explanation." And this is so in a twofold sense. Pure experience cannot be verbalized, and it is impossible to return back farther; one has already gone too far in describing it. What is meaningless cannot be verbalized. Or does even this hide some meaning in itself?

> I rose, I left. Arrived at the gate; I turned back. The garden then smiled at me. I then leaned against the gate and looked for a long time. The smile of the trees, of the massive laurel, that *meant* something; that was the true secret of existence. I recalled that one Sunday, not more than three weeks ago, I had already noticed a sort of guilty air in things. Was it addressed to me? I felt, to my annoyance, that I had no means of understanding it. No means. And yet it was there, waiting, and it was like a look. It was there, on the trunk of a chestnut tree . . . it was *the* chestnut tree. Things, one would have said, were thoughts stopping on their way that forgot themselves, that forgot what they wished to think and that remained like that, wavering, with a queer little sense that was beyond them. This little sense irritated me, I was *unable* to understand it even if I had remained one hundred and seven years leaning on the gate; I had learned about existence all that I was able to know.[15]

Whence that smile, that secret, that "queer little sense"? Is it then impossible to experience pure, simple being divested of all meaning? This evasive reference, that smile of things remains always. Even when they have run back into the stream. Even when color, form or movement is going to escape from the thing, when it flows out of it, half coagulates in it, and even almost becomes a thing.[16] Even in naked sensation intentionality speaks out and there is a thematization. It is in these problematics that James' own argumentation finds its (hidden) continuity.

In the *Principles* he passes without evident connection from the discussion of the *thing* to that of the object of experience, of that which is experienced. But we are now able to see the connection.

8. Subject and Object in Experience

We constantly use the word "object," but what does it really mean? What ought this word mean in psychology? James asks himself this question (I, 275 ff.) and then makes a distinction between "topic" and "object," between *subject* and *object* of thought. In common parlance the word is used without reference to the act of knowledge, it is a term for individual existing things. When I say, for instance: "Columbus discovered America in 1492" and I ask someone what is my object, he will probably answer: "Columbus or America," or perhaps "the discovery of America." We always name the substantive nucleus of experience. But this is really not the object; it is a "topic," a subject, that with which we are concerned. I am dealing with Columbus. *He* is my subject. In another connection "America" might be the subject, or "the discovery of America" or "the year 1492." The "object" of my thought, however, is nothing more nor less than the entire content of that thinking.

Keeping to that example, the object of my consciousness is nothing more nor less than: "Columbus-discovered-America-in-1492" taken in its complete totality. To this object belongs everything that is present with it in experience, in its original circle of marginal relations that surround the nucleus like a horizon. If we continue to think about Columbus, for instance, and think that "he was a courageous man," the psychologist says then that Columbus is still the *subject*. The thought *concerns* Columbus. But *the object* of our second thought, now at the moment that I think of it is once more nothing more nor less than the whole: "he-was-a-courageous-man."

> The object of every thought, then, is neither more nor less than all that the thought thinks, exactly as the thought thinks it, however complicated the matter, and however symbolic the manner of the thinking may be (I, 276).

Strictly speaking, it is impossible for me to describe completely this thought-of whole, this object of thought. The only thing I can name is the subject, the thematic nucleus. We must not allow ourselves to be fooled by the sentence that expresses the object. And let us say once more this is so precisely because we want to understand words as communications concerning a subject and because a sentence, considered afterwards, seems to be composed of elementary "ideas."

The object is an undivided, if articulated, whole, as we have seen in Chapter V, 4. Let us think, for instance, of the following: "the-pack-of-cards-is-lying-on-the-table"; here we can distinguish time elements in our thinking. It is not necessary that an object be a simultaneous whole. It often happens that I do not have everything present together in time. Thinking goes on in parts of time. But when I try to loosen those parts of time from one another, and distinguish them from one another, I am unable to find even one that is so short that the whole object is not present in it in one way or another (I, 279). The whole is contained in every part, even if it be only in the way that the part thinks the whole. We also do not think in words; and in reality we scarcely ever think in sentences. We do express the progressing articulation of developing thought in sentences and words, but the expression of thinking as executed is always a *paraphrase*.

9. Thinking Is Accomplished in Paraphrases

When we wish to make something clearer we paraphrase it; literally, we talk around it, not in order to evade the matter but precisely in order to clarify it. By repeating a sentence in another form, by embroidering a theme we make the object of thought clearer to the listener or reader. We can content ourselves with simply naming subjects, but when I paraphrase something, I want to enable another to follow the development of my thought, to experience *what* I think.

The same thing applies to the description of a situation or of a thing. We thereby try to evoke something and make it present. Here also a simple naming gives the subject, but it does not give the object. "Not long ago I was in this or that park and saw a beautiful tree there." This is a description which, because it is sufficient to *name* what I met with, will not be of further interest to anyone.

We all know those two kinds of description from experience.

When we ask someone interestedly: "How did you make out with the dentist?" he might answer: "the dentist let me in, used the drill and he was occupied with me for a quarter of an hour." When we ask again: "Did it hurt?" he replies: "a little." That is all he says. This is a "naming" description. But one who paraphrases, and hence wishes to make the experience become present, begins with: "What an atmosphere! You enter, you go and sit down in a strange shining seat, and immediately an unpleasant feeling comes over you. You lie backwards somewhat helplessly and are now at the mercy of a devotee of technology, etc."

Or let us consider the description of a perception: "I see a tree, a clock, a man, or any other thing you wish. I see something that runs on wheels, a bird that flies," and I usually imagine that I have thus adequately described my perception, that I am naming the subject of my perception. But a complete analysis of a perception requires the description of the object.

We see therefore that that which I call subject is definitely not given in reality in the way I call it. I name it and intend the complete thing that exists before all in itself, for example, a book. But it is an old question whether I am allowed to say that I see a book lying there when I see one lying there. For what do I see? I see the surface, the cover on which are golden letters. Can I say then that I see that *this* is a book?

Before me stands a box. It is impossible for me to see all around it at once. Neither can I imagine one instance in which it would be possible for me to have a simultaneous all-around view of it. At most I could make a glass box and thus see all sides at once. A complete simultaneity of all aspects is an impossibility. And yet I say that I see a box, and I mean the whole thing, rectangular in shape, a cube that I can open, etc. *Perception, too, is accomplished in paraphrases.* It too has its subject and object. In the object I thematize the subject which can never appear to me otherwise than in a perspective way.

10. The Perspectivity of Experience

Merleau-Ponty studied these problems extensively, and he tells us: "To see is to enter into a universe of beings that *show themselves,* and they would not show themselves if they were not capable of being hidden behind one another or behind me."[17] Our relation to things is already expressed in what a child does when it plays "look-look" in a box. The child holds his hand before his eyes and at the same time looks above then. He shows *and* hides himself, just as things show *and* hide themselves in our dealings with them: they have always aspects "behind the hand," they never appear as they are in their fullness, but only "perspectively." For we always see from one standpoint or another. But the thing, the subject, is a thematization of the object-of-my-perception. We should try to understand that seeing which always takes place from one particular viewpoint nevertheless is not imprisoned in its own perspective.[18]

The chess board that lies between my opponent and myself is for both of us the same board, though it is evident that every piece that stands on it is seen from a different side. Though the object of our perception is different, the subject is the same. I can see how a thing looks different to another who is in another place, although I do not presently see it the way he sees it. Does this rest on an experience? Not in the sense that I have ever met with the "real thing" in my experience. I can never see more than three sides of a cube. If I say that I have acquired the complete image of a cube with front and back, bottom and top and the sides as a result of a series of sense perceptions that flow into one another, this is not correct. For every one of those sense perceptions that flow into one another is itself in perspective. The form of a cube as such, of which all the surfaces are equal in size, whose corners are all rectangular and the ribs identical in length, I can in no way perceive. How then did I arrive at that knowledge? From the beginning I have seen more in the perspectives than only this one-sided form. Using an expression borrowed from James, I have a *conception* of the cube. This I *can* have because the perspectival forms point beyond their arbitrary shape. The perspectival form is the way the thing appears, it is that thing itself, as I thematize it in that form (with its context) .

There is no reason for breaking up the two and saying that the one, the form, is the *sign* of the other, the thing. There is no need for me to infer the thing from the form; the thing is given *in* the form. The one aspect is implied in the other, but only to the extent that the perspectival form appears in a context. It is thus able to point beyond its limitation. Thus also is the continuity of possible forms visible in the accidental perspectival form. Hence when we say that we grasp things, subjects, in the accidental forms of the objects of perception, this is so because those forms appear in a context, in a referential coherence. If we now return to the terminology we introduced above and identify "subject" (topic) with "theme," we see again how closely theme and field are connected: *the theme of perception is that which becomes thematic as condensation of the field.* A theme limits itself, closes itself, segregates itself *within* a field.

We did not have to borrow our examples from perception. Perspectivity occurs in all forms of experience. The term means only that experience is *person-related* (involved in a person) ; it means that it shows up in what appears in experience from the standpoint of the person; but, at the same time, in virtue of the context, it is transparent towards the unity of the thing that is thematized, passing through retention and "protention" of the varying perspectives, as *the same.* And this takes place pre-reflectively. It is not a rational activity, not a fully conscious construction that comes about here; although the way of describing it might suggest that. But we shall deal with this in our ninth chapter.

11. James' "Object of Thought" and Husserl's "Noema"

Let us recall James' definition: the object of every thought is everything that thought thinks, precisely as it thinks it. What we have just seen shows that "thinking" must not be understood here in the narrow sense. James' definition applies to all experience. Regarding this point we have now once more a fundamental agreement between James and Husserl, as was also pointed out by Gurwitsch.[19] Already in the *Logische Untersuchungen*, we find that a distinction is made between the "Gegenstand, so wie er intendiert ist" (the thing or object in the way it is intended) and the "Gegenstand, welcher intendiert ist" (the object or thing that is intended) .[20] It is evident that this is identical with James' distinction between "object" and "topic." But it is clear from the context that Husserl here is thinking more of the fact that *one same* thing can be intended in various ways: perceiving, representing, remembering, etc. Hence we could here refer to James' opinion that "it makes little or no difference in what sort of mind-stuff, in what quality of imagery . . . thinking goes on, so long as we think *the same*" (I, 269) .

But Husserl, in this connection, speaks also of

> the real consistency of the outward (actual or possible) knowledge-connections of the act itself (dem reellen Bestand des Aktes selbst ausserliche [wirkliche oder mogliche] Erkenntniszusammenhange) : when I imagine the German emperor, it is irrelevant, in respect to the intended 'Gegenstand' (subject) whether or not I recall at the same time whose son he was.

Hence we can say that the above example is in line with James' distinction.

But all doubt is removed when we study Husserl's reflections as given in his *Ideen*.[21] Husserl calls "noema" the object of an act. The noema of judgments, that is, of a concrete experience-judgment, is the "judged as such," but this is nothing other than what we ordinarily call judgment. If we wish now to understand what the problem is, we must not confuse the judgment with that which is judged. The things in question, particularly the subject-things, are "that which is judged." The whole that is formed from them, the totality of that which is judged, taken exactly with the characteristics and specific givenness that is present in lived consciousness, this totality forms the complete noematic correlate, the meaning (the term being taken here in its widest sense) of the judgment-experience. Now the object, the complete noematic correlate is certainly the same identical thing in the statements of James and Husserl. Even Husserl's words: "genau so genommen (wie) es in Erlebnis 'Bewusstes' ist" is identical with James' "exactly as the thought thinks it."

One of the ambiguities we found in James was his use of the term "thought" and the difficulty to find out whether he meant by it "consciousness" or more strictly speaking, "thinking." His theory we have applied to the whole field of the phenomena of consciousness. It is clear that Husserl intended the same universality. For example, he defines the noema of perception as "the perceived as such" (das Wahrgenommene als solches) and compares it to the noema of remembering, judging, etc.[22]

Every psychological method of examination makes more or less use of that. Thus in the Rorschach test we are not content with the interpretations formulated by the person who is taking the test. We try afterwards to find out how he came to that interpretation. The reason is that we are not interested only in "subjects," but we are principally interested in the "objects" of his experience. Sometimes the psychologist is much more interested in the marginal than in the thematic. But in any case it is a question of getting hold of experience as it is experienced. For this characterizes the person with his perspective. It pictures his situation.

It may be true that the noematic description of any kind of experience is an open, endless project, because the description of the field of experience necessarily gets lost in the indefiniteness of the marginal and hence must constantly be taken over again. Nevertheless what that description aims at is nothing less than to express as adequately as possible what is given with absolute and unassailable certainty in experience. The noema has a truth in itself that cannot be assailed by anything. This thought is much older than phenomenology and much older than James. For example, we read in the third Meditation of Descartes: "Now, in, respect to ideas, if we consider them only in themselves, and we do not refer them to other things, they cannot, properly speaking, be false; for whether I imagine a goat or a chimera, it is not less true that I imagine the one as much as the other."[23] The noema, whatever it may be, is in itself something that is given, and has its own character of reality and its own character of truth.

Hence we find in Husserl, a few centuries later, the fundamental methodical principle of phenomenology: "No theory that can be conceived can make us doubt that every dator intuition is a legitimate source of knowledge, in the way that it presents itself, but also only within the limits in which it presents itself."[24] There is a reality of mythical things just as much as there is a reality of chairs and tables. I can say after all what an angel is like (in my experience, *when* I experience such a thing). It matters not for the present moment whether angels *exist* or not. If I have an idea of them then this is a source of knowledge, of lawful and psychologically important knowledge. Of course, I cannot borrow from it a knowledge regarding the *conditions* under which such an idea arises. But an analysis of the conditions presupposes the idea itself and the noematic description of it, if it is to be meaningful.

We are still speaking in the spirit of James. What an experience is, and to what it can be developed or reduced, are two things, not one (I, 279). Hence it is our psychological duty "to cling as closely as possible to the actual constitution of the thought we are studying" (I, 276). Husserl expresses the same idea.[25] Both thinkers are of the opinion that psychology may not and cannot neglect a descriptive orientation.

12. Terminology

In order to get a better survey let us once more gather the meanings that have been given to various terms. James made a distinction between the *topic* and the *object* of experience; we spoke of *subject* and *object*. They are respectively "that about which we are concerned" and the "actual whole of experience." These do not stand against or alongside each other: we considered that the *topic* or *subject* was a thematization of the *object*. Hence the subject can also be called *theme;* as such it is part of the object: the *subject* is the thematized part of the *object*. The actual whole of experience we too have called *noema,* in line with Husserl. The *theme* then is a differentiation within the *noema*. The non-thematized part James calls *margin* or context. And so we can speak of *thematic* and *marginal* experience.

Hence when we describe experience we have at our disposal a diversity of orientations. A *noematic description* tries "to cling as closely as possible to the actual constitution of thought"; to the question what is the "the perceived as such," (Wahrgenommene als solches) the answer is: "we get the answer in pure surrender to what is essentially *given*"[26] (erhalten [wir] die Antwort in reiner Hingabe an das wesensmässig *Gegebene*).

Hence it is also possible to have a *thematic description,* that describes more specifically the theme, the noematic nucleus, as "objective or concrete sense" (gegenstandlichen Sinn). Then, with respect to that, the rest, the "remaining" part of the noema, appears as the margin. Every thematic description encounters this margin, discovers the context as a territory that constitutes the meaning of the theme. In other words, the margin appears in a thematic description as the *horizon* of the theme.

According to Husserl, James was the first, as far as he knew, who concentrated his attention on the phenomenon of *horizon.*[27] James not only described it but also found a term for it. A spoken sentence is surrounded by a fringe, it sounds within a frame of vague relations that surround the meaning as with a horizon (I, 276). Husserl uses the term in the same sense.[28] But he gives it a wider application when it appears that in horizons others are implicated and that finally any worldly given carries with it the world-horizon through which it becomes known as worldly.[29] We have still to see how the problem that is here indicated also comes to the fore in James.

13. Reality and Illusion

When James demands that one should stick as closely as possible to the actual constitution of experience, this demand contains more than a principle for a noematic description. There is in it a criticism of many theoretical constructions and it also contains a view regarding the reality of experience.

With respect to the critique, it would be a major task to describe all the cases in which psychology arrived at absurd construction. This task we do not intend to undertake since one example will suffice. How many have maintained that we *cannot* see spatial depth, and hence also do not see it in spite of the evidence of experience, *because* our retina is two-dimensional! But no argument can prove that an experience that actually occurs does not exist (II, 221 Note).

James himself sometimes forgets his own mandate. He does this, for example, in accord with current ideas, when he defines illusion as a phenomenon that results from a discrepancy be-

tween perception and knowing (II, 86). When we put a stick
into the water, we see a break in the stick where air and water
meet. This is an illusion. We know that the stick is straight, but
we see it as crooked. Here then we have a case of illusion, of a
discrepancy between perceiving and knowing. And our difficulties
begin when we now ask ourselves how we know that the stick is
straight. For that knowledge is based on other sense perceptions,
for example feeling the stick with our hand, but nothing as yet
gives me a guarantee that touching the stick and concluding from
it that the stick is straight, is not itself an illusion.

Let us now leave the problem for a while and turn to the
phenomenon known as "constancy of size." When I hold my
hand close to my eyes I do not see it to be larger than when I
hold the hand at a distance of three feet. But a photograph of
these two situations shows us that a camera, and hence also the
eye, halves all linear sizes when we double the distance. If we
accept the definition of illusion just given, we shall no doubt
consider that the constancy of size is evidently an illusion. For
I *know* that my hand should be "smaller" at a distance from
me than when it is close. And yet I see it in its constant uniform
size. Here then is another discrepancy between perceiving and
knowing.

But psychology *here* never speaks of "illusion." The definition that is based on discrepancy is a definition *ad hoc;* it is used
only when it suits the situation. It is a definition that does not
define the true psychological criterion for distinguishing between
reality and illusion. Reality and illusion as experiences must be
distinguished on the basis of intrinsic characteristics of those
experiences themselves.[30] When their actual constitution indicates no distinction, a distinction has no psychological meaning.

Illusions are not inventions of psychologists; there is a perception that we experience directly as illusional. Hence we see constantly how difficult it is for us to stick to what is given. When I
travel on a road and see a flat stone lying at a distance and it is in
reality a patch of sunlight, we have nevertheless a real experience. I see that stone, because my whole field of perception and
motorial field give to that patch of light the meaning of a stone

lying on the road.[31] The whole context leads to that. I already prepare myself to stop soon on that stone and feel it under my feet. I already direct my step to the thing I see at a distance. When I come nearer to it, I see that it is not a stone but a spot of sunlight. The illusion is removed before I have had the chance to test it with my foot. This transition has been accomplished completely within the sphere of the visible. In reality there was no illusion.

The stone on the road was an image that fitted in the situation just as constancy of the size of my hand fits the figure of my body. The road, the distance, the difference of the intensity of light together with the surroundings and the form in this context, made me see a stone. This is a perception of reality, independent of the question whether this reality will stand the test of a logical analysis. That is the way it is perceived. The logician who analyzes what reality really is makes use of that primary experience of reality.

When I come near, there might be a moment when I perceive that stone stone as something that is deceptive; this is no ordinary stone, it is something else that presents itself that way. At that moment I can speak of an illusion, of an object of experience that shows itself as something that is not like the other things around me in its constitution; in the way it presents itself it deceives me. This then makes me doubt and I ask myself what can that be? My experience then suddenly changes in conformity with the new situation: it is no object at all, it is a patch of sunlight. I have re-discovered reality.

So long as the object appears to me as something that is deceptive, as an illusion, I want to tread on it, to touch it, to grasp it. This is the true foundation of those definitions of the illusion which desire to appeal to something that is tangible. Our ineradicable tendency to take into our hands whatever is illusional and to examine it more closely presupposes that the thing as it appears to us demands that control. Here is no question of truth or falsity in the sphere of judgment, but we ask whether it is *given* as real or as deceptive.

The illusion is not a discrepancy between perceiving and

knowing, but an incompatibility in perception itself that can lead to a discrepancy of knowledge. This "knowing" is not the scientific, rationally purified knowing, for the latter does not at all operate in our daily experience of reality. It is a knowing of what is familiar, as I have learned to know it and that has become "self-evident."

This is why the "breaking" of a stick in the water is for me an illusion; it conflicts with the network and coherence of the things with which I am familiar. Constancy of the size of my hand does not conflict with that network; hence it is no illusion. However, if I wish to define illusion according to a scientific knowledge about things, I shall be obliged to call all perception illusional, for scientific knowledge teaches us that everything "is" different from the way we perceive it.

That is why our perception of individual things addresses itself to the context and to the probability on which it it is based, our familiarity with that context and on the human world in general. "Perception," says James, "is of definite and probable things" (II, 82). Experience of the real, and of the illusional as something within that reality is based on a "belief," on a doxic confidence.

14. Experience of the Real

Everybody knows the difference between imagining something and believing that it exists. It is with this that James begins his examination of reality (II, 283 ff.). No one objects if I amuse myself picturing to myself that my horse that is in the stable suddenly acquires wings, rises in the air, and briskly flies around. I can even imagine this very vividly (II, 289). But I do not believe that this is really my old horse that is in the stable; I do not believe that Pegasus actually exists. There is a difference in what I imagine and what I experience with a doxic confidence in reality.

We could consider the first as the foundation of the second. There are representations of winged horses, but I do not believe in the reality of such horses when I see them. There is, on the other hand, a perception-image of a horse which I also can call a representation (Vorstellung) but on that occasion I believe in the reality of what is represented. Must I say then that there is a representation that acquires reality-value when I *confirm* the reality of the represented thing?

But it makes no difference whether I believe that things have their character of reality from themselves or because I attribute reality to them: in both cases the descriptive distinction between representations of real things and representations of fictitious things remains the same. I "believe" with respect to the first; I do not believe in the second. I can at will represent to myself any kind of man who does not exist. I can give him eyes of any color I wish. But when I represent my father to myself, his eyes are blue. I am limited by reality. In this case the representation is characterized as the representation of something real. This reality is *such*, not otherwise. It is this certainty that James calls "belief" and we have chosen to call "doxa."

We can thus distinguish between fictitious representations and "doxic" representations. However, when they are taken simply as representations (Vorstellung), as a general way of experience, both the doxic *and* the fictitious representations are real. Nevertheless, when taken in that abstract way, the represented is in general an antithesis of the real. For though a doxic representation is a representation of the real, it is nothing more than a *representation* (Vorstellung) it is not the real itself.[32] The represented also "is," but this *to be* is the *to be* of a level other than the *to be* of the real which, as we express it then, "is really there." This distinction becomes clear to us through the "sense of reality," although here we must not take the term "sense" literally. For "reality" is not a quality of what is experienced in the same sense that "red" or "round" or "near" are qualities. Still less is the character of reality something that is originally discerned by a rational judgment. For there is question here of a doxic confidence that is already present in experience itself as confidence, as a pre-reflective certainty, although I can later also pronounce judgment about it. This doxic confidence, says James, is something that according to its inner nature shows kinship with the emotions (II, 283).

It is rather a "feeling" than a perception or a judgment. And we see that James' reasoning is in complete accord with what has been said about illusion from the standpoint of phenomenological psychology. It is a feeling that tells us: this *is*, these things are *real*. Until now James has not given us a satisfactory definition of "the character of reality." Before reproaching him for it, let us realize that it is not at all easy to make a definition. It is difficult for the philosopher to say precisely what he means by "Sein" (to be), because he must always make use of "to be" in order to say what he means by it. It is equally difficult for James to say what "doxic confidence" precisely means. It is therefore better to follow him as he paraphrases that matter than to ask him for a strict definition.

There are many degrees of certainty ranging from a mere supposition to the highest form of evidence. They are all doxic forms. There is a straightforward, "Yes, that is so and not otherwise" and a "Yes, it might be so." These are degrees of reality in the "phenomenal world" that are guides for our conduct, our hesitation, or purposive certainty. And we might thus conceive the idea that doxic confidence has something to do with a "consent." And yet we cannot really say that it is that, for it does not consist in the fact that I agree with reality and that *therefore* it is a reality. It is not because I say, "Yes, this is truly an ashcan" that the thing acquires the character of reality. And yet: "Consent is recognized by all to be a manifestation of our active nature. It would naturally be described by such terms as 'willingness,' or the 'turning of our disposition' " (II, 283). And that to which this is directed *is* the real (II, 295).

James, nevertheless, does try to give us a better definition. He appeals to Stuart Mill and Brentano, who, we must say, are not more successful than James himself. Mill asks himself what is the difference between thinking a reality and merely representing something to oneself. We all know that the distinction is fundamental and that no one lets himself be deceived about it. And yet one cannot say more about it than that the distinction lies precisely in the "belief," in that nucleus of our spiritual (mental) functions. James then remarks that Mill's conclusion evidently expresses that " 'belief', the sense of reality, feels like itself—that is as much as we can say" (II, 286). Shall we do better when we follow Brentano?

Every object, says Brentano, is conscious in a twofold way, as conscious phenomenon *and* as object of a new act, for example, a desire. Something is given, *and* I direct myself towards it in a particular way.[33] James adds: I first experience the object as such; in the second place I can ask the question: is it a real something; and when I reply "yes" to that, I evidently have then a "belief."

It would be naive to think that that object itself, and what James means by "belief" are superimposed. We must be on our guard here against exchanging logical and psychological levels. From the psychological standpoint we are not concerned with *first* experiencing something and *after that* confirming it as a reality. Still less can there be question of a *judgment* although the above sentence seems to suggest that. The whole is already taking place in experience *before* all reflection.

And so we have to admit that doxic confidence is a fundamental datum that cannot be defined, a foundation on which doxic modifications become possible. First of all James does not yet say this. The psychological contraries of "belief" are not "disbelief" but *doubt* and *examination* (inquiry). In James they appear as phenomena that belong to the same order. We shall see later that he does not maintain this point of view; that is why we now speak of doxic modalities in the sense given to them by Husserl.

Husserl introduces doxic modalities as being characteristic of acts.[34] Hence there belongs to experience, for example, a doxic certainty, "it is so"; and then, we find, correlatively in the noema, the character of reality of what has been experienced (sensed). The same takes place in the remembrances, representations and ideas that have a relation to what has been experienced or can be perceived; they are "being-placing" (Seinssetzende) or *thetic* acts. But the certainty, the doxic confidence that accompanies them can pass into doubt, suspicion, question, uncertainty—and correlatively there appear in the noema modalities of being, of "possible," "probably," "doubtful," "can be doubted," etc.; as, for example, when what is experienced in doxic confidence as that and that, or so and so, acquires an illusional character. In such a series, the doxic confidence must be considered as a non-modalized primitive form, as the most basic doxa (Ur-doxa), whereas the other forms must be considered as doxic modalities, as modifications of the most basic doxa (Ur-doxa).

In *Erfahrung und Urteil,* Husserl defines the Ur-doxa more closely as world-consciousness as the universal foundation of confidence in the "self-evident" pre-given world, that is presupposed in all action and equally as much in every cognitive taking-of-a-stand. When I grasp some other object in my field of perception, for example when I am looking at a book on my table, I then notice something that *is* there for me, something that for me was already existing, that was already there in my room, even when I was not yet tending to it; just as this room "was already there" as an existing part-structure in that familiar whole which I call the world.[35] If I doubt, if I question, I do it nevertheless within that Ur-doxic whole. The Ur-doxa is the basis and horizon of all doxic modifications.

It is not necessary to do violence to the texts in order to explain James' thoughts in that sense. For him as for Husserl, experience of reality is a fundamental phenomenon of experience that cannot be reduced to a more fundamental structure.

15. The Coherence of Experiences

The fact, however, that the experience of reality cannot be reduced to something else does not mean, according to James, that one cannot ask further questions about it. And so, for example, the question under what *conditions* we consider something as real is significant.

James introduces here an experiment in thoughts. Suppose that there is a man, an adult with a mature mind but "tabula rasa," a man without any experience. Suppose that this imaginary man receives the impression of a burning candle. Suppose further that this impression is purely subjective and that there is really no candle there. Does this man experience his impression as a reality? Does he believe that the candle is present? But, asks James, must I not precisely reverse the question? Could there be any sense in doubting about the reality of the candle? Seeing, where there is as yet no experience, must here coincide with "belief," with the acceptance of the candle as a reality. Are we then not allowed to say generally: every object, every experience, that is not contradicted by or contrary to other phenomena is ipso facto posited as a reality? (II, 288) .

It is my experience that makes me reject definite things as unreal, whereas I take other things as real precisely on the basis of this experience. If I have not yet had any experience, my first experience must of itself have for me the character of reality, because it gives no occasion for doubt. Hence the character of reality of things is connected with the relations of those things with other things in the world of experience which, as we have already seen, always appear as an *outside* world.[36]

Let us return once more to the illusion of which we spoke above. I deny the reality of the broken stick in the water because it does not agree with other experiences, for instance, with the fact that when I take the stick out of the water, the stick is once more straight and whole. Why do I refuse to admit that the stick breaks every time it is in the water? It is the connection and coherence of my experiences and my general confidence in the reality of the world that here give me the "decision." Everything that comes up in the mind we hold to be true until we notice that it is in conflict with the coherence of experiences.

A dream-candle has existence, that is certain, but not the same existence (existence in itself namely, or *outside my mind*) that candles possess when we perceive them in our waking hours. A dreamhorse has wings; but neither horse, nor wings agree with any horses or wings that are known to us in our memory. That we are capable at any moment of our choice to think of the same thing we were thinking about earlier, is the fundamental law of our mental constitution.[37]

But when we now think that this cannot be reconciled with other ways, we must then make a choice and determine which way we shall maintain, for we cannot go on thinking simultaneously in ways that are mutually exclusive.

> The whole distinction of real and unreal, the whole psychology
> of belief, disbelief, and doubt, is thus grounded on two mental

facts—first, that we are liable to think differently of the same; and second, that when we have done so, we can choose which way of thinking to adhere to and which to disregard (II, 290).

The latter sounds rather simple, as if we had a completely free choice of *what* is accepted as reality. When James said this, it was because he was impressed by the diverse *orders* of reality.

16. Orders of Reality, "Worlds"

The things we renounce, that do not fit into the coherence or texture of our experiences, we usually do not consider to be realities. They are treated as superfluities, as *null*. But the philosopher attributes also to the things of the imagination a certain reality, namely their own proper imaginary reality (II, 291).

Whoever wishes to describe experience in the most simple terms, James says later,[38] and at the same time wishes to make as few assumptions as possible must presuppose at least three things:

(1) Developing fields of experience that possess a certain mutual continuity;

(2) Nothing should be postulated that is not given by way of nature in those fields, neither a pure ego, nor material substance;

(3) All the usually presupposed fields are incomplete, and refer to a complement that lies outside their content. Finally we have a multiplicity of fields that exclude one another more or less, and yet are continuous in various ways.

Here we are concerned with the third point. For this implies also a connection between reality and imagination, and hence a certain *order,* in which they are connected (cohere).

Does James now see only different, coexistent and equivalent realms of experience, or does he see them in a hierarchical or foundational order? We spoke earlier of a theme, a field and a horizon and saw that the last term although rarely used by James, meant something real for him. We can now restate that question in the following manner: Do James' coexistent fields of experience have a *common* horizon? Do the individual fields of experience refer to a fundamental context or texture that encloses all the fields? We now encounter one of the problems which James did not solve. Two answers can be drawn from his work. The one is expressed in the title *"A Pluralistic Universe"*; the other we shall now examine.

There are more than the two worlds of reality and of imagination. The philosopher strives not only to give to every object of his thought the exact place in one or other of those worlds; he tries also to determine their mutual relations within the whole of the world that *is* (II, 291). The various worlds, or orders of reality, are therefore rather sub-universes, in spite of the unconnectedness that is attributed to them in daily life.

But which now are those worlds? The following, according to James, are the most important:

(1) The "sensible" world, the ordinary world of everyday life, in which things have all sorts of qualities such as: heat, color, sound, life, weight, electricity.

(2) The world of natural science. That about which science speaks does not exist in the "sensible" world, but the reverse is also true. He who uses a scientific concept refers to a sub-universe other than the universe of the ordinary man.

(3) A third sub-universe is that of ideal relations and abstract truths, expressed in logical, mathematical, metaphysical, ethical and esthetic judgments.

(4) The world of group-idols, of the opinions and prejudices that are characteristic of particular (cultural) groups, opinions that are considered as self-evident by one group and equally non-self-evident by another.

(5) Supernatural worlds, of heaven and hell, of the mythologies, of the Iliad, etc.

(6) The world of personal conceptions, of which there are as many as there are men.

(7) The worlds of insanity and madness, indefinite in number.

James did not consider his summing up to be complete. On the contrary, he was interested in the most important worlds, and wanted to shed light on their significance. With respect to the latter we must now name two points. Every object of experience acquires its own place indicated for it in such an order and every order acquires, in itself, a consistent structure. If there is no room for the winged horse in the everyday world, if it has no reality in that world, then another, namely the world of myths, is ready to take it up. In this world, the winged horse has then its own reality. In this world it "exists" in a context that has its own legitimacy: a legitimacy that cannot always be reduced to that of other orders of reality. And so we are obliged to say that declarations concerning different worlds are made from different standpoints; they have different horizons. But this means that it is impossible to describe "reality" without more ado. That which we describe is at the same time dependent on the horizon in which we see it.

17. *Description and Horizon*

It is useful to show the significance of the horizon by using two examples taken from scientific thought. The great psychologist of the sense organs, Hering, in his *Grundzuge der Lehre von Lichtsinn* begins with a description of what we see when we open our eyes. In a book written at a later time the French philosopher Nogué, without any dependence on Hering, gave a short description, also from the "naive" standpoint of the opened eye. It is interesting to put the two passages alongside one another. How readily we describe only that which we "want" to see, as the saying is.

Hering has the following description:

> When we open our eyes in a room in which there is light, we see before us a variety of things that are spread out in space; these are circumscribed or contrasted with one another through a variety of colors, taking color here in the widest sense, hence also black, gray, white, in fact all that is dark or bright. It is by the colors that the contours of those objects are filled out; they are the stuff out of which that which appears to our eyes constructs itself before us. Our *world of vision* consists purely of various patterns of colors, and the things as we *see* them, that is, the "Sehdinge" (sight-things) are nothing else than colors of diverse kinds and forms.[39]

Now let us close our eyes once more and open them again, this time as suggested by Nagué.

> If we open our eyes on the world, it appears to us as an empty milieu at the centre of which we are placed, and which contains a multiplicity of objects that are situated in various places. According to the disposition of the surrounding decor, that milieu is said to be more or less narrow, or more or less spacious, it gives room, it is free or is occupied, filled with things or beings that take that place and leave open only a restricted portion . . . that milieu, that void, where we are and that is filled with sensible objects, is what we commonly call space.[40]

Both authors ask us to do the *same* thing: to "open our eyes." And yet how different is that which is seen as suggested by Hering and by Nogué! Hering sees immediately "Sehdinge" (sight-things) that must be distinguished from the real thing. For Hering these "Sehdinge" are purely visual data, they are that which one "perceives really and exclusively with the eyes." They cannot be touched, heard, smelled or tasted. Hering does not see *things,* with which we can deal. Evidently, he considers them as *not given.*

Nogué, on the contrary, immediately sees a world of things that are both visible and audible. They are given in a way that permits us to handle them. The very first thing he notices is the spacious quality of space, the "empty space," *in* which one can enter. I am at a distance from something else. I must move in order to reach it. There is or is not room in that space. It is full or empty. There are things that are in my way, or that leave me room to pass between them. There is a depth in that world that is entirely absent from the description given by Hering, and that will not return to it without great difficulty.

Whereas the visibility as known to Hering is the visibility of a "Sehwelt" (sight-world), of a world that appears to the eye, the visibility according to Nogué is that of things themselves; they are not "Erscheinungen" (appearances) but visible objects. Hence Hering writes a "Lehre vom Lichtsinn" (Theory of the sense of light). He aims at physiology and it is with the eye of a physiologist that he sees the world. Nogué, as he himself says, cannot prevent himself from seeing the emptiness of the space that, for him, stands at the centre, in connection with the mobility of the observer who as an indigent being looks for what is absent in that space.

But what then is the true connection? Does Hering describe only that which he sees because he aims at physiology? And is Nogué different because he has a biological prejudice? Or do both *see* it the way they describe it? Both can maintain that they have given "unprejudiced" descriptions of what appears when one opens one's eyes. Is it not evident that we originally and primarily see only shaped colors? The rest must then in some way be added afterwards. But it is just as evident that we find ourselves in a space from the very beginning, a space we can and must pass through in our search for a prey.

But if we say: he sees it that way, hence it is that way, we have to add that every way of seeing things has value only within a particular horizon. To see is to thematize; and that means then to thematize within a field, within an order of reality. The descriptions of Hering and Nogué are not descriptions of things as they exist, rounded in themselves, but of things in their horizon. It is the horizon that determines the meaning as meaning within a certain order of reality. And once again is raised the question of to what extent those horizons themselves and the worlds they contain are ordered towards one another?

18. The Life-World as the Fundamental Order of Reality

According to James, the various worlds have only a rather loose inter-connection. On the contrary, it is one of Husserl's fundamental theses that there are no horizons that exist alongside of and free from one another; he maintains instead that they are differentiated by and are based upon an ultimate, or rather, a first general horizon, namely that of the *"Lebenswelt"* (Life-world), the world within which all that is human originally has its meaning, the foundation that is shared by all who are called "man," the foundation that makes possible an understanding between the most different races and peoples.

The fact that it is self-evident for a people I have never met that what is hard is hard, what is heavy is heavy, that to slap one is to cause pain, refers me to our common world of experiences and contexts, and of interconnections of experiences. It is this world, "in which we are already living, and which gives the foundation for all achievement of knowledge and for all scientific determination" ("in der wir immer schon leben, und die den Boden für alle Erkenntnisleistung abgibt und für alle wissenschaftliche Bestimmung").[41]

To us, human beings of these times, the world appears as already affected and influenced by the results of centuries of scientific thought. This made James believe that theoretical views had changed the very appearance of reality. We have then the more reason to ask with Husserl for the pre-predicative originality of the "Life-world," in which such influences are not yet present. Naturally this is a task that is practically never finished, no less than James' parallel search for a pure experience.

This means that this project, precisely on account of its indefiniteness, remains always actual. Merleau-Ponty's phenomenology of perception is a result of this fact; the same can be said of Haering's question about and return to the foundations of scientific thought in everyday experience; and similar to it are James' attempts, before these two, to put order in the orders of reality itself. This he does in two ways: First, by establishing that every man lets one world prevail over another and then calls this world one of "practical realities" (II, 293). The latter then constitutes the system of relations to which the other worlds are oriented. Are we totally free here in our choice? According to James, we are when properly considered. All that arouses our interest we consider to be the real (II, 295). And thus the "choice" is determined by interest, and one gives the preference to the sensible world, another to scientific reality, etc. (II, 294). "Reality" is then simply dependent on our emotional and active life (II, 295).[42]

On closer inspection, however, that choice is limited: *for we do not escape from the original reality of sensation* (experience)[43] (II, 299). If we keep in mind that James has rejected a "sensationalistic" doctrine of experience (sensation); that, as we have seen, he considers that sensations are already related to and involved in things, we are permitted to waive the fact that he falls back on Hume in his discussion of this orginal reality. *"Sensible objects are thus either our realities or the tests of our realities"* (II, 301). Here we have nothing but the primacy of the "Life-world" (Lebenswelt)! For Husserl also the reality of perception characterizes, in the first place, the "Ur-doxa." It is to this world that all others are oriented.

This is confirmed by the second manner in which James arrives at an ordering. It is, he tells us, "our own reality, that sense of our own life which we at every moment possess" that constitutes the ultimate orientation for our doxic confidence (II, 297). *But what else is this proper (our own) reality than our corporeity?* If we remember that "life" and "body" really hang together, we see that the "Life-world" is that world, that order of reality, in which we live through the body.

Every horizon is involved in and refers to the Ur-doxic horizon that is given as "Life-world" together with corporeity. If there is a question of reality, then this defines *the* reality. *"Whatever things have intimate and continuous connection with my life are things of whose reality I cannot doubt"* (II, 298). Everything that is declared, described and analyzed by scientific thought, is involved in and refers back to that reality. A more real reality than this does not exist for us. Regardless of how often someone in school tells us that the sun "in reality" does not turn around the earth, every morning we *see* that the sun rises.

Whenever someone wished to show why, and in what respect such things can be explained in another way, we have to go back to those connections and attitudes that belong to the reality of life. The teacher may tell us that the earth, in reality, turns around its own axis. This he must explain by means of things taken from my natural everyday world. I must first compare the earth to a ball and allow the ball to turn within my fingers, before I understand what the cosmologist means by the turning around of the earth. I realize then that his explanation of the course of the sun is logical in his system. But I can never *see* that the sun stands still. The first reality that is the foundation of all scientific thought is that of the Life-world. Hence there is a character of reality of that which we call a thing, an original fundamental content of the thing-concept, that can never be taken away by any explanation in terms of natural science.

We get a better idea of James' opposition to association theory and his preference for a description of experience when we study them in that connection. For we must then say that it is unreasonable to want the phenomenal world to arise genetically from an analysis of that same world. That which is the foundation of every analysis cannot itself be reduced to that which is constructed and comes into being only in that analysis. The doctrine of experiences (sensations) is one way in which we can describe the phenomenal. The opinion that those sensations (experiences) came first and that the phenomenal was constructed out of them, is unreasonable. For although it is possible to come from the phenomenal thing to a sensation-concept (experience-concept) the reverse is not possible.

That is why it is not strange that the definition of "reality" encountered such difficulties. For every definition *presupposes* the reality of the Life-world, and it can be explained only by this world. James told us that doxic confidence, the confidence in the self-evident reality of the Life-world must properly be considered as a feeling.

If we anticipate his theory concerning emotions, which we shall deal with later on, we are then permitted to say: *doxic confidence is the way we participate in the Life-world through the body, and experience this participation.* James says the same thing when he declares that the most fundamental reality is the world of "practical realities." For "practical" refers to the action, the activity of the body.

We meet here the great theme of "action," of corporeity, in the psychology of James. It is this theme that is finally decisive for his psychology, although he did not develop it extensively. We call real that which we deal with corporeally; that to which we also *want* to turn; and we must add: to which we also *must* turn, for it is unreasonable to deny the fact that our own reality, the feeling of our own life and existence, coincides with the experience of corporeity.

This then is a conclusion we are permitted to draw from what has gone before: the Life-world, the concrete, real world of our daily experience has precedence over all others. When someone says, "glass is not glass, but something else," he starts from everyday reality in order then to say something about it. What he has said we can accept or reject. But in order to agree or disagree with it, one has to start from what can be handled, from a thing that is given in this corporeal world.

When someone says, "matter does not exist, for matter is principally empty space between atoms," he must then, in order to introduce his subject, have recourse to a piece of that non-existing matter, take it and say, "look, *that* which I show you does not exist." Primarily *that* remains the given (datum). The reason is that our existence is a corporeal existence; it is not that of a pure spirit who considers appearances as appearances, but the corporeal existence of vulnerable man, bound to space and time.

19. Consciousness and Things

Consciousness is directed to things. Thus, following James, did we begin the argument developed in this chapter. But what *is* that "thing"? Not something that already exists independently of us, and is then simply registered in perception. We grasp "things" with our awareness of identity which conceives "the same" in the constant changing stream of experience.

Let us recall what we saw in Chapter IV. We must then say that the developing individual *can* attain this within the frame of a community that shows him the way, and that gives testimony in language of its traditional "conceptions." It is the language that gives us an ontology; a sedimented ontology, an explanation of the world, in which things are fastened; a fixation that has allowed the original flux and change of the stream of experience to coagulate. At first this seemed to be a falsification. But the fixation that finds its "precipitation" in language, already belongs to the characteristics of experience. The "unanalysed bloom" of sensation (experience) is a hypothetical limit.

Experience, from the start, concretizes *things,* and it is mean-

ingful to the extent that it shows directedness. Before all reflection there is already articulation in the stream of experience,
there are orderings and differentiations and there are connections
by which the one refers to another. This appeared also to be so in
the "nausée" described by Sartre: the "conception" of the "ut-
terly meaningless" is mentally impossible, because it *is* already
meaningful.

So the substantive tendency of experience is a fundamental
characteristic. We saw in the previous chapter how that tendency
expressed itself in thematization, which does not merely delimit
themes in the field of experience but polarizes that field and also
the margin, so that it shows relevance with respect to the theme.
In order to see what then occurs (in the measure this can be
explained) we have tried, following James, to understand as
adequately as possible the field of experience as object of experience; and we have seen the necessity of using noematic descriptions as starting points in our analysis of thematizations.

This problem flows over into that of the reality of experience.
Orders of reality seemed to be ordered in turn towards a fundamental order, the order of the "Life-world." Here meaningfulness
and thematization in a definite direction are already pre-ordered
by the inevitable reality of the body. Corporeal reality is *Ur*-
reality (original reality).

That is why it is difficult to understand thematizations here as
activities; these are already pre-given in movement and perception, in the "paramount reality of sensation," in which the given,
in its connection with the body, appears in thing-structures.
When consciousness is directed to things, when, to express it
more exactly, it is originally as Ur-doxa, experience-of-things, this
means *that intentionality is based on corporeity.* But then the
doctrine of experience necessarily has its foundation in the theory of the body. That James too reached that conclusion we shall
see in the following chapters, although this may already be evident from what we have said above.

NOTES

1. E. B. Titchener, "Functional Psychology and the Psychology of Act; I," *Amer. J. Psychol.*, vol. 32, 1921, p. 235 Note.
2. Cf. also James, "The Thing and Its Relations," in *A Pluralistic Universe*, p. 358.
3. *Ibid.*, p. 348.
4. Cf. above Note 16, p. 173.
5. James, *A Pluralistic Universe*, p. 548.
6. Cf. above, pp. (130 ff.)
7. Perry, *Thought*, vol. 1, p. 457: "An idea is an idea, effectively and not merely nominally, when and in so far as it is convertible, directly or indirectly, actually or hypothetically, into perceptual experience."
8. James, *A Pluralistic Universe*, p. 250.
9. That James is extremely modern in his theory concerning brain activity may be reckoned among his great merits. The following passage concerning the field theory is also "up to date": "The amount of activity at any given point in the brain-cortex is the sum of the tendencies of all other points to discharge into it, such tendencies being proportionate (1) to the number of times the excitement of each other point may have accompanied that of the point in question; (2) to the intensity of such excitements; and (3) to the absence of any rival point functionally disconnected with the first point, into which the discharges might be diverted" (*Principles*, vol. 1, p. 567). This contains James' physiological theory of association.
10. E. Severance & M. Washburn, "The Loss of Associative Power in Words After a Long Fixation," *Amer. J. Psychol.*, vol. 18, 1907; M. Basset & C. Warne, "On Lapse of Verbal Meaning with Repetition," *Amer. J. Psychol.*, vol. 30, 1919; V. Don & H. Weld, "Lapse of Meaning with Visual Fixation," *Amer. J. Psychol.*, vol. 35, 1924.
11. J. P. Sartre, *La Nausée*, 62nd ed., (Paris, 1948), p. 162: ". . . C'était la pâte même des choses, cette raçine était pétrie dans de l'existence. Ou plutôt la raçine, les grilles du jardin, le banc, le gazon rare de la pelouse, tout ça s'était évanoui; la diversité des choses, leur individualité n'était qu'une apparence, un vernis. Ce vernis avait fondu, il restait des masses monstrueuses et molles, en désordre—nues, d'une effrayante et obscène nudité."
12. *Ibid.*, p. 163.
13. *Ibid.*, p. 164.
14. *Ibid.*, p. 164: "J'avais beau répéter: 'C'est une raçine,' ça ne prenait plus. Je voyais bien qu'one ne pouvait pas passer de sa fonction de racine, de pompe aspirante, *à ça,* à cette peau dure et compacte de phoque, à cet aspect huileux, calleux, entêté. La fonction n'expliquait rien: elle permettait de comprendre en gros ce que c'était qu'une

raçine, mais pas du tout *celle-ci.* Cette raçine, avec sa couleur, sa forme, son mouvement figé, était . . . au-dessous de toute explication."

15. *Ibid.,* p. 171: "Je me levai, je sortis. Arrive à la grille, je me suis retourné. Alors le jardin m'a souri. Je me suis appuyé à la grille et j'ai longtemps regardé. Le sourire des arbres, du massif de laurier *ca voulait* dire quelque chose; ç'était ça le véritable secret de l'existence. Je me rappelai qu'un dimanche, il n'y a pas plus de trois semaines, j'avais déjá saisi sur les choses une sorte d'air complice. Était-ce à moi qu'il s'adressait. Je sentais avec ennui que ju n'avais aucun moyen de comprendre. Aucun moyen. Pourtant c'était là, dans l'attente, ca ressemblait à un regard. C'était là, sur le tron du marronier . . . c'était le marronier. Les choses, on aurait dit des pensées qui s'arrêtaient en route, qui s'oubliaient, qui oubliaient ce qu'elles avaient voulu penser et qui restaient comme ça, ballottantes, avec un drôle petit sens qui les dépassait. Çam'agaçait ce petit sens: je *ne pouvais pas* le comprendre, quand bien même je serais resté cent sept ans appuyé à la grille; j'avis appris sur l'existence tout ce que je pouvais savoir."

16. *Ibid.,* p. 164.

17. Merleau-Ponty, *Phénoménologie de la Perception,* (Paris, 1945) , p. 82.

18. *Ibid.,* p. 81: "Il nous faut comprendre comment la vision peut se faire de quelque part sans être enfermé dans sa perspective."

19. Gurwitch, *The Field of Consciousness,* pp. 185 ff.

20. Edmund Husserl, *Logische Untersuchungen,* Bd. 2/1, (Halle, 1922) , p. 400.

21. Husserl, *Ideen,* vol. 1, p. 194.

22. *Ibid.,* p. 182.

23. Rene Descartes, "Méditations," in *Ouvres et Lettres de Descartes,* (Paris, 1949) , p. 178: "Maintenant, pour ce qui concerne les idées, si on les considère seulement en elles-mêmes, et qu'on ne les rapporte point à quelque autre chose, elles ne peuvent, à proprement parler, être fausses; car soit que j'imagine une chèvre ou une chimère, il n'est pas moins vrai que j'imagine l'une autant que l'autre." Cf. W. James, *Principles,* vol. 1, p. 187, the discussion of introspection, and the quotation from Brentano, *Psychologie vom Empirischen Standpunkte,* (Leipzig, 1874) , pp. 181 ff.

24. Husserl, *Ideen,* vol. 1, p. 43, where Husserl calls this the "Principle of all Principles." In my "Postscript" for *Persoon en Wereld,* p. 252, I took over this phenomenological principle regarding the theory of knowledge and introduced it into phenomenological psychology. Our study of James also prompted us to do this. Delfgaauw criticized this "Postscript" and in it he doubted "if this can be called the fundamental principle of phenomenology." He also states that this principle, in any case, does not cover the later development of phenomenology. We reply

to the second point that this later development would then be no longer a phenomenology; and to the first, this, "kann uns keine erdenkliche Theorie irre machen" (no imaginable theory can destroy the truth of that). Cf. B. Delfgaauw, "Verantwoording der Phaenomenologische Psychologie," *Nederl. Tijdschr. Psychol.,* vol. 9, 1954, p. 82.

25. Cf. Husserl, *Ideen,* vol. 1, p. 183.

26. *Ibid.,* p. 183.

27. Edmund Husserl, *Die Krisis der Europäischen Wissenschaften und die Transzendentale Phänomenologie,* (The Hague, 1954), p. 269.

28. Cf. Husserl, *Ideen,* vol. 1, pp. 48 ff, 80, 99, 129, 164 ff.

29. Husserl, *Krisis,* p. 267. Cf. the study of H. Kuhn. "The Phenomenological Concept of 'Horizon'" in Marvin Farber, ed., *Historical Essays in Memory of Edmund Husserl,* (Cambridge, Mass., 1940), pp. 106-123.

30. Merleau-Ponty, *Phénoménologie,* p. 340.

31. *Ibid.,* p. 343.

32. Let us not forget, however, that "real" here means: as reality that is *experienced*.

33. Brentano, *Psychologie vom Empirischen Standpunkte,* pp. 266 ff.

34. Husserl, *Ideen,* vol. 1, pp. 214 ff.

35. Edmund Husserl, *Erfahrung und Urteil,* (Hamburg, 1948), pp. 25 ff. Cf. also *Krisis,* pp. 105 ff.: "Erfasse ich in Sonderheit in meinem Wahrnehmungsfeld, z.B. auf ein Buch auf dem Tisch hinsehend, irgendein Object, so erfasse ich ein für mich Seiendes, das schon vorher für mich seiend, schon 'dort' war, 'in meinem Studier-zimmer,' auch wenn ich noch nicht darauf gerichtet war."

36. Cf. above, pp. 90 ff.

37. Cf. above, pp. 119 ff.

38. In a psychological course, 1895-96, quoted by Perry, *Thought,* vol. 2, p. 365.

39. Ewald Hering, *Grundzüge der Lehre vom Lichtsinn,* (Berlin, 1925), p. 1: "Wenn wir im beleuchteten Raume die Augen aufschlagen, sehen wir vor uns eine Mannigfaltigkeit räumlich ausgedehnter Gebilde, die sich durch die Verschiedenheit ihrer Farbe voneinander abgrenzen oder abheben, wobei das Wort Farbe im weitesten Sinne genommen und auch Schwarz, Grau, Weiss, überhaupt judes Dunkel und jedes Hell darunter verstanden ist. Die Farben sind es, welche die Umrisse jener Gebilde ausfüllen, sie sind der Stoff, aus dem das unserem Auge Erscheinende sich vor uns aufbaut; unsere *Sehwelt* besteht lediglich aus verschieden gestalteten Farben, und die Dinge, so wie wir sie *sehen,* d.h. die *Sehdinge,* sind nichts anderes als Farben verschiedener Art und Form."

40. Jean Nogué, *L'activité Primitive du Moi,* (Paris, 1936), pp. 123 ff.: "Si nous ouvrons les yeux sur le monde, celui-ci nous apparaît

comme un milieu vide au centre duquel nous sommes placés et que fer-
ment une multiplicité d'objets situés en des lieux différents. Suivant la
disposition du décor environnant, ce milieu est dit plus ou moins
resserré, plus ou moins spacieux, il offre de la place, it est libre, ou bien
il est occupé, encombré de choses ou d'êtres qui prennent de cette place
et n'en laissent disponible qu'une portion restreinte. . . . Ce milieu, ce
vide, où nous sommes et que viennent peupler tous les objets sensibles,
tel est ce que l'on nomme le plus communément *espace.*"

41. Husserl, *Erfahrung und Urteil*, p. 38. Cf. also Alfred Schutz, on
"Multiple Realities," *Phil. Phenomenol. Res.*, vol. 5, 1945; "Common
Sense and Scientific Interpretation of Human Action," *Phil. Phenome-
nol. Res.*, vol. 14, 1953; "Symbol, Reality and Society," in L. Bryson, ed.,
Symbols and Society, (New York, 1955). Schutz develops here, better
than we have seen elsewhere, the relationship between James and
Husserl concerning the matter of the "Lebenswelt."

42. Th. L. Haering, *Philosophie der Naturwissenschaft*, (Munich,
1923).

43. Cf. James, *Pragmatism*, pp. 264 ff.; *Will to Believe*, pp. 117 ff.

VII ATTENTION AND CHOICE

1. Experience and Interest

James presupposes a spontaneity of conduct; this is in accord with his opinion that it is necessary to speak of a psyche when there is purposive behavior that is variable with respect to the means that are used for the attainment of a goal. Man *chooses* his means, and to some extent also his ends. He is interested in one, and pays no attention to another. The various worlds of which we have spoken in the previous chapter possess reality for the man who addresses himself to them; and that reality disappears when his inner attention to them disappears (II, 293). It makes no difference that everyone has his own particular habits of attention. What we are concerned with is the fact that *choosing* (selecting) occurs in experience. The phenomena of attentively turning toward things and of perfectly conscious willing are special forms of that. They betray a partisanship, an interest.

According to James, the fifth great characteristic of the stream of experience is the fact that it is always more interested in one part of the object than in another, accepts or rejects a part, and thus chooses (I, 284). Not everything that at the moment could reach me actually does reach me. Not everything that stimulates my senses at that moment is also sensed by me. This means that the stream of consciousness makes a choice. This choosing is a "structuring." James, although not expressing it that way, seems to believe that this coincides with the setting of thematic boundaries, with the differentiation of a theme within the field of experience.

This is an activity. I can, for example, be listening and pass by what I "see" at the same time. It is possible for me to thematize within a sense-modality, for instance when I try to hear one melody after the other while "hearing" a double melody. Two melodies are played simultaneously and their melodies harmonize so perfectly that they form a unity. This whole we can analyze while listening and break up into two melodic lines in such a way that, at a certain moment, we recognize one of the two melodies and do not at all hear the other. In order to hear one melody pregnantly the other must drop back into something that takes place in the background. After that we can let the first drop back in its turn and thematize the other, and the first becomes now inaudible; so inaudible that if one does not remember its name, it is necessary to thematize it anew in order to know which one it was.

In such a way the stream of experience constantly achieves "structures," and these are certainly not confined to the sphere that usually is classified under "attention." James also considers the "figures" of Gestalt psychology to be the result of accentuating activity. When a metronome is ticking with equal intervals, it is almost impossible to hear a completely homogeneous regularity. We group the ticks and make of them measures of ¾ or ¼. The ticks are structured into larger unities and these sometimes are made into elements of even larger unities.

When, at night, I hear the large clock striking twelve, I count the strokes in groups of three or four. But I do not merely *count* them by threes or fours; I *hear* them in groups of three and four. And it also seems to us then that the intervals between the third and fourth strokes are somewhat longer than the pauses between the second and third: every group of three (or four) also divides itself phenomenally in time from the following groups. The universality of the distinctions of *this* and *that, here* and *there, now* and *then,* is the expression of our constant selective structuring, of our selective interest.

Helmholtz says that we notice only those sensations which are signs to us of *things*. But what are things? Nothing . . . but special groups of sensible qualities, which happen practically or aesthetically to interest us, to which we therefore give substantive names, and which we exalt to this exclusive status of independence and dignity. But in itself, apart from my interest, a particular dust-wreath on a windy day is just as much of an individual thing, and just as much or as little deserves an individual name, as my own body does" (I, 285) .

As we have already said: the selectivity of the stream of experience betrays intentionality; selection is thematization. And if we re-introduce here the views of James regarding "conception" which we have already discussed, we notice again the "closedness" of James' phenomenological system. Man does not only choose his worlds, but also his "things" (objects) . And this choosing is a *doing*. But this brings up a problem: is this "doing" not actually a "happening"? And is interest perhaps not so much a *chosen preference* as a *forced specialization?* Let us pursue the examination of this problem.

2. *The Senses as Filters*

The senses are themselves already selective organs. The spectrum, for instance, that the eye is able to perceive is but a fraction of the total electro-magnetic spectrum. The visible spectrum is but an infinitesimal part of what lies beyond infrared and ultraviolet, Roentgen rays and radio waves. All the rest we have left out of consideration but not by our own choice; the eye acts here as a filter; it selects and orders things. This selection could have been different from what it actually is; but *this* is the way it is and must be accepted by experience as something that is given that way. From the indistinguishable continuum of wavelengths that reach the organism, and that in themselves possess no qualitative differences or nuances of color, the eye grasps a few and transforms them into colors. The same is done by all the senses, and they thus constitute a large and varied filter that reacts upon a part of the infinite number of physical variables, and "leaves" the rest "out of consideration" (I, 254) .

James does not draw this conclusion but we can safely anticipate that this filter-activity is not a personal activity. There is at work here a mechanism for which no man has any responsibility. Hence he has not made any choice in that respect either to accept or reject.

But if James still looks upon the grouping-phenomena as

results of an activity, Gestalt psychology has since dispensed us of any responsibility in that regard. The organization of data that are filtered by the senses takes place according to definite rules that were still unknown to James, but which we have learned from Gestalt psychology; thus the closed contour is for us the boundary of a thing enclosed within that contour, and that contour never belongs to the background from which it divides the thing. But once more: this is not on the basis of *our* choice. If we fail to study Gestalt psychology, we do not even know that this occurs, still less *how* it takes place. The organism "does" it for us.

And is this then not true also of the next-in-line higher phenomenon which James calls the "phenomenon of constancy"?

> The mind selects again. It chooses certain of the sensations to represent the thing most *truly*, and considers the rest as its appearances, modified by the conditions of the moment. Thus my table-top is named *square*, after but one of an infinite number of retinal sensations which it yields, the rest of them being sensations of two acute and two obtuse angles; but I call the latter *perspective* views, and the four right angles the *true* form of the table, and erect the attribute squareness into the table's essence, for aesthetic reasons of my own (I, 285).

But do *I* do it? Or are those phenomena of constancy also autonomous filter-effects? For here also I do not know *that* I do it, nor *how*. And is it not necessary to apply here the rule of Geulincx: *ego non facio id, quod quomodo fiat nescio* (I do not do that which I do not know how I do it)? But then, all that has been said in the previous chapters concerning thematization becomes doubtful to the extent that in that matter we always presupposed the activity of a person.

3. Attention as Voluntary Filter

James first of all reaches another conclusion. Perception implies a twofold choice. From among all present sensations we choose that which is meaningful with non-present connections (perspectival and "true" form); and we consider the latter as those that pre-eminently represent objective reality (I, 286).

What someone is aware of depends on his experiences with the things; but this experience was itself already determined by his attention.

I am in a certain sense delivered to my impressions, to my milieu, first to my parents, then to my teacher and finally to society; and so I am formed, molded, becoming finally what I am, not of myself, but made by all who have influenced me. But, says James, if that is so, we must nevertheless take account of the fact that personal experience is formed with the help of the selection of the person himself, who to a certain degree decides *himself* what he will accept or reject from among the impressions that are offered to him. This is determined by his interest.

Of how many children is it not said that they "never listen"? But if a child did this always, how then could a child become itself? He "listens" to and hears that in which he is interested. Interest in this connection does not mean "that alone that is pleasing to the child" but: that to which the child opens himself.

We are indeed exposed to impressions that literally come down upon us, without our choice; but the *ordering* of those impressions, and hence their *meaning*, is our own work. Hence it is unreasonable to plan a program for a good education in the sense that everyone will have to go and look at the Acropolis. This in itself has absolutely no formative value. It is possible for someone who has no opportunity to go to Greece to learn more from pictures than the man who runs around and through the buildings.

There are people who are unable to see what is picturesque in Paris but notice only that the social conditions are so far behind those of the orderly Netherlands. Experience is formed with the help of personal choice; but naturally, not purely and solely by that. I can experience something only when there is something that can be experienced. But experience is not a passive undergoing of impressions. If this were so, education and formation could never be anything but training.

James attributes great importance to personal selectivity. This is also evident from the way he thinks and reasons. Isn't his whole course of reasoning concerning discrimination built on selectivity? " . . . all Reasoning depends on the ability of the mind to break up the totality of the phenomenon reasoned about, into parts, and to pick out from among these the particular one which, in our given emergency, may lead to the proper conclusion" (I, 287) .

It is not otherwise in the matter of art. The artist selects, rejects, brings parts into harmony. And higher still, in the field of ethics, the choice is sovereign. We see then "that the mind is at every stage a theatre of simultaneous possibilities. Consciousness consists in the comparison of these with each other, the selection of some, and the suppression of the rest by the reinforcing and inhibiting agency of attention" (I, 288) .

4. Spontaneous Attention (Turning-Toward) or Autonomous Organization?

So once more, my experience interests me, and hence it pleases me to pay attention to it (I, 402) . What is this "attention"? Everybody knows it. We speak of attention when the psyche places before itself vividly and clearly one from among a variety of simultaneously possible objects of thought (I, 403 ff.) . But upon closer examination we learn that it is always a matter of *physiological* processes, and, in particular, on two levels:

(1) the attuning of the senses, and

(2) the previous preparation starting from higher nerve centers in regard to interesting things. Wherever we speak of attention, we may safely assume that there is activity on both levels (I, 434 ff.) .

Hence the question comes up once more: is this so-called voluntary attention truly spontaneous? Or is it an autonomous organization that is taken care of by brain processes? We think of the phenomenon of choice, and especially of attention, as a power, even as something spiritual. But perhaps, is it not rather a result of the brain processes that are active at a particular time, and that are determined by the total activity of the brain? Is the thing that draws our attention not always the one that takes the initiative? Is attention not *drawn?*

The whole process of involuntary choice is explained when

we admit that at a certain moment something occurs that interests us so much that the experience of something that is connected with it is thereby called up. And this, through the very associative connections of the brain processes, is what fixates our experience. This fixation *is* attention, and it is coupled with a vague feeling of activity (I, 449). Hence we can explain the concentration, the fixing of our attention on something, by the fact that we press the right button and when the desired attuning of the nervous apparatus has taken place, then it automatically makes a selection.

When properly considered it is only the *effort of concentration*, and not the having-attention, that deceives us, making us admit a spontaneous power. We imagine that we can do better when we *will* it. But the fact is that we feel effort only when there is a conflict of interests. When the ideas A and Z both "clamor for attention," when they try to push one another away from the foreground, and we give preference to A, we have the feeling of an effort of the will every time that Z comes forward. But this need not mean more than that there is a "struggle" between various brain processes, of which one brakes the other. And this braking could be experienced as a feeling of effort (I, 453).

If so, effort and spontaneity of concentration would then be nothing but epiphenomena accompanying phenomena that possess no activity of their own. They express that something takes place but they themselves cause nothing new:

> Attention may have to go, like many a faculty once deemed essential, like many a verbal phantom, like many an idol of the tribe. It may be an excrescence on Psychology. No need of it to drag ideas before consciousness or fix them, when we see how perfectly they drag and fix each other there (I, 452).

But more things are involved in this doubt about the spontaneity of attention. For is it not necessary to extend the argumentation to all phenomena in which consciousness seems to be *active?* But again one thing is certain: our whole feeling of reality, all that which in human life we consider as properly human, depends on the feeling that in life things are really *decided.* Human society depends on whether they are decided or not. "This appearance, which makes life and history tingle with such a tragic zest, *may* not be an illusion" (I, 453).

But at the time that James writes this, he already has his doubts about consciousness. This he recounts a little later in an article entitled "Does Consciousness Exist?" (1904). There he says that already twenty years before (in 1884) he had begun to ask himself whether consciousness actually existed. An article that appeared two years later, in 1886, and which maintained that consciousness does not exist,[1] he considered important, although he was still incapable of accepting that view (I, 305). "Seven or eight years past," he tells us in 1904, "I have suggested its non-existence to my students, and tried to give them its progmatic equivalent in realities of experience."[2]

This was already anticipated in the *Principles*, although James attributes the reasoning to "opponents": "*The consciousness doesn't count*, these reasoners say; it doesn't exist for science, it is *nil;* you mustn't think about it at all" (I, 454). But James' own explanation concerning attention with respect to the powers of learning already shows some progress in that direction.

5. Consciousness and the Body

We have come to the point where James' psychology still shows only a shaky balance. It is based, on the one hand, on the description of experience from within; on the other on the physiology of the brain; so we must now see where the centre of gravity is to be found. The problem has sounded more or less loudly in all the preceding chapters. It is now impossible to avoid it. If experience has no decisive significance for corporeal happenings, if the science of experience *must* borrow its arguments primarily from corporeal events, it then finds itself in an extraordinary situation. Every description "from within" then describes "appearances" and nothing more. If this is actually James' final view, then the whole relationship with phenomenology comes to nought. Then, finally, it is not without reason that James has been called the forerunner or even the founder of behaviorism. Here we seem to have reached the point where this fact appears clear as daylight. Consciousness is reduced to an epiphenomenon of corporeal events. If so, *behavior,* and not *experience,* constitutes the object of psychology.

NOTES

1. P. Sourian, "La Conscience de Soi," *Rev. Philos.,* vol. 22, 1886, pp. 449–472.

2. William James, *Essays in Radical Empiricism,* (London, 1912), p. 3.

VIII EXPERIENCE AND BEHAVIOR

1. "Does Consciousness Exist?"

"Experience" and "thing" are names for two kinds of objects that are placed opposite each other both in philosophical and everyday thought. Spirit and matter, soul and body, are constantly considered as equivalent, but radically different substances. So does James begin his considerations concerning consciousness.[1]

But Kant undermined the soul, and introduced the transcendental ego. Since then the bipolar relation has been out of balance. Consciousness became empty, a "Bewusstheit" (thing-like consciousness) or a formal "Bewusstsein überhaupt" (consciousness as such). And, says James,

> I believe that 'consciousness,' when once it has evaporated to this estate of pure diaphaneity, is on the point of disappearing altogether. It is the name of a nonentity, and has no right to a place among first principles. Those who still cling to it are clinging to a mere echo, the faint rumor left behind by the disappearing 'soul' upon the air of philosophy. . . . It seems to me that the hour is ripe for it to be openly and universally discarded.[2]

Surely this denial of consciousness has only a limited meaning for James. *The* consciousness is not there, there is no *something* that we must call consciousness; but there is indeed a function that we can call by that name; we see clearly then that there is no consciousness-*substance* that we can put alongside the substance of things. It is the Cartesian duality that James here radically and definitively rejects. There is only one "primal stuff," only one matter, from which both experiences and things are constructed: "pure experience" is that primal stuff.

And let no one say now that there is a fundamental difference between the thing I perceive and the representation of that thing.

> When I now think about my hat that I left a moment ago in the cloakroom, where is the dualism, the discontinuity between the hat that is thought of and the real hat? It is with a true *absent hat* that my mind is occupied. I practically take account of it as of a reality. If it were present on the table, the hat would determine a movement of my hand; I would remove it. Likewise the hat that is conceived, the hat in a thought will determine in a moment from now the direction of my steps. I will go to fetch it. The idea I have of it will continue until the hat is a sensible present, and will harmoniously fuse with it.[3]

Idea and hat have the same "primal stuff." It is not that one is consciousness and the other material reality. Consciousness is a fiction, while concretely, ideas and thoughts are fully real.

Consequently, we cannot say that consciousness is consciousness of itself. But is this not in complete disagreement with the presuppositions which James constantly used when he described the stream of experience?[4] Do we not find here a re-orientation of his thoughts? This is not the case in so far as he *bases* the denial of consciousness as substantivity *precisely on the description of* the *stream of experience.*

Let others have their own ideas about that, he tells us; I speak now only for myself and I notice that

> The stream of thinking (which I recognize emphatically as a phenomenon) is only a careless name for what, when scrutinized, reveals itself to consist chiefly of the stream of my breathing. The 'I think' which Kant said must be able to accompany all my objects, is the 'I breathe' which actually does accompany them. There are other internal facts besides breathing . . . and these increase the assets of 'consciousness,' so far as the latter is subject to immediate perception; but breath, which was ever the original of 'spirit,' breath moving outwards, between the glottis and the nostrils, is, I am persuaded, the essence out of which philosophers have constructed the entity known to them as consciousness.[5]

This conclusion was already contained in the *Principles:* our whole feeling of spiritual activity, or what usually passes for such, is in reality a feeling of corporeal activities the exact nature of which men do not take into consideration (I, 301 ff.) . The ideas developed in that article of 1904 certainly tally with the *Principles*. This problem came up already when we discussed the question of attention. We shall meet it again when we examine more closely James' theory about the emotions, and his discussion of the will.

It is therefore the stream of consciousness itself that James refers and consigns to the reality of the body, and the unreality—hence also inactivity of consciousness. This, of course, leads to difficulties, especially when James later inclines to the view (which he then again rejects) that what seems to be active in experience is not truly that which is active.[6] After all, is this view not the foundation of his constant reduction of phenomena to the activities of the brain processes, although these are not given to us in experience, although we are not aware of them?

James gives no clear solution to that dilemma. We must even ask ourselves whether he ever realized sufficiently that he placed a burden of insoluble contradictions on the foundations of his psychology. Or must we say that he is one of the few who accepts that situation and refuses to cover it up with theoretical constructions?

When James repudiates consciousness, this does not mean that he denies the existence of experience. On the contrary, it is on the basis of experience that he does not want to hear about it any more. According to James: *Experience does not refer beyond itself to a transcendental subject or to a substantial soul; experience refers to the body.* The science of experience becomes the science of *behavior* (conduct) .

2. *James' Functional Behaviorism*

James' analysis of the stream of experience might make us look upon him as a psychologist of consciousness who is interested in the structure of (isolated) experience. Our second chapter already taught us that he did not want to be that kind of psychologist. He was interested in a *functional* psychology, which conceives consciousness as a biological phenomenon, and examines the role of consciousness in behavior. It fulfills its role principally in adjusting man to his milieu. Hence he expressly warns his readers once more:

> When, in our last chapters, we entered an original forest of pure inner processes, we must not forget that the final result of all those processes must be some form of corporeal activity. The nervous system, considered physiologically, is nothing but a machine that translates stimuli into reactions; the intellectual part of our existence is connected only with the 'central' part of the activity of that machine (II, 372).

Intellectual performances, and experiences in general, are then seen in their natural connection only when we realize that they are an intermediary phase between stimulus and reaction. It is this connection between stimulus and reaction, rather than experience, that is the decisive phenomenon: there is never any sense impression that does not, immediately or later, lead to activity—or it must be impeded by a stronger impression.[7] And so the chapter concerning movements is based on the fundamental view that every experience produces a movement (II, 372).

But then is it the *experience* that produces the movement? "All action is thus *re*-action upon the outer world."[8] "Every current that runs into it from skin or eye or ear runs out again into muscles, glands, or viscera, and helps to adapt the animal to the environment from which the current came."[9] The whole nervous system *is* nothing but a system of connections between a sensory starting point and a terminus in a muscle or gland (I, 103). *But then the connection between a sense and an effector is an autonomous reaction-circuit* (Cf. I, 24). This conclusion became one of the fundamental principles of behaviorism. We shall see in a moment how this conclusion makes it useless to introduce consciousness in behavior-psychology.

There are other points, connected with the latter, that makes James a forerunner of behaviorism. We saw in Chapter III,[10] that James took a stand against the representative theory of knowledge. His later philosophical considerations went farther in the development of that theme. The theory of "pure experience" is one of its consequences. And so we hear him say once more that pure experience does not know a duplicate of the outer world in an inner world of representations.[11] Hence this characteristic doctrine of behaviorism too is found in James. Let us add that James, at least in a sketchy way, constructed a theory of the conditioned reflex to explain effects of learning.[12] Hence we understand why he has justly been called the one who prepared for behaviorism. But that he was not a behaviorist, in fact that behaviorism is in conflict with James' fundamental ideas, we shall realize only if we examine what that theory does with James' declarations.

3. Radical Behaviorism

The essential formulation of the fundamental idea of radical behaviorism given by Tilquin correlates well with the summary we have given of James' ideas:

> Man is, and is nothing but an organism (materialistic monism) who in order to live must adjust himself to his milieu (biological dualism). The adaptations are made by responses executed as a reply to changes of environment (principle of adaptation). Every stimulus arouses a response, every response proceeds from a stimulus (principle of the functioning of the nervous system through complete arcs).[13]

And yet we already see a difference. If behaviorism excludes all Cartesian dualism[14] because it does not agree with the postulate of materialistic monism,[15] it follows that it differs greatly from the basis upon which James rejects that dualism: namely the testimony of *experience*. James remarks: "the constitution of reality which I am making for is of psychic type."[16] Reality for James is *experienced* reality. And thus James and behaviorism part already where they seem to meet.

Behaviorism rejects consciousness with an angry, materialistic earnestness. "Mind is behavior, and nothing else," says Lashley,[17] and he thus plays into the hands of Watson. If one accepts that such things as "conscious phenomena" take place, one must say, nevertheless, that they cannot be used by *science*. For the first demand of every science is that the data must be verifiable and

controllable. Introspective data are *not* verifiable; they belong to
the subject in whom they appear. They are personal data.[18]

When someone says that he has pain, it is impossible for me to
control his *feeling*. The most I can do is to use what he tells me as
an indication and then find out whether definite and clear bodily
phenomena take place on the occasion of the noise he makes.
These I can define particularly by the fact that another can also
witness them. But a feeling of pain, of joy, of anxiety cannot be
described exactly as a *feeling*. This does not yet mean, however,
that "feelings" do not exist.

Behaviorism begins as *methodical* behaviorism. There are
indeed conscious phenomena but what does that give us? What
can we do with them in science? But this methodical behaviorism
that refuses to base its investigation on introspective data, necessarily leads to an *ontological* behaviorism: consciousness is not
only meaningless for scientific investigation, but it does not *exist*.
Just as chemistry does not know alchemy, as astronomy does not
know astrology, and psychology does not know telepathy, so also
the behaviorist does not recognize phenomena of consciousness.
These antiquated ideas disappear with the development of science.[19]

Never during his investigations did the behaviorist come
across those spiritual things.[20] Situations, contents or phenomena
of consciousness do not exist because nervous processes do not
end or begin in the brain! When a process seems to have its
origin in the central nervous system, the energy that is necessary
for it must come originally from the outer world and be carried
to the central nervous system. The law of the conservation of
energy says that no new energy is ever created. Hence when I
think I do something, because I "will" it as a spiritual being and
that I put into motion my muscles by means of the immaterial
will and thus produce energy that was not present, I am then
saying something that is contrary to the law of the conservation
of energy.

Let us assume, says Watson, that there is a visual representation that does not arise as a result of something that has actually
been seen. Is this then a process that arises *centrally*? This can't

be. An image that arises in me when I am daydreaming *cannot* originate in the brain that lies under my skull. For my brain is only a central circuit or switchboard in which the incoming energy is changed into outgoing energy, in which sense stimuli are changed into motor currents. The so-called visual representation is nothing but a *fiction*.

All the investigations and theories of the introspective psychologists that are consecrated to images or reasonings are the formation of a fundamental error. They rest on illusions that dominate common thought. We believe in representations because we *say* we have them. But they are not there. At most, there are stimuli-reaction circuits that correspond to that so-called "representation." The reaction circuit of the afferent periphery with the motor periphery is a closed arc that is given objectively.[21]

Probably someone will object that that closedness of the reaction arc is not clearly present in higher psychic phenomena. I could be calmly sunning myself in the park and suddenly recall that I must give a lecture at the college at ten o'clock. Where does that remembrance originate if it has to come from the periphery? We shall then have to say that there are postponed reactions. To think, to remember, are postponed reactions. We consider learning and memory principally in connection with the past. To remember, for instance, is to retain a concept or an ability which one acquired earlier. Such a definition is attuned to the past. Is it not possible to define it differently? Is it not possible to say: "memory" is the collective name for all the phenomena of reactions that are postponed for different lengths of time? I learn a few lines which I shall be asked to recite this morning. If I remember those lines, it means nothing other than the fact that I am able to postpone my reaction to a later time.

The so-called inner processes are only a matter of postponed reactions. We shall have to examine to what extent incoming stimuli can make the central nervous system an occasion for continued circular processes that do not directly lead to motor reactions. This means that we do not have to admit that later reactions are put in motion by "psychic energy." After all, what could such a "psychic energy" be? It either has no relation to anything that is material and yet is able to influence (bodily) matter; or it is a physical energy, and in this case it is, by definition, not a "psychic" force. In both cases the concept of a psychic force is superflous for an objective study of behavior, and it is even harmful for it causes confusion.

But then is what we call thinking not an activity that appears precisely to the extent that one *renounces* bodily reactions? Have we not here a purely inner, spiritual activity?

If one has already proclaimed that the inner activities of which introspective psychology speaks do not exist, then one must of course continue to formulate things in that radical fashion. What else is thinking except an *implicit behavior* that is distinguished from explicit behavior only by the fact that it cannot be seen by the naked eye? Thinking is a verbal substitute for an activity. To think is to speak softly in such a way that another is unable to notice it. Thinking is a muscular preparation that consists of slight movements of the larynx that are intermediaries between stimuli and explicit reactions. Here, of course, we have only an hypothesis but it is objective nevertheless.[22]

Moreover, the spoken language itself already bears the character of a postponed reaction, a substitute. "Come," I say, "let's go fishing this afternoon." I am then already actually fishing. But since I am not yet near the lake, I do it in word only, but will do it later in reality.

If we reduce "inner processes" to material activities in that fashion, there is no longer any need for the concept of "consciousness," namely, for the simple reason that the term then represents no reality whatsoever. There is no consciousness. No one, says Watson, has ever seen, touched or tasted consciousness. It is impossible to put it under a microscope. It is not possible to prove that it determines behavior. This is the essential point. The behaviorist will accept consciousness as soon as someone proves its existence, in the way the other sciences prove the existence of their own objects.[23]

This short survey of some of the fundamental ideas of Watson's radical behaviorism is sufficient for our purpose. James

238 *On the Way Toward a Phenomenological Psychology*

reduced the stream of experience to the corporeal activity that so clearly and constantly accompanies the phenomena of life and whose name has been decisive throughout history in all European thought for the concept of a soul or spirit, namely *breath*. But what he says is that *breathing* is properly and really corporeal activity, although this is also experienced and conceived as something spiritual.

This experience itself remains something real for James. Contrary to his position is the reasoning of behaviorism that states that corporeal activities are physical and thus must be understood as belonging entirely to physical functions and subject to purely physical laws. Behaviorists do not admit that physical energy can be transformed into psychic phenomena and vice versa. Hence it is impossible that conscious phenomena should exist. There are then no conscious phenomena.

4. An Extraordinary Outcome

Consciousness is a fiction. The reasoning that leads to that conclusion is forceful. And yet there are some questions that clamor for an answer. For instance, *what is fiction?* Repeatedly Watson uses terms like "fiction," "error," "illusion," "prejudice." But what kind of "processes" are they? Must we say that the thinking and reasoning of a scientist who says: "what another scientist maintains is a 'fiction' and is simply a behavior that consists in movements of the organs of breathing"?

Man has modes of behavior that manifest a definite biological usefulness. We eat to keep alive. When I now say to someone that I am hungry and am going to eat, this communication, this verbal reaction can be considered as an anticipatory substitute for eating itself. It is the substitute for the fulfillment of a biological need. If we reduce the "inner processes" in general to postponed bodily reactions, we must also be able to point to an actual reaction at the end of the postponement. What happens then, in that respect, to that remarkable group of "purely reflective" actions?

I declare that the declaration of Mr. James is nonsense. What then am I doing, behavioristically speaking? What biologically useful behavior am I postponing when I declare that another declaration is nonsense. Is the thinking and reasoning of science also a behavior that has a biological meaning? When Euclid constructed his axioms, and hence postponed a certain behavior, *what* was it that he postponed? Suppose he had not "thought" but had *acted,* what then would he have *done* in place of writing down those axioms? What is the biology of chemistry?

To express this more generally: *does scientific thought come under (the heading of) behavior in the behavioristic sense?* Is the practice of science or of theorizing in science once more a behavior that is of the same nature as eating, running, etc.? If so, we must say that it is a strongly determined breathing, caused by logical stimuli, truth stimuli, esthetic stimuli, etc. How does behaviorism explain the origin of science? Why did someone begin to practice science? It is easy enough to speak about an "urge for knowledge." But what is the biological meaning of such a thing? Or must we accept with James that there is question here of accidental variations in human hereditary genes?[24] (II, 636 ff.) .

Whatever way one replies to these questions, there is one detail we must keep well in mind. It is: whether the practice of science does not presuppose reflection and "consciousness" in order for us to reduce it to something else. Watson agrees on this point. The behaviorist has consciousness like anybody else; but his science can be outside "consciousness" in a psychological sense. The "observation" of consciousness is no more the task of the psychologist than that of the practitioner of natural science. *For them consciousness is the instrument with which all scientists do their work.* We might call this the return to a non-reflective and naive use of consciousness.[25]

A remarkable issue! Within psychology the existence of consciousness is denied. And yet we need consciousness as the original instrument of scientific thought. Hence whether behaviorism represents itself as a methodological or ontological behaviorism, it cannot do without recognizing that which Watson calls "the naive use of consciousness as an instrument."

Nevertheless, does the scientist not implicitly admit the existence of consciousness since he makes use of it? Does Watson not

expressly recognize its existence? Hence does he not posit dualism
while refusing to stand up for it? Watson would reply that in
regard to scientific knowledge the world is one: the *world of
objects* is not twofold. But he would admit without difficulty that
in the presence of this unique world there are *subjects* that know
it. And he would add that the subjects cannot be known scientifically except as objects.[26]

No double world is permitted to exist. How "self-evident" has
that explanation of our attitude toward the world now become!
There stands an inkwell on the table. It *stands* there really, and I
"have" a perception of it. This is the duplication which behaviorism, and James likewise, justly reject. For what is duplicated
demands a *being* duplicated: that of the matter and that of the
mind. But "consciousness" is the name of a function. "That
function is knowing."[27] In the terminology of Watson: the subject is always "examining objects";[28] there is question of consciousness only in so far as objects are given to us. The observation *of* this consciousness is a meaningless project; just as it is
senseless to desire to see seeing. Watson predicates nothing more
nor less than *intentionality;* consciousness is essentially and exclusively the being-conscious-of- (something). The generality of
the term "consciousness" expresses exclusively that there are
more ways of "examining objects." And in this respect the doctrine of Watson is rather limited.

5. James' Doctrine of Pure Experience

Radical behaviorism tries to overcome Cartesian dualism by a
materialistic monism; the solution that James looks for
seems—and we say this with all prudence—to be in the direction
of a spiritualistic monism, although it proclaims itself as a radical
empiricism.[29]

Someone is sitting in my room reading a book. What he sees
he considers real; it is present; there is a collection of individual
objects in a world of things. What he perceives are those things
themselves that are there. Are these also *once more* in his mind?
When a thing is in two places, this must be in the way a dot can
be on two lines: as a *point of intersection.*

If then "pure experience" of the room is that kind of point of intersection of two groups of experiences, we should then be able to count this experience, as it were, twice, one time as belonging to this, then again as belonging to the other group; and one could say that that experience exists twice, although considered properly there is but one.[30]

The one experience forms a part of diverse contexts that can be considered independently of one another with respect to the history of the room and that of the reader. Hence there is no reason for duplicating things.

All that is given us in experience has one and the same "primal stuff," namely, the *pure experience itself*.[31] What is given *is* experience; experience is datum, is *what is given*. Hence it is also more exact to speak of data in the plural. To the question of what a certain experience is made of, the answer must be: "It is made of *that,* of just what appears, of space, of intensity, of flatness, brownness, heaviness or what not."[32] The same applies to concepts, memories, imaginations; in one context they count as things, in another as conscious-states.[33]

Experience has no inner duality; when we divide it into consciousness and content we do not by subtraction but by addition, namely by adding other groups of associated experiences. We must, of course, distinguish between the knower and what is known but not as if we had an absolute and real opposition. For here precisely the same applies: an experience that in one context functions as knower is something-known in another context. Knowing is a relation between experiences and this relation is itself an experience.[34] Radical empiricism maintains that the relations that connect experiences are themselves experienced relations and every experienced relation must be considered as truly "real" as other content-experiences.[35]

This short summary of the doctrine suffices for our purpose. It is immediately clear to what insoluble difficulties it inevitably leads. Let us, for instance, merely ask how James *now* will have to formulate the problem regarding the relations between experiences and brain-processes.[36] His physiological realism on the one hand, and the doctrine of pure experience on the other, both carried to the limit, find themselves alongside each other in his "system." They seem irreconcilable. This is characteristic of James.

We shall try to bring about a synthesis, although this is not the right name for it. But we can somewhat understand that contradiction when we realize that James in all his theories adheres to the following proposition: *the access to phenomena lies in experience: the basis of the phenomena lies in the body.*

The core of experience is one's body.[37] His view is unambiguously expressed in this long passage:

> The world experienced (otherwise called the 'field of consciousness') comes at all times with our body as its centre, centre of vision, centre of action, centre of interest. Where the body is 'here;' when the body acts is 'now;' what the body touches is 'this;' all other things are 'there' and 'then' and 'that.' These words of emphasized position imply a systematization of things with reference to a focus of action and interest which lies in the body; and the systematization is now so instinctive (was it ever not so?) that no developed or active experience exists for us at all except in that ordered form. So far as 'thoughts' and 'feelings' can be active, their activity terminates in the activity of the body, and only through first arousing its activities can they begin to change those of the rest of the world. The body is the storm centre, the origin of co-ordinates, the constant place of stress in all that experience-train. Everything circles round it, and is felt from its point of view. The word 'I' then, is primarily a noun of position, just like 'this' and 'here.'[38]

6. The Body as the Origin of Reality

James points to the body as the source of reality. But "source" here has two meanings. First, the body is the centre, the point of intersection of reality. "I" is a positional noun. It can be understood in a limited, spatial sense. The body is then the localization-zero-point to which all experienced spatial relations are directed. But one does not have to limit oneself to this. The body also defines the "now," it is the temporal source to which the past and the future, in retention and "protention" are directed. It is at the same time the "place of action" (transaction). If James had known the terminology now in use he could have said also: the body is the core-of-the-situation. After all, his definition does not differ greatly from what Marcel tells us: "c'est par rapport à lui en tant qu' il est mon corps que tout existant se définit et se situe."[39] (It is in regard to it—in as much as it is my body—that every existent defines and situates itself.) The body is the point of intersection of the coordinates of experienced reality. This is the first meaning of "source."

Secondly, the body is also for James something more than a "source" in that first meaning. It is more than a *centre* of ordering and activity, more than a point of orientation for a description of experienced reality. It also constitutes the effective foundation for it. It is by the structures and functions of the body that we experience things in the way we experience them. But in particular it is that which takes place in the central nervous system that constitutes that foundation. Experience, in a certain sense, is a translated mirroring of what takes place there. It is "translated" because we do not experience the processes that occur in the central nervous system as processes, but as a direct and spontaneous being-with-the-things, our connection with the physical reality is not experienced by us in the way it must be thought by us.

The problem in which James became entangled is the psychophysical problem. We cannot blame him for it for what psychologist since Descartes has *not* been misled by it? What we could accuse him of is that he tried to solve it in too simple a manner, hence also in a way that was illogical. For the physical reality that leads to experience is itself a construction on the basis of an experienced reality.

Brain processes and experience are not so directly connected from a theoretical standpoint as James makes it appear. The phenomenal brain is itself primarily one that is exhibited in the world of experience, that as such cannot act as a foundation of that world. On the other hand, the physical operation of the brain is not experienced as such. James' doctrine about the body shows then an ambiguous structure. On the one hand he makes important contributions to a phenomenology of corporeity; on the other he lets it flow over into physiological considerations which he mixes up with his phenomenology.

But this should not blind us to the fact that, unshackled by that ambiguity, he attributed so central a place to the body in the matter of behavior. James' theory about the body constitutes the core of his psychology. It is the centre of the world of experience; and in the physical world, it is the foundation of experience.[40]

7. The *"Objective"* and the *"Subjective"* Body

In the theory of "pure experience" there is also an attempt to reduce the phenomenal body and the real physical body to *one* denominator. For the sake of convenience we shall speak of the *subjective* and the *objective* body. The terms, in this respect, will not easily lead to misunderstanding.

We saw previously that James wished to reduce the Cartesian dualism of spirit and matter, soul and body, to simple, pure experience in various contexts. "Thoughts and things are absolutely homogeneous as to their material, and . . . their opposition is only one of relation and of function."[41] Now, one of the most current objections to that doctrine rests on the fact that our affections are, nevertheless, given as inner phenomena, as conscious phenomena, that differ really from spatial, material things.[42] But the material things "outside," and the "inner" phenomena are after all only two groups in which we classify our experiences in accord with the way they influence our other experiences. Take the experience of "hardness." As an "external phenomenon" "hardness" is strong, energetic and aggressive; it dents things because it is impenetrable. But as "an internal phenomenon" taken as "sensation," that same "hardness" is in no place; it thinks nothing and without difficulty penetrates into other "sensations" (feelings).[43]

If we consider affections or emotions, it can then be shown that:

(1) the current conception of them rests on a too hasty and incorrect conclusion; that on the contrary;

(2) the ambiguity of the "affections" illustrates very nicely the proposition that we are here in the presence of a selective classification.[44] In regard to the first point James refers to the *Principles*. We shall deal extensively with that in the next chapter. Let us now consider the second.

A feeling of pain, for instance, is a local feeling; we can always speak of it in an objective or a subjective sense. We can say that we have the sensation of "pain" but also that a definite part of our body hurts. And such a way all the adjectives that express an evaluation are ambiguous. Is the brilliancy of a diamond a quality of the thing itself or is a feeling of our mind? The various satisfactions that a thing gives can be conceived, piece by piece, as "affections"; in combination we call them the beauty of the thing itself.

So too do sensations individually already have that ambiguity. We can say that warmth affects us pleasantly but also that the heat *is* pleasant. We even go so far as to speak of a hard road, a dizzy height, a cheerful morning or a somber sky or air.[45] It is especially with those appreciative qualities that we are concerned in our relations with things; it is the dangerous, the beautiful, the rare, the useful in things that attracts us.[46] It is these qualities that *corporeally* speak to us in those "emotions."

Our very body is pre-eminently characterized by that ambiguity. I sometimes handle it exclusively as a part of the outer world. But at other times I consider it as "mine," I classify it with the "self" and then definite local changes in it are counted as spiritual events. Breathing is my "thinking," sense adaptations constitute my "attention," kinesthetic changes are my "efforts," visceral disturbances are my "emotions."[47] If "subject" and "object" are really separated by "the whole diameter of being," if they have really no attributes in common, why then is it so difficult to distinguish, in respect to a given known material thing, what part is observed by a sense and what part is "added subjectively"?[48] The distinction between subjective and objective has no real meaning in primordial, pure experience.

But then this must also be true of the body. The one particular thing that can be said about it is that it is constantly experienced. It forms a continuous core of sensations, whereas the surrounding world changes gradually but continuously.[49] It also presents itself constantly as *the same;* I find it always as given, together with other, more changing experiences. As "subjective" body, as "mine," it is a reality of experience. It is a fact that I have my other experiences not only in the familiar direct experience, but can also bring them in relation with other experiences and thus acquire a knowing-about them; now this must be true also with respect to my own body. But does this not mean, when logically reasoned out, that the subjective body becomes objective if it becomes involved in another context of experiences?

As we have stated before, James nowhere gives that doctrine explicitly. But it follows logically from what has gone before. Subjective body and objective body *are* identical. We are in the presence of one and the same reality of experience, but in diverse contexts. The body too is such an intersection point of lines that cross one another. The *same* body that is *my* body in the context of my perspective experience, and the permanent core of the "self," is in the context of scientific knowledge a (living) thing.

Hence the coordination of experience with brain processes does not take place directly but indirectly. The bridge is not formed by an "intersection-point" that is common to experience and brain processes; the coordination is postulated on the basis of the identity of the body in both series. *And only where the two series cross, in the experienced body, lies the identity of the "physical" and the "psychic" and nowhere else.*

It seems to us that such a formulation of the "psychophysical relation" according to the ideas of James is considerably more powerful than, for example, the isomorphic hypothesis of the Gestalt theory notwithstanding all the problems that still remain. For the latter theory postulates the existence of a structural identity between physical processes and experiences; that they coincide with each other according to structure. But this is not only something that cannot be proven, but it is also an unacceptable hypothesis.

From the formulation according to the mind of James it follows already that such a theory is improbable. Crossing lines diverge outside the intersection point; this point is the "experienced" body. Every arrangement of points on that one line in respect to points on another line remains arbitrary because they no longer coincide; but more than that: the divergence of the lines is here the expression of an irreducible discrepancy.

8. The Principle of Complementarity

The considerations we have just expressed follow so evidently from James' ideas that we can simply ascribe them to him. If we then look from the standpoint of our present general scientific thinking at the doctrine of James, we see that he introduced the principle of *complementarity* in his formulation of the connection between the "physical" and the "psychic."

The principle which was first formulated by Niels Bohr as a consequence of experiences in the field of atomic theory contains the following:[50] The facts and relations in two different experiments must, under definite conditions, be described with the help of two different models and theories, each one of which has validity for one of those experiments but also excludes the other at the same time. This is not a question of "preliminary" imperfections of scientific theories, but of a fundamental principle of scientific knowledge: when one asks the same question in two different ways, nature can give different answers. These answers are complementary.

The seeming contradiction expresses the fact that only both answers taken together can give the complete answer; that every answer has validity only within a limited context. The classical war between the wave theory and the corpuscular theory of light is an example about which we have all heard. Sometimes light phenomena manifest themselves in physical experiments as wave phenomena that have all the properties that belong to these; at another time the same light seems to consist of loose light-quanta or "bodies." These diverse and mutually exclusive kinds of phenomena do not accidentally and arbitrarily replace each other; they show a connection with the particular kind of experiment to which they are subjected.

Since Bohr brought this principle to men's attention it has been seen that the principle can be applied to many fields of scientific thought. Thus, the view of those who for a long time thought that biology, the science of living organisms, would finally be reduced to chemistry or physics is seen to be incorrect in the light of that principle. For the physical and chemical "questions" that are addressed to the dead cell can never be "answered" in the way a living cell can do it. Biological knowledge of the organism on the one hand, and physico-chemical knowledge of it on the other hand, are complementary. These two kinds of knowledge can ask the same question on the basis of vital functions; but they ask their questions in a different context and get different answers.

Let us now allow James to express himself once more. "There is no thought-stuff different from thing-stuff, I said; but the same identical piece of 'pure experience' . . . can stand alternately for a 'fact of consciousness' or for a physical reality, according as it is taken in one context or in another."[51] In other words: depending upon the context of the questions we address to experience, this experience replies that it is "subjective" or "objective," "psychic" or "physical." Of itself it does not belong to one or other of those two series; it is only on the basis of a particular questioning that it does. Phenomena can be questioned in their mutual connection, or in connection with the (experiencing) person. These two kinds of questioning are complementary, just like the resulting words.

9. Experience and Phenomenon

We must now go one step further. One of the ambiguities of James' doctrine of "pure experience" is that the term "experience" is indifferently used for *experiencing* and for *that which is experienced*. We have seen also that James expressly desired to identify the two. On the other hand, he gives himself much pain in the articles collected in his *Essays* to define the "function of knowing," the connection of the *experienced* with *experiencing*. James gets into trouble when he once more conceives that intentional relation as *experience*, and in fact as one that is of the same order as the experiences that are mutually involved in that relation. We shall not enter into the logical difficulties that arise because of that artifice. We can put them aside *because that identification does not agree with James' own principle of complementarity.*

To avoid confusion we reserve the term "experience" for the

relation of a "person" to a phenomenon. This is the way we spoke in the second chapter in conformity with the *Principles* and it is in this sense we have used the term up to the present chapter: in an experience, someone who can say "I" is conscious of something that he can distinguish from himself. The "something" that is experienced we call "phenomenon." If one says that this "phenomenon" is also experience one then forgets that "experience" and "phenomenon" truly have their point of intersection in the "given" (datum), but that they belong to different contexts. And so though we are unable to distinguish experience and phenomenon in and concerning the "given" as soon as we consider the "given" there exists a discrepancy between the two, *either* in the connection of intentional relations *or* in the connection of time-spatial relations of the phenomena among themselves.

Herein also lies the reason why James was unable to attain to a phenomenology in the strict sense of that term: he identifies the intentional relation with a temporal-spatial relation[52] and he did not see that all that is "given" necessarily presupposes the being-given-to-someone. Hence we shall not follow James in this respect, but shall give preference to a more phenomenological manner of reasoning implicitly contained in the *Principles*. But when we ask ourselves why James arrived at that identification, a superficial knowledge of the *Essays* will suffice to show us that James wished thereby to attack the dualism of Descartes. However, what he achieved in that respect remains unchanged if one maintains the distinction between experience and phenomenon.

10. *"Physical" and "Psychic"*

James' "world of pure experience," of which the body is the source, is nothing else than that order of reality which was called the "Life-world" in Chapter VI.[53] It is the world of ante-predicative and pre-reflective experience, in which, according to Husserl, the constituting subjectivity and the constituted "objectivity" cannot yet be distinguished. It is that world, in which experience and phenomenon find their point of intersection in the "given" that is ordained to the body.

This world is the "given" upon which every scientific interpretation is based and that precedes it; it is that which is presupposed in every explanation of the "given" into a physical and a psychic "sphere," and hence in turn cannot itself be considered as a *synthesis* of "material" and "spiritual" phenomena. On the contrary, the difference between "physical" and "psychic" arises in the reflection about that world; it first appears as a difference on the basis of the diverse questions that are addressed to the same data (givens) in diverse contexts.

This takes place in the doxic certainty that those concept-horizons cannot be reduced to one another; what remains obscure and pre-given is that they cross one another in the datum (given) itself. It is in a dogmatic confirmation of critical thought that the philosopher first hypostasizes "subject" and "object" and constructs an absolute opposition, that the psychic and the physical appear as independent and parallel. They become "substances" that have no longer any connection, and *can* no longer have it because their connection in the construction of the opposition of the subject-object was already removed. Only then does the problem arise how the one series can be *brought* into connection with the other, how they "correspond."

Descartes who maintained a most radical opposition between them tried to re-establish the connection that had been removed by a miracle of interaction that was unacceptable in his system. Later strict parallelistic solutions of the psychophysical problem are equally unsatisfactory, first of all because they are evidently insufficient as an explanation of the Life-world. A materialistic or spiritualistic monism leads to the same evil.

For instance, behavioristic monism leads to an absurd interpretation of behavior and corporeity. It gives no solution of dualism, because it is itself determined by dualism. The concept of corporeity and materiality which it uses is after all *the same* as that of Descartes. The simple rejection of the concept of spirit cannot be called a solution of the problem.

In phenomenology an attempt is made to bring back the problems to the original form in which they arise in the Life-world. This must, among other things, result in an expression of the psychophysical problem that leads to the view that there is no question here of a problem about being but of a problem about knowledge. "Physical" and "psychic" are forms under which the same "given" (datum) appears in complementary questionings concerning the time-spatial and intentional relations. This questioning causes them to diverge. It is the questionings that cannot be reduced the one to the other. They cross one another where the question is addressed to the datum (given).

11. My World and Our World

In the questioning concerning the Life-world, experience and phenomenon find again their identity in the given that is ordered to the body, to the "origin" of the coordinates of experienced reality. My body is the origin of a field, *not of the Life-world in its totality*.

We are making premature abstractions when having made a description on the basis of our corporeity, we let it result in a theory that identifies our own corporeity with *the* corporeity. I find myself in the Life-world as one of many "I-bodies" within the social world. In the Life-world there is given an ordering of things to all possible or actually present "I-bodies" as so many origins; a co-ordering of the same things in respect to diverse bodies. He who fails to take this into consideration and then asks further questions quickly gets entangled in solipsistic problems, problems which James knew how to avoid.

What else is your body than a perception in *my* field of experience? This question James addresses to himself in order to bring himself back to proper proportions, on the basis of the same reality of experience:

> In that perceptual part of *my* universe which I call *your* body, your mind and my mind meet and may be called conterminous. Your mind actuates that body and mine sees it; my thoughts pass into it as into their harmonious cognitive fulfilment; your emotions and volitions pass into it as causes into their effects.
> But that percept hangs together with all our other physical percepts. They are of one stuff with it; and if it be our common possession, they must be so likewise. For instance, your hand lays hold of one end of a rope and my hand lays hold of the other

end. We pull against each other. Can our two hands be mutual objects in this experience, and the rope not be mutual also? What is true of the rope is true of any other percept. Your objects are over and over again the same as mine. . .

Practically, then, our minds meet in a world of objects which they share in common, which would still be there, if one or several of the minds were destroyed.[54]

Your body, which you move and feel from within, must be at the same place as your body that I see from outside or touch. "There" means for me where I put my finger. When I put my finger on your body and you do not feel the touch of my finger "there" in my sense, where then do you feel it? Your inner body-consciousness meets my finger *there;* it is *there* that you resist my pressure, or withdraw, or remove my finger with your hand.[55]

This does not mean that James thereby *proves* the sociality, the intersubjectivity of things and the world—although he thinks he does. He *indicates* them, he points to the pre-givenness of the social Life-world, from which every fancied proof must start. He starts from the givenness of the *alter ego* (of the other self) as we already noted in Chapter II, 1.

Once more is his view so different in meaning from the ideas expressed by Merleau-Ponty? The phenomenological world is not pure being, but the meaning that transpires at the intersecton of my experiences and those of another, by the concatenation of the ones with the others; hence it is inseparable from the subjectivity and the intersubjectivity that form their unity by taking over my past experiences into my present experience, or the experience of another into mine.[56]

But the Life-world is the reality that is ordered to the body, to our bodies, to "I-bodies." If we call this world that of the Ur-doxa, the fundamental order of reality, we have said at the same time that the doctrine of experience comes down to a doctrine about the body, to a doctrine of behavior.

12. Experience and Behavior

James, like phenomenology, combines extreme subjectivism with extreme objectivism.[57] Berkeley's saying *esse est percipi* (to be is to be perceived) of which we spoke in Chapter III, 9, was already accepted implicitly in the *Principles;* and James maintained it explicitly later on. *Esse* (to be) is *sentiri* (to be felt) he says first of all in regard to situations of consciousness;[58] they *are* to the extent that they *are felt,* and are what is felt there. This applies also to the experience of activity: "The *percipi* in these originals of experience is the *esse.*"[59]

And, finally, this is true of things. The physical has no other content than the psychic. Subject and object flow into one another. It was Berkeley who first remarked: "Esse ese percipi."[60] Our sensations are not small inner duplicates of things, they are the things themselves to the extent that they are present to us.[61] And yet we cannot say that James maintains an idealistic position.

A conceptual system, a theory, in order to be accepted as true, must at least accept the reality of sensible things, by explaining them as influences upon us (II, 312). In other words, a theory must take for its foundation the reality of the Life-world, the reality as it is primordially experienced.

Reality is accessible to scientific investigation, to a systematic questioning about and search for the relations that are not themselves given in direct experience. The experienced reality can be grasped as an orderly, time-spatial whole of time-spatial processes, that are subject to laws that can be formulated. This way of looking at things, by reducing what is immediately experienced to time-spatial structures, opens up a new point of view that leads to knowledge that is complementary with respect to the knowledge that is given by the analysis of immediate experience. This "nature-knowledge" is not *less* but also not *more* valid than the phenomenological. However, one must avoid, without more ado, conceiving the contents of one of the two series of knowledge on the basis of the other. They converge towards the world of experience. Each has its own validity within its own framework.

And so we see that James plainly accepts the validity of the scientific knowledge *alongside of* descriptive knowledge. In fact, he does not hesitate to affirm at the same time the freedom and the necessity of behavior and experience. He takes the stand that when I experience myself as doing something, I also actually am doing it. He also takes the stand that the influence of the "psychic" upon the "physical" is impossible and he bases himself on the same reasons as those that had already been given in Helmholtz.[62]

When subjectivism and objectivism imply each other in this way, they no longer merit those names. In James they signify no longer metaphysical interpretations of what reality ultimately is; they are names of various contexts of knowledge concerning the same things. Those contexts already exist undivided in the Lifeworld. Here intentionality and casual connection coincide. Here also experience appears as based on behavior. And that is why both descriptive and explanatory psychology must, in their divergent contexts, make behavior and the body the central theme of their investigation.

NOTES

1. William James, "Does Consciousness Exist?", *J. Phil.,* vol. 1, 1904, quoted as reprinted in *Essays in Radical Empiricism,* (London, 1912), pp. 1-38.
2. James, *Essays,* pp. 2 ff.
3. William James, "La Notion de Conscience," *Arch. Psychol.,* vol. 5, 1905. Quoted as reprinted in James, *Essays,* pp. 206–233; see pp. 215 ff.: "Si je pense en ce moment à mon chapeau que j'ai laissé tout à l'heure au vestiaire où est le dualisme, le discontinu, entre le chapeau pensé et le chapeau réel? C'est d'un vrai *chapeau absent* que mon esprit s'occupe. J'en tiens compte praitquement comme d'une réalité. S'il était présent sur cette table, le chapeau déterminerait un mouvement de ma main: je l'enlèverais. De même ce chapeau conçu, ce chapeau en idée, déterminera tantôt la direction de mes pas. J'irai le prendre. L'idée que j'en ai se continuera jusqu'à la présence sensible du chapeau, et s'y fondra harmonieusement."
4. James, *Essays,* p. 6.
5. *Ibid.,* p. 37.
6. "The Experience of Activity," in James, *Essays,* p. 168.
7. James, *Will to Believe,* p. 113, cf. *Talks to Teachers,* pp. 170 ff.: "A belief as fundamental as any in modern psychology is the belief at last attained that conscious processes of any sort, conscious processes merely as such, *must* pass over into motion, open or concealed."
8. James, *Will to Believe,* p. 114.

9. James, *Talks to Teachers*, p. 26.
10. James, *Essays*, pp. 11 ff.
11. James, *Talks to Teachers*, p. 27.
12. *Ibid.*, p. 38.
13. A. Tilquin, *Le Behaviorisme*, (Paris, 1950), p. 27.
14. *Ibid.*, p. 45.
15. *Ibid.*, pp. 29 ff.
16. Perry, *Thought*, II, p. 764.
17. K. S. Lashley, "The Behavioristic Interpretation of Consciousness," *Psych. Rev.*, vol. 30, 1923, p. 240.
18. J. B. Watson, *Psychology from the Standpoint of a Behaviorist*, (Philadelphia, 1924), p. 1; *The Ways of Behaviorism*, (New York, 1928), pp. 6 ff.
19. Watson, *Psychology from the Standpoint of a Behaviorist*, pp. 348 ff.
20. *Ibid.*, p. 2.
21. J. B. Watson, *Behavior, An Introduction to Comparative Psychology*, (New York, 1914), pp. 17 ff.
22. *Ibid.*, pp. 19 ff. It does not matter that this hypothesis has been refuted. For one can use the vocal organs to repeat known texts while thinking of something else. But the behaviorist then looks for another bodily equivalent of thought. What is at stake is to define the "inner" phenomena as bodily activities.
23. Watson, *The Ways of Behaviorism*, pp. 3 ff.
24. James, *Will to Believe*, p. 55: "Take science itself! Without an imperious inner demand on our part for ideal logical and mathematical harmonies, we should never have attained to proving that such harmonies lie hidden between all the chinks and interstices of the crude natural world. Hardly a law has been established in science, hardly a fact ascertained, which was not first sought after, often with sweat and blood, to gratify an inner need. Whence such needs come from we do not know: we find them in us, and biological psychology so far only classes them with Darwin's 'accidental variations.' "
25. Watson, *Behavior, An Introduction to Comparative Psychology*, p. 27.
26. Tilquin, *Le Behaviorisme*, pp. 79 ff.: "Cependant le savant n'admet-il pas implicitement l'existence de la conscience puisqu'il s'en sert? Watson n'en reconnaît-il pas expressément l'existence? Dès lors n'est-ce pas, tout en refusant de prendre parti, poser le dualisme? Watson répondrait qu'au regard de la connaissance scientifique le monde est un: le *monde des objets* n'est pas double. Mais il reconnaitraît sans difficulté qu'en face de ce monde unique il y a des *sujets* qui le connaissent. Et il ajouterait que les sujets ne peuvent être scientifiquement connus qu'en tant qu'objets."

27. James, *Essays*, p. 4.
28. J. B. Watson, "Psychology as the Behaviorist Views it," *Psychol. Rev.*, vol. 20, 1930, p. 174 Note.
29. James, "A World of Pure Experience," in *Essays*, p. 41.
30. James, "Does 'Consciousness' Exist?", in *Essays*, pp. 11 ff. Cf. Ernst Mach, "Antimetaphysische Vorbemerkungen," in *Die Analyse der Empfindungen*, 1st ed., (Jena, 1885). James read this work and underwent its influence.
31. James, "Does 'Consciousness' Exist?", in *Essays*, p. 4.
32. *Ibid.*, pp. 26 ff.
33. *Ibid.*, p. 15. Cf. also the article of 1895, "The Knowing of Things Together," *Psychol. Rev.*, vol. 2.
34. James, "Does 'Consciousness' Exist?", in *Essays*, pp. 4, 9, 25.
35. James, "World of Pure Experience," in *Essays*, p. 42.
36. Cf. his notes, in Perry, *Thought*, vol. 2, pp. 368 ff.
37. James, "World of Pure Experience," in *Essays*, p. 65.
38. William James, "The Experience of Activity," in *Essays*, p. 170, Note. Also *A Pluralistic Universe*, p. 380, Note.
39. Gabriel Marcel, *Être et Avoir*, (Paris, 1935), p. 10. Cf. Maurice Merleau-Ponty, *Phénoménologie de la Perception*, (Paris, 1945), p. 402: "I *have* the world as unfinished individual, through my body as a potency of that world." (*"J'ai le monde comme individu inachevé à travers mon corps comme puissance de ce monde."*)
40. Cf. Husserl, *Ideen*, vol. 2, pp. 158 ff: "Der Leib als Orientierungzentrum."
41. William James, "The Place of Affectional Facts in a World of Pure Experience," *J. Phil.*, vol. 2, 1905. Reprinted in *Essays*, pp. 137-154.
42. *Ibid.*, p. 138.
43. *Ibid.*, p. 139.
44. *Ibid.*, p. 141.
45. *Ibid.*, pp. 142 ff.
46. *Ibid.*, p. 150.
47. *Ibid.*, p. 153.
48. James, "Does 'Consciousness' Exist?", in *Essays*, p. 29.
49. James, "World of Pure Experience," in *Essays*, p. 65.
50. Neils Bohr, "Das Quantenpostulat und die Neuere Entwicklung der Atomistik," *Naturwissenschaften*, vol. 16, 1928, pp. 245 ff; "Wirkungsquantum und Naturbeschreibung," *Naturwissenschaften*, vol. 17, 1929, pp. 483 ff. In the second article Bohr proposes some applications of the principle to psychological problems to which psychology had until then paid too little attention.
51. James, "The Place of Affectional Facts in a World of Pure Experience," in *Essays*, pp. 137 ff.

52. James, *Essays,* p. 25. Cf. "Consciousness connotes a kind of external relation," in *Ibid.,* pp. 55 ff.
53. We have shown earlier that this can be said (cf. above pp. 211 f.) although James now and then contradicts himself regarding that point. For instance, we saw (pp. 116 or 32) that James is inclined to identify "pure experience" with "pure sensation."
54. James, "World of Pure Experience," in *Essays,* pp. 78 ff.
55. Ibid., pp. 84 f.
56. Merleau-Ponty, *Phénoménologie,* Avant-Propos, p. xv: "Le monde phénoménologique, c'est, non pas de l'être pur, mois le sens qui transparaît a l'intersection de mes expériences et de celles d'autrui, par l'engrenage des unes sur les autres, it est donc inséparable de la subjectivité et de l'intersubjectivité qui font leur unité par la reprise de mes expériences passées dans mes expériences présentes, de l'expérience d'autrui dans la mienne."
57. *Ibid.,* p. xv.
58. James, "How Two Minds Can Know One Thing," in *Essays,* p. 127.
59. James, "The Experience of Activity," in *Essays,* p. 168.
60. Cf. for example *Principles,* vol. 2, p. 290, Note: " 'The candle exists' is equivalent to 'The candle is *over there.*' And the 'over there' means real space, space related to other reals. The proposition amounts to saying: 'The candle is in the same space with other reals.' It affirms of the candle a very concrete predicate—namely, this relation to other particular concrete things. *Their* real existence, as we shall later see, resolves itself into their peculiar relation to *ourselves.* Existence is thus no substantive quality when we predicate it of any object; it is a relation, ultimately terminating in ourselves, and at the moment when it terminates, becoming a *practical* relation."
61. James, "La Notion de Conscience," in *Essays,* p. 212.
62. Herman von Helmholtz, "Über das Ziel und die Fortschritte der Naturwissenschaft," *Vortrage und Reden,* Bd. I, (Braunschweig, 1884), p. 352: "Ist aber das Gesetz von der Erhaltung der Kraft auch für die lebenden Wesen giltig, so folgt daraus, dass die physikalischen und chemischen Kräfte der zum Aufbau ihres Körpers verwendeten Stoffe ohne Unterbrechung und ohne Willkür fortdauernd thätig sind, und dass ihre strenge Gesetzlichkeit in keinem Augenblicke durchbrochen wird."

IX THE BODY, BEHAVIOR AND REFLECTION

1. The Spontaneity of Behavior

There is irrefutable evidence that we act, do, are busy with and thereby really influence things and change them. We are the cause of numerous events; this is the way we experience it and hence we are permitted to say that it is so.[1]

> No matter what activities there may really be in this extraordinary universe of ours, it is impossible for us to conceive of any of them being either lived through or authentically known otherwise than in this dramatic shape of something sustaining a felt purpose against felt obstacles and overcoming or being overcome. What 'sustaining' means here is clear to anyone who has lived through the experience, but to no one else . . . If there is anything hiding in the background, it ought not to be called activity, but should get itself another name.[2]

With these words James underlines once more the lawfulness of a way of looking at things that takes behavior seriously and conceives it as an actual activity of a person. It can also be considered as the epiphenomenon of "real," physical events that occur independently of experience. But these "real" events are first constructed on the basis of behavior, and on that account must be called differently. They presuppose conduct.

But this does not mean that experience can always, and without any exception, serve as a standard for the genuineness of experience. In the way we speak about our conduct there may appear unjustified substantizations, so that we speak of *the* will or *the* emotion, that would thus function as the cause of behavior. There is then a need for closer examination of things. For much of what we do and the way we do it, remains hidden to our own direct experience.

The body has already at its disposal definite possibilities that do not become conscious as such in our self-awareness. It is senseless to say that when we slip and are about to fall, we restore our balance because we "will" it; for this happens of itself. Or we must define that "willing" quite differently than it usually occurs. Only the fundamental datum, namely that our activity is truly our own activity, must be accepted without more ado, but it then remains for us to specify what that "own" means here. Hence our fundamental theme in this chapter will be the relation between behavior, body and the experience of behavior.

2. Habit, the Plasticity of the Nervous System

James' theory about habits seems primitive to us today. No wonder. For it is only after him that the investigation of the formation of habits received an extraordinary development. Hence we shall leave out the details and limit ourselves to some fundamental ideas that are of particular significance. They concern the possibility and the function of habit which, as James began to notice, has so great a dominion over our life (I, 104 ff.) .

The possibility of acquiring habits must be explained by the plasticity of organic matter, of the body; and in particular by the plasticity of that part that directs our behavior, namely, the nervous system.

If you buy a new suit, it feels unfamiliar. Wear it for some time and it adopts the shape of the body. Things adjust themselves to their use and their environment. And this is the way with everything. One must "break in" shoes by wearing them, break in a car by running it. At a certain moment we can say that the matter has developed into a *habit*.

An instrument that has been used for some time adjusts itself to the hand of the one who uses it, and it is then often easier to handle than a new instrument. The best violins are not only those that have been built by great makers of violins but those that have, in addition, been played by great violinists; that is, the violins that have preserved good habits from their good "education."

Habit in this broad sense presupposes a structured matter that possesses plasticity. Such a body will keep its integrity when strong forces are exercised upon it. It is capable of such things because it partly yields to those forces, changes its form and changes only gradually and because it also exercises a counter-force. Hence plasticity means that something has a structure that is sufficiently weak to undergo changes of form, and yet is also strong enough so as not to yield all at once. Every relatively stable phase of equilibrium in such a gradually transformable structure is characterized by what can be called a new set of habits.

Organic matter, particularly nervous tissue, seems to possess an extraordinary plasticity as to its inner structure. And so we can say unhesitatingly that the phenomenon of habit in living beings is the result of the plasticity of the organic matter (I, 105). This applies to the whole body but is particularly true of the brain.

Now what are the forces that influence that plasticity? They are principally the forces of currents of activities that reach it from the sensory organs and that seek a way back to the periphery. On that occasion they leave traces of themselves in the paths they happen to take. Currents of activities thus unavoidably deepen the old paths, or create new pathways. To sum up: the plasticity of the brain expresses itself in this that once good pathways have arisen they do not easily disappear (I, 107).

If we call such a path an *organ* and the current of activity that inaugurates or forms it the *function,* we can then repeat the famous French formula: (la fonction fait l'organe) "function creates the organ" (I, 109). Truly, says James, a short summary of the doctrine concerning habits is given in the saying that our nervous system directs itself according to the ways in which it is used (I, 112).

Man is born with the inclination to do more things than what he has ready-made circuits for at the time of his birth (I, 113).

He is a being who is eager to learn. He can form many habits, because and to the extent that he has a most plastic nervous system at his disposal.

3. Habit, the Autonomy of the Body

The plasticity of the nervous system makes possible the birth of new, not inborn automatisms. Hence habit formation has a twofold effect that explains the *function* of habit.

(1) Habit simplifies the movements that are necessary for the attainment of a particular result; it makes the movements more accurate and lessens the fatigue (I, 112). One who begins to learn to play the piano moves not only his fingers up and down but his whole hand, his arm and even his whole body. But he learns to restrict his reactions to some particular organs. To learn is to organize by regulation, says Buytendijk.[3] The regulation or management finds expression in the habit.

(2) Habit diminishes the conscious attention with which our actions are executed (I, 114). Habit formation ends in unreflective daily actions. Regarding the things we do the whole day long through habit, we do not know how we do them and often not even *that* we do them. A number of people cannot say what stocking or shoe or trouser-leg they put on first. In order to answer that question they must first clearly represent that action; and often even this is not sufficient, they must *perform* the action. And so also when we are asked which half of a double door we open first, or in what direction the door of a vehicle opens, it is often impossible to give an immediate answer, but our definite activity regarding such things never fails.

No one can describe the sequence in which he executes the daily repeated and interconnected habitual actions. Even when I desire to describe a habitual activity in its various phases and do it on the basis of presently executing it and try to *notice* what I actually do, the character of habit influences me so greatly that I am constantly inclined to forget what I am doing.

Habit formation is the means by which the body not only is manageable and becomes a live instrument, but it dispenses us from the necessity of paying attention to everything we do. For the body knows the patterns according to which we act. "I don't have to represent the word to myself in order to know it and be able to pronounce it," says Merleau-Ponty. "It suffices that I possess its auricular and sonorous essence as one of the modulations, one of the possible uses of my body."[4] Even when I read a foreign language I do not have to represent to myself the sound and the pronounciation of one word after another; this I do only when I am learning the language.

When we observe that a child is learning to read, we see that it is still occupied with acquiring patterns which later, when they are ingrained, will no longer require any attention on the part of the speaker. We have at our disposal whole sentences, whole thought-developments in the form of patterns of behavior that are ready for use. It costs the experienced politician no effort to give an "improvised" political speech; for "to improvise" does not mean to think of something new, but to order in another connection what is ready for use. Find the "dominant point of view" and the "inspired speech" flows forth automatically. But when I ask him about it afterwards, he then reproduces through habit almost the identical talk.

We are often unable to recall whether we have done something that we do through habit. For instance, we do not know whether we have closed the window in the kitchen, or turned off the gas. And then when we are in bed, we try in vain to imagine whether we did it or not. If we say: I must have done it, we express our confidence in habit, confidence in the body that knows how and what.

"To will" does not enter into that kind of behavior. It operates of itself; that is, the body operates with an autonomy that requires scarcely any reflection. If we try to make voluntary movements in the sense that we foresee from phase to phase what is possible, what we desire, and then execute the action, we make no smooth movements but produce a series of shocking, unadjusted, not-fluently-connected, jerky movements. The role of reflection, of knowing and willing, is much smaller in our behavior that we habitually imagine. *Habitually!* We are accustomed, we have the habit, of speaking of our behavior as if it flowed constantly from our knowledge and our volition, as if we reflect before we do something, and as though what we do results from that reflection, and is therefore adapted to a situation. But in reality there appears to be in our "doing" a far-reaching autonomy of the body with respect to reflection.

4. Chain Reactions, the Theory of the Automaton

James' reflections concerning habit led him gradually to a direction which, as we shall see, did not please him. If a chain of successive nerve processes A,B,C,D,E, etc. is necessary for the execution of complicated actions, it follows that habit formation consists in the fact that every element automatically puts into motion the following link (I, 114). Or, the sensation, caused by the first part of the action is the occasion for the start of the second part of the action. The habitual action occurs as an automatic chain-reaction.

James shows in his chapter concerning the function of the brain how he represents to himself the birth of such acquired chain-reactions on the phsyiological level (I, 24 ff.). This comes down to a theory of conditioned reaction. Elsewhere he expresses his thought more clearly: *"Every acquired reaction is, as a rule, either a complication grafted on a native reaction, or a substitute for a native reaction, which the same object originally tended to provoke."*[5]

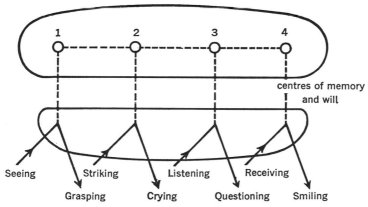

Figure 3. Talks to teachers, p. 41.

Let us examine the second case. When we show a new toy to a child, he tries to grab it. We slap his hand and he cries. We tell him: "ask for it" and he asks. He receives the toy and he smiles. Figure 3 illustrates how James imagines all this as four successive simple reactions.[6] But they can be arranged in a new way, as in Figure 4. The child then has learned something. To ask and to smile are substitutes for the original reaction of grasping. The other partial reactions are left out. The whole rests on an organization of processes and articulations in the brain. The motor chain-reactions, in which one line of an action without the intervention of the will or of knowledge sets in motion the next link, rests on the same organizing ability of the brain or, as James told us, on the plasticity of the brain.

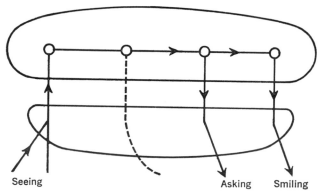

Seeing   Asking   Smiling

Figure 4. Talks to teachers, p. 42.

But when we say that the spinal cord is a machine that has a number of reflexes, why not say that the brain is that kind of machine but that it has many more reflexes and that herein lies the only difference? (I, 129). Does the theory of habit, via the doctrine of the conditioned reaction, not lead to a theory of automatism that has the same onesidedness as behaviorism? Is then the *reality* that is hidden behind behavior not the activity of the brain? Suppose we confine ourselves to one same level, the level of the body. Can we not satisfactorily describe all the outwardly observable phenomena of intelligent behavior on that level? (I, 128). This question of behaviorism James had proposed to himself.

In a sense, he tells us, I cannot escape from that conclusion. For I started from the view that there is always a parallelism between the happenings in consciousness and the happenings in the brain. Hence it should be possible in principle to describe the phenomena of consciousness as brain-phenomena. For after all we have to admit that the complexity of the brain machinery must be of the same order as the complexity of consciousness. But if we accept that, why not be radical? The hemispheres are machines. What then is the function of consciousness? Mechanically speaking there is none (I, 128 ff.).

Descartes has the merit of having been the first to dare to accept a completely autonomous nervous system that is capable of executing complex and apparently intelligent actions. But, with a perfectly arbitrary self-limitation, he applied that idea only to the animal and not to man. Should we re-assume that limitation? Must we not say with Hodgson that no single experience can have any causal efficacy? Must we not compare experiences to the colors of a mosaic? The small stones are kept in place by one another and not by the colors (I, 130).

Therefore we should not hesitate to apply those ideas to the most exclusively "human" achievements, for instance to the writing of "Hamlet." Naturally it must be possible to describe the composition of a play like "Hamlet" in terms of Shakespeare's brain. We could similarly write a complete biography of those two hundred pound proteins that we call Martin Luther, without implying that he had inner experiences. But does that make sense? Must we not admit that for psychology an irreplaceable point of view is contained in the vision which our daily self-interpretation possesses regarding the origin of a work of art as a *personal creation?* (I, 132 ff.).

James expresses this even more explicitly and convincingly in another place:

A Beethoven string-quartet is truly, as some one has said, a scraping of horses' tails on cats' bowels, and may be exhaustively described in such terms; but the application of this description in no way precludes the simultaneous applicability of an entirely different description.[7]

Psychology, like physics, must maintain a certain naïveté. When it notices that in its field of investigation ideas *seem* to operate causally, it is best to speak that way about them. It gains nothing when it breaks away from common sense in this respect, and if it does, it loses in any case the naturalness of language (I, 137). It is then necessary to come to the conclusion that the theory of automatism that is imposed on the psychologist is irresponsible and unsuitable in the present state of psychology (I, 138).

When James wrote this, he had not yet discovered the principle of complementarity. That is why his own conclusions appear unacceptable. For throughout the *Principles* he himself constantly returns to the discussion on the level of brain processes, that is, on the level where the theory of automatism has its irrefutable advantages. It is only when we accept the principle of complementarity that we can agree that the theory of automatism and the descriptive doctrine of consciousness are mutually complementary visions regarding the one same reality.

5. Homeostasis: The Organism Maintains Norms

The too quick identification of the bases of habits with the fundamental properties of all matter, as was done by James, prevented him from developing his own view. For his own view ought to read: *Behavior, though it is based on the properties of the body, already manifests purposiveness before all reflection.* Behavior chooses detours where it could have gone by the shortest road. It shows therefore the variability of the means for the attainment of the one same goal. It shows adjustment to varying circumstances and situations. It betrays control over the body. We already saw in Chapter II how he thus defines the reason that led him to speak about the psyche. That this "psyche," at least in great part, is corporeity and not a "spirit" is an evident conclusion.

Habit is an adaptation to ever new projects and leads to

having command over a long period of time. Habit precisely pleads for the "psychic" character of the body. But James had also maintained that physical laws are nothing but the unchangeable *habits* which the elementary parts of matter possess in their mutual action and reaction (I, 104). It is then no longer enough to add that the habits in the organic world possess greater variability since they are, in nature, identified with the "habits" of inorganic matter.

But if we wish to maintain the continuity of organism and nature, we shall not be able to avoid defining that continuity *starting from the organism* and not vice versa. If we wish to start from the properties of matter, we then witness a breach, there is no continuity. The "habits" of inorganic matter are, after all, not habits in the same sense as when we speak of habits of organisms. For in the latter case a habit is the expression of a regulative adjustment that finds its source in the organism. This may not be said about physical "habits." We can, of course, maintain that internal-regulative adjustment is present in dead matter, *on a null level*. The desired continuity is then preserved: dead matter is a particular case of living matter, because its properties and functions are more limited than those of living matter but not vice versa.

The activities of, and the events in, living matter in an *organism* are not totally dependent on the material conditions in the environment of the organism. This is evident in all those actions by which organisms, regulating their own function, maintain a norm and thus make known their relative substantivity in respect to the material environment. In this way there arises, in a certain opposition to the external milieu, an "internal milieu" which, as it is provided with its own internal communication-and-reaction system, is symbolized by a Jordan curve: an organism, as a closed figure, splits the world into two realms, the inner and the outer.[8] Every point of the curve can be connected with another point along a path that lies completely within the curve. An organism is a system with a relative autonomy.

Claude Bernard summarized all this in a famous declaration: the stability of the internal milieu is a condition for their independence from the external milieu.[9] About seventy years later Cannon introduced here the concept of homeostasis.[10]

Homeostasis is the general property in virtue of which organisms strive to keep constant the conditions of life. The organism possesses mechanisms by which it maintains internal norms, such as a constant body-temperature or a constant sugar content in the blood. It is clear that its own regulation of temperature, that guarantees an internal level of temperature which is favorable for physiological functions, protects the organism against the consequences of external changes in temperature; and it thus enables the organism to move in environments that differ in temperature.

The idea of homeostasis was first applied only to the internal vegetative functions of the organism. The "keeping the conditions of life constant," however, is not confined to that level. The maintenance of norms takes place also in behavior, taking this term in a broader sense. The reflexes too can be considered as homeostatic phenomena, as means for the maintenance of norms. They too take place through an internal regulation by means of a mechanism that is inborn and is fixed in the structure of the organism. The same is true of instincts that have a congenital foundation and are behaviors that are characteristic of a species and show a rather firm invariability. In principle, instinctive actions occur blindly, automatically. They enable the animal to maintain its life without foresight or insight, simply "in virtue of its nature."[11]

It is reasonable then to speak of a hierarchical arrangement of homeostatic levels in which every higher level presupposes the lower. Instinctive actions, for example, presuppose an organism that regulates its own processes of material variations and has motor reflexes at its disposal. The "freedom" that the organism thus possesses with respect to the environment gives opportunity for the play of free, spontaneous behavior. This behavior itself also demands regulation. It must be adapted and maintain a certain norm if the organism is to attain a relative autonomy. Hence animal behavior manifests the existence of native patterns of behavior that are connected with the maintenance and propagation of the organism.

Let us take one example. The diggerwasp *Sphex flavipennis* instinctively seizes grasshoppers, paralyzes them so that the immovable insect remains alive, it puts it in a hole dug in the ground, and lays an egg on top so that the emerging larva will have food at its disposal. This entire behavior is not based on motherly care but on instinct. The behavior shows a purposiveness that is antecedent to all reflection and is based on the properties of the body, on homeostatic properties that are absent from inorganic matter, that is, which function on the "null-level."

6. Regulation on Higher Levels

When new habits are acquired this takes place on a new homeostatic level. Habit is not something pre-given, it is not an inborn pattern that is enclosed in the organism, it is not something particular that belongs to the species, but it is an individual adaptation of a particular organism to particular situations that leads to an automatization of movements and behavior. Habits too maintain norms; but they are the individual norms of individual organisms. Thus arises a new level of freedom: namely that of the variability of behavior within a species or group. The fact that habits of a variety of specifically similar organisms, of animals or men, can manifest agreement among themselves should not deceive us. This results from the correspondence of body structure and body functions, of fundamental tendencies and social environment. But habits result always from an *individual* adjustment.

James chose his examples principally from this group. The absence of clear distinctions between the "habits" of inorganic matter and the self-managing organisms on the one hand, and between diverse homeostatic levels on the other, prevent him from sufficiently differentiating his machine-theory of the nervous system. *Every higher homeostatic level signifies a higher level of "freedom," of emancipation of the organism with respect to the laws of inorganic nature.* Every higher level signifies an enrichment of what James called plasticity, a broadening of the possibilities of adjustment to ever more variable situations, and a greater variability of behavior. It is only when this becomes an individual variability that it makes sense to speak of a *habit*. And this always transcends the level of instinctive behavior.

We have mentioned the diggerwasp *Sphex flavipennis*. Fabré, the entomologist, who studied insects for many years, made the following experiment with that wasp. One of its activities consisted of dragging its booty to the hole it had dug in the ground. But before depositing the prey into the hole the wasp made an inspection of it. During that inspection Fabré pulled the grasshopper a couple of inches away from the rim of the hole. The wasp, re-discovering its prey, dragged it once more towards the hole and made another tour of inspection. Fabré pulled the grasshopper back once more. The same ritual was repeated forty times. Fabré then gave up his trials.[12] Blind instinct had won a victory over his patience. The behavior, with all the purposiveness contained in it, manifests here such a fixed concatenation of phases that it is necessary to speak of an automatic chain of reactions. The completion of one phase invites forcibly the start of the following phase.

It is this way also that James imagined the course of actions done through habit. But he was wrong. Experiments with rats have shown that these animals are well capable of learning to find their way in a maze. At first the animal does not yet know the way; next it learns to know it a little, although it makes repeated mistakes. The number of errors diminishes and finally the rat knows the way. It has developed a motor habit that avoids useless effort.

According to a theory like that of James one could conceive motor habit as a chain reaction, a chain of successive movements each one being prompted by the sensation of the previous one. But MacFarlane has shown convincingly that a rat that had learned well the path through a maze by running through shallow water still continued to follow the same "way" in that maze when there was high water covering so that now it unexpectedly had to swim.[13] But the latter requires entirely different patterns of movement than the first.

The adjustment of the animal to the given situation, the

formation of a habit with respect to the maze was not confined to an automatization of a pattern of movement. The animal learned a *way* in a *space* with which it became acquainted. With respect to the knowledge which guides behavior, the homeostatic reactions that belong to a lower level and the elementary patterns of behavior such as reflexes and instinctive behaviors have themselves become a plastic nature. The animal makes *use* of those properties, it "chooses" the means that are at its disposal for the organization of a behavior of a higher order. It is able to do that because evidently the homeostasis on a lower level is for this animal not merely a stabilizer of patterns of behavior on that level but the animal knows how to organize the stabilized function in a higher order. It organizes its own behavior.

This must be reflected in the nervous system. Evidently centers that are on higher nervous levels regulate the connections of activities on lower levels. When such forms of regulation that imply an integration and organization become habitual they evidently can acquire a form of coordinated activities similar to what we see in activities on the lower level. And so a habit often appears to us as if it were a mechanism of the same order as reflexes and instincts, although this is not the case. For a habit can in turn be unlearned. But a habit in its turn creates an order in which a voluntary action, an action with true intentions and purposes, becomes possible.

We are still within the realm of the possibilities of the body. Reflection, or a "soul" did not yet seem necessary. And hence James declared: behavior rests in great part on the "wisdom" of the body itself.

7. To Will

We say that the body is governed by the will. Desire, wish and will are situations of experience known to everybody and cannot be made clearer by definition. We can, of course, ask ourselves what the will "does." And then it appears that the one immediate result of "to will" lies in bodily movements, which on that account are called voluntary movements (II, 486). And yet we cannot maintain that all movements arise from the will. Voluntary movements are, with respect to reflex movements or to instinctive and emotional movements, *secondary functions,* they are not *primary* functions of the organism. James considers this a very important point in the theory concerning "willing." This guidance of movement which we call "to will" is preceded by the involuntary, spontaneous movement on the basis of pre-given bodily organization. In other words, a voluntary movement is an organization on a higher level, that already presupposes an organization on a lower level. A true voluntary movement presupposes, for instance, that the person who acts *can foresee what he will do,* and how could he do this if he did not yet know that he is able to do it? But then he must have learned the latter through experiences he has acquired about his own body (II, 487).

A voluntary movement presupposes a familiarity with one's own body. Let us suppose that after birth we suddenly become fully mature and conscious. How would we then know what we could do with one arm? How could I know that I can voluntarily manage any part of my body. Voluntary movements are forms of organization on the basis of an organization on a lower level of which I have knowledge. This means that there must be present in my memory a store of images of various possible movements and these images (ideas) rest on experience. Hence the experience of our own corporeal possibilities is the first condition for the possibility of willing something (II, 488). Experiments show the correctness of that view. In order to execute successfully a series of voluntary movements it is necessary that they be guided by guiding sensations (II, 490), whose significance must be known.[14] This means that, if we *will* to make a movement, there must be an idea (image) of the movement based upon experience (II, 492).

But now we are faced with an interesting problem when we wish to define more closely what "to will" a movement consists in. Must something else other than that image of a movement stand before our mind when we will to execute a movement. In other words, is "to will" more than having an image, an idea of a movement?

No, says James, nothing else has to be before my mind than

the kinesthetic representation of what the action should be. From the periphery, however, I receive sensations of the effects of what I do. I know "about" where my arm is and the "about" is sufficiently precise to be able to react to that. But something like a "fiat" is not necessary for the execution of a movement. A voluntary movement is possible when we have the experience of what the body can do in virtue of its own organization.

A voluntary movement is guided in its execution by the sensations of movements that let me know how the movement is progressing. I judge that the course of the movements is good by the experience that I have of my movements and by the representation of the movement that guides that specific movement. This *representation consists in an anticipation of a series of sensations of movements.* According to James the anticipatory representation of a melody of sensations of movements determines *what* a movement will be. But what now determines *that* there will be a movement?

Here is the question. Is the representation of the movement a sufficient reason for the eliciting of the imagined movement, or is an extra antecedent necessary, such as a fiat, a decision, a consent, an act of the will? (II, 522). The answer is: this is not always necessary. There exists an *ideomotor activity* by which the very representation of the movement provokes the movement. The condition for this to occur is that there are no conflicting representations that impede the execution of the representation of the movement.

We know what it means to leave our bed on an ice-cold morning in a room that is not heated. The thought of getting up is simply unacceptable as long as we lie under the warm covers. Time goes on. I try to stretch it: five more minutes! But I realize at the same time: "I *must* get up, I can't wait any longer." But do I do it? Is it possible for me to indicate the moment when I make a decision of the will and get up as a consequence of it? Is it not rather a fact that I suddenly notice that I *am* up? I suddenly stand beside my bed. Did I then *will* this in the explicit intellectual sense of: It must be done, so be it? That which has guided my movement is the representation: "I must lie here no longer," which for one fortunate moment has not been blocked by any antagonists. This rising was an ideomotor process (II, 524 ff.).

This we can call a "decision." But there is no explicit "I will let it come to pass" in this experience. Still mindful of the freezing temperature, the thought of the duty of rising may become so pungent that it determines action in spite of inhibition. In the latter case, I have a sense of energetic moral effort, and consider that I have done a virtuous act.[15]

It seems to James that the situation thus described contains in miniature the data of the whole psychology of "to will" (II, 525). Movements result from representations. But then is it not difficult to explain why every representation does not lead to a movement? Well, says James, I am not so sure of that. When I have a representation of a movement and yet do not do anything, I can, as a rule, notice at least a *beginning* of a movement, which is then blocked by another. There is in man a natural tendency to translate images of movements into actual movements. It is, for instance, impossible to prompt a child that is just learning to talk to repeat some words after us and then wait until he says them after us and *not* at the same time repeat the same words again with the child. At least we shape our mouth according to the word which we want the child to repeat. When one has urged someone to jump over a ditch and he hesitates it is almost impossible for us to encourage him and *not* at the same time to make an initial movement for jumping with him.

Every representation of a movement to some extent causes the actual movement and this is the stronger the less it is hindered by contrary ideas (II, 526). Movement is the natural and immediate result of feeling, irrespective of the quality of the feeling. This is true of reflexes, of movements of expression, and just as true also of voluntary movements. Ideomotor activity constitutes the fundamental pattern also for those actions where a special "fiat" is still necessary.

8. Blondel's Analysis of Voluntary Movement

One of the difficulties to which James' ideas would lead us is that no element of voluntariness remains in voluntary movements, if the latter is conceived as the natural and normal result of a representation of a movement. This, moreover, is a difficulty that we find not only in James. There are therefore reasons for asking what is meant by "voluntary." Here also there could be question of an unjustified substantization. It could be that the "will-act" which at first sight seems necessary for a voluntary movement is not at all independent, nor one that *really* needs to be distinguished from the movement. Blondel, in his analysis of voluntary movement was influenced by James, and he arrived at making a distinction between four moments.[16]

(1) A voluntary movement presupposes motor mechanisms on lower levels, motor habits, by which limbs and their articulation can move with more or less independence from one another. Hence body-control is presupposed.

(2) A voluntary movement presupposes the representation of a movement that invites it and in which the actual movement is anticipated. It is clear that a mountain climber, during his ascent, knows moment after moment where and how he will place his foot.

(3) A voluntary movement presupposes an affective urge that sees in the imagined movement a means to attain the desired goal.

(4) A voluntary movement presupposes agreement with the affective urge that determines the action. But this motivation can be *rejected* for the sake of another.

But what does this "rejecting" mean? Does it not mean simply, as in the case of failing to get out of bed on account of the cold, that one thought comes off second in the presence of another? Does it not mean that one urge overcomes and represses another? The "voluntary" movement then, also for Blondel, does not yet presuppose any "will." It presupposes no purely "psychic" activity that is non-corporeal.

We can say with Buytendijk, and James would have agreed, that nowhere do we find the least suggestion for the idea that those functions which we call "psychic" navigate like a "demon" in any phase of life.[17] *The "psychic" is a way of naming corporeal action considered from some particular definite standpoint.* What is that standpoint?

We have seen that the organism must be represented by a Jordan-curve; it has delimited and isolated itself; it has emancipated itself toward a relative independence. It is not, as behaviorism proposed, a simple conductor of action-currents; it regulates its guiding properties from inside out. It was this that James meant when he spoke of the selective activity of the stream of consciousness. The organism is a (within certain limits) self-attuning instrument. It "receives" and reacts in various ways on account of diverse dispositions, feelings that are regulated from within and in such a way that norms are maintained on that occasion. The activities of the organism appear then not as a straight, unambiguous independence from the events in the environment. Hence, with respect to those events, the activity (at least in part) is unpredictable. They are therefore not purely accidental phenomena but functions of outer happenings and inner dispositions. They appear as *spontaneous,* no as forced (determined) ; as *variable* and yet determined by a norm. They appear as *meaningful,* as the results of free deliberation, choice and decision. Behavior appears as activity that is directed from within. From this standpoint we say that they are *psychically* determined.

"To will" is the way self-experience conceives and expresses those phenomena. "I will" is not a reference to the activity of my "psyche" as an independent substance but it is my expressed knowledge of my disposition. The analysis of experience gives me an insight into the structure of any movement in which inside is complementary to that which the organic consideration of that movement provides: namely, a movement that is guided by the person in which a decision is spontaneously made on the foundation of an evaluation.

We must say then that what we rightly call a "voluntary movement" can nevertheless be an *involuntary* activity, namely an ideomotor activity. The confusion arises because of the traditional, mythologizing burden attached to the term "to will" which obscures the phenomena instead of clarifying them.

9. Emotion: Experience of Bodily Reactions

James, with relentless stringency, goes on to show that experience points and refers to the body, and that it does not arise from an autonomous psyche or an immaterial soul. We notice that his considerations are leading him to a fundamental position which we can provisionally define as follows: *in experience the body comes to itself.* Experience, seen in this way, is the realization that the body has of its own action. This is James' doctrine contained in his controversial theory of the emotions.[18]

An emotion is a complicated phenomenon. James had already noted immediately that emotions are often awakened by things with which we have no practical purpose. For example, something ridiculous, or something beautiful are not necessarily things with which we *do* something. We laugh about something or stand still admiring it. This points to the varieties of the situations in which emotions arise; and the variety of behavior with which emotions are coupled.

Experience tells us that emotion does not simply coincide with some actual bodily behavior. I can become more angry when I recall an insult than when I received it. And we are more emotional at the sight of a mother who is dead than at one who is still alive (II, 442 ff.). And yet we must maintain that it is corporeal man and not the spirit that becomes emotional. Man's emotion is an emotion of the body. This is most evident when we first confine ourselves to the consideration of the lower emotions such as hatred, lust, fury.

In our everyday attitude we imagine that the psychic perception of some event arouses a psychic affection that is called an emotion. We then also believe that that psychic situation causes some bodily expression. James' theory, on the contrary, maintains *that the bodily change immediately follows upon the perception of the event and that the experience of those changes, while they are taking place, is the emotion* (II, 449).

Everyday experience tells us: we lose a fortune, we are sorry and we cry; we meet a bear, have fear, and run away; we are insulted, become angry and strike someone. But James tells us that if we express it in a popular way that sequence is wrong; it is more exact to say that we feel sorry because we cry, are angry because we strike, fearful because we tremble. Without those corporeal conditions that immediately follow upon the perception, this perception would be purely cognitive, it would be pale, colorless and without any warmth of feeling. It could then be that we see a bear and judge that it is best for us to run away; that we are insulted and consider it proper to strike; but then we would not *feel* fear or anger (II, 450).

James' theory is usually expressed in the popular form which he himself mentioned and discussed: we have sorrow *because* we cry. But it is important to show that this is not a correct expression of the actual content of that view, which we ought rather to formulate this way: sorrow is the way we experience crying. Crying is the primary emotional phenomenon; "sorrow" is the way we realize this. The important point is the primacy of the bodily reaction.

When we see a bear, or receive an insult, we begin with bodily reactions that follow upon those things; the noticing of this *is* an emotion. In that reaction which we note as an emotion, we find already the answer that the body gives to the situation, and hence this reply is not primarily determined by the noticing of the reaction. When someone makes me angry, and I *feel* furious, my reaction to his conduct is already underway, it has perhaps already been completed. It is only when I run away that I notice my fear of the bear. The experience, however swift it might be, comes afterwards; just as I *feel* the pain only after I have withdrawn my hand from a hot stove.

It is only afterwards when I describe it, that my own behavior appears to me as a rational order of noticing, reflecting, deciding and acting. When I am back and safe, I say to myself, "Yes, I saw the bear, and thought then, I better run now, for otherwise it will be too late." It is true in a certain sense that by saying: "I saw him, and thought, I must not stop, let me clear out," I give a meaningful interpretation of what I did when I ran away. But at the moment *that* I ran away, that kind of process surely did not take place. In the situation itself I acted without any reflection, literally inconsiderately; and in critical situations so much so that I "have no time" to become emotional. This does indeed come later, as a slowed-up resonance.

Behavior is already attuned meaningfully before all reflection. The body reacts in the behavior and in the internal changes of disposition that belong to it. The experience of those changes of disposition is the emotion. Emotion is the experience of the resonance that an event arouses in our body; a resonance that can be described in physiological terms.

The body reacts to that which causes the emotion by a higher secretion of adrenalin, by changes in breathing, etc. To some extent these internal processes lead also to external perceptible phenomena: the person becomes red or pale, perspires, shivers or trembles. These are phenomena of an internal change of disposition. They betray that the organism is preparing itself for a new action. It is in a state of disturbance.

These internal changes are felt and this feeling is the emotion. The body is the sounding board.

> Our whole cubic capacity is sensibly alive; and each morsel of it contributes its pulsations of feeling, dim or sharp, pleasant, painful, or dubious, to that sense of personality that every one of us unfailingly carries with him. It is surprising what little items give accent to these complexes of sensibility. When worried by any slight trouble, one may find that the focus of one's bodily consciousness is the contraction, often quite inconsiderable, of the eyes and brows. When momentarily embarrassed, it is something in the pharynx that compels either a swallow, a clearing of the throat, or a slight cough (II, 451).

When we imagine a strong emotion and then try to remove from our experience of it all feelings of corporeal symptoms, what remains? Nothing! No "mind stuff," from which an emotion could be constructed. What remains is only a perception, a cold, neutral, intellectual situation (II, 452). What *is* fear, when there is no accelerated heartbeat or short breathing, no quivering lips or impotent limbs, no chicken-heartedness or rumbling bowels? Take away those corporeal conditions and the emotion disappears. Every emotion presents the same picture. A disincarnate human emotion is a non-entity. Are we not immediately calm when the symptoms of anger or fear suddenly disappear? They were not symptoms, they were the emotion itself.

Once again let there be no misunderstanding. The theory does not say that emotions are "nothing but" corporeal conditions, but it says that the body echoes to events that vitally concern us; the emotion is the way we experience that vital involvement of our body.

10. Lotze and Horwicz

James' theory of the emotions caused great excitement in its time. It found defenders and enemies. This we shall pass by, as well as the attempts that have been made to prove or disprove the theory experimentally.[19] We are interested in the meaning of the theory in itself, and in connection with James' fundamental ideas. In this respect some historical observations are important.

Titchener has shown conclusively that the theory was not new.[20] But in regard to that we may agree with Stumpf: perfect originality in matters that were always open to introspection can indeed be used to show the subtlety of the author, but it could not plead for the thesis he defends.[21] There were forerunners. Two of these, who were read by James, we can mention here.

On the flyleaf of James' copy of Lotze's *Medicinische Psychologie* is the following annotation: "Emotions due to bodily reverberation, 438."[22] When we read that paragraph it seems that James' expression is not a summary of Lotze's ideas, but a conclusion. Lotze himself, in accord with the common conceptions of his time, looks upon corporeal expressions as accompanying phenomena, although there is already in his description a suggestion that it is more than that. There are states of mind, he tells us, in which we reach movements that meet in a particularly adapted way the psychic urge for activity. So does a rhythmical impression arouse a lively sentiment which we strengthen further by executing the work rhythmically.

Also where a sentiment is aroused primarily by the observation of intellectual attitudes, sensible feelings endow it with their own coloring; the slowing down of those feelings hinders the formation of the state of mind.

> We have different thoughts and strivings when we are lying down that when we are standing up; a constrained position of the body dampens our attitude; when we are stretched out in an easy and nonchalant way, it is difficult for us to pay attention, and anger is appeased by giving a rest to the body; the hand that straightens out the wrinkles in one's forehead also quiets the sorrow that was expressed by them. It would be difficult to determine the boundaries of that influence, but it is undoubtedly far reaching.[23]

It is so far reaching, James concludes, that the feeling itself disappears with the phenomenon of its expression. So Lotze attributes to the bodily attitude and to the "corporeal feelings" a constitutive function in the states of mind which, when one puts less stress on "the psychic" than Lotze did, can reasonably inspire a theory like that of James.

Horwicz, whose work, as we have recalled, James was acquainted with, teaches that emotion has its basis in the autonomy and spontaneity of the organism that is directed to self preservation. Emotion, he tells us, "is the becoming aware of usefulness or harmfulness" (ist das Innewerden des Nutzens oder Schadens) [24] and thus he goes back to the very old idea of the opposition between the pleasant and the unpleasant; this fundamental opposition of the emotions is connected with the biological "intentions" of the organism. And, he tells us, an emotion is a *noticing* of the useful and the harmful. Does this not take place primarily through the body?

That "inner becoming aware" (Innewerden) is the most elementary form of consciousness, more a brooding suspicion than a knowing. It is not purely receptive and passive. An emotion does not have to become a striving, since it is always that already.[25] It is true that Horwicz later speaks of a retroactive effect of the emotions upon glandular secretions, and that he considers external expressions as consequences of emotions. But these reasonings are cancelled out when we survey once more with James the relation of body and soul.

282 On the Way Toward a Phenomenological Psychology

It is this that constitutes the originality of James' theory of emotions. A certain connection between emotions and the body had been known for a long time and it had been repeatedly described. But the theory was always burdened with the difficulties of the psychophysical problem. James' orientation concerning this point enables him to formulate old data within a new context: "If our hypothesis is true, it makes us realize more deeply than ever how much our mental life is knit up with our corporeal frame, in the strictest sense of the term" (II, 467).

11. Emotion and Feeling (Sentiment)

James at first confines his theory of the emotions to the lower and more coarse affective phenomena. As regards the "more subtle emotions" or feelings (sentiments), such as the moral, intellectual and esthetic feelings, it is necessary to say that James' treatment of them is inadequate (II, 468 ff.). And it is easy to see why. Being struck by the insight into the relations found in emotions, James generalizes them and tries to reduce other feelings to the same. But the direct corporeal involvement on the basis of vital interests is much less significant in respect to feelings and it may not appear at all. Hence the emphasis falls rather on the difference than on kinship. For although James, on the one hand, expresses the opinion that the feelings are also in great measure determined by the body, he also says the following:

> The bodily sounding-board is at work, as careful introspection will show, far more than we usually suppose. Still, where long familiarity with a certain class of effects, even aesthetic ones, has blunted mere emotional excitability as much as it has sharpened taste and judgment, we do get the intellectual emotion, if such it can be called, pure and undefiled. And the dryness of it, the paleness, the absence of all glow, as it may exist in a thoroughly expert critic's mind, not only shows us what an altogether different thing it is from the 'coarser' emotions we considered first, but makes us suspect that almost the entire difference lies in the fact that the bodily sounding-board, vibrating in the one case, is in the other mute. 'Not so very bad' is, in a person of consummate taste, apt to be the highest limit of approving expression. 'Rien ne me choque' is said to have been Chopin's superlative of praise of new music. A sentimental layman would feel, and ought to

feel, horrified, on being admitted into such a critic's mind, to see how cold, how thin, how void of human significance, are the motives for favor or disfavor that there prevail (II, 471).

Similarly, James elsewhere makes a distinction between the emotions and the tones of feelings.[26]

But under the pressure of criticism, in that same article, he also comes to a further and closer specification. We do indeed run away from a bear, but not when it is firmly bound by chains or when, being expert shots, we are hunting and have a good gun. The stimulus for bodily changes that is experienced as an emotion is not simply a thing or happening; it is a situation. The emotion is the observation of the *resonance to* the *meaning* of things; that meaning depends on the situation in which they appear.[27]

This we can express in another way: in the emotion there is a resonance of the *value* with which something appeals to us; some values are *vital* ones; reactions to them are prefigured in the body; other values are social or humane, intellectual, moral or esthetic; they appear on a higher homeostatic level; the reactions to them are not innate but are taught by others, or are developed personally. Such values do not have so direct a hold on the body, but affect more our being-a-person. This coincides with what James says elsewhere:

> If we were radically feelingless, and if ideas were the only things our mind could entertain, we should lose all our likes and dislikes at a stroke, and be unable to point to any one situation or experience in life more valuable or significant than any other.[28]

A feeling also demonstrates the participation of a person. This we saw in Chapter VIII, 7, where we followed James in a consideration that aimed at showing that we must understand the qualities in which we experience the world through our involvement in that world.

It is not the emotion, but the feeling that is the *general* occurrence; the emotion is *particular*. Emotion is a special class, a particular modality of feeling, of affective participation. In emotion and feeling we see the person participate in the other's values, and we see his resonance to that participation. As James had already said, feeling is a function of values, and in this light his choice of the term "feeling" for experience in general assumes a new importance. In Chapter V, 7, we saw James compare "feeling" to "being in a mood": in feeling things appeal to us with respect to their value, and we notice our resonance to that value.[29]

Intellectual, moral and esthetic feelings can then be rated somewhat higher, as is done also by Lotze and Horwicz, because they are indeed "higher" feelings. They become possible on a higher level of homeostatic organization when the "cruder" feelings—emotions that are more connected with the body's vulnerability—are already fully in function. The fact that the higher organization now begins to govern the lower and thus even takes it up into itself is something that will occupy our attention later.

12. The Function of the Stream of Experience

It has become clear to us in our study of the phenomena of willing and feeling or emotion what James meant when he said experience points and refers to the body. After all he meant the same thing that was expressed years later by Merleau-Ponty:

> Our body, to the extent that it moves itself, that is in the measure in which it is inseparable from a view of the world and is that view realized, is the condition of the possibility, not only of geometric synthesis, but also of all the expressive activities and all the acquisitions that constitute the cultural world.[30]

The body is the source of reality. And the reflection that sees itself in the contemplative, action-less experience, as a source of a higher order, discovers upon closer insight its deeper source in the corporeal. James' doctrine of corporeity is a pre-view of phenomenology; and it is one that, in spite of all objections one may level against it, is based on a purer realization of the significance of the corporeal than many later phenomenologies of the "spirit."

The stream of experience has two functions that strike the eye: "it leads to knowledge and it leads to action."[31] A long Western tradition is inclined to see in the rational function that leads to knowledge the most real aspect of experience. But how can this view be maintained in a time when the doctrine of evolution has taught us that man has had ancestors who were not yet men? Experience must have a meaningful place in the scope of evolution; it must have its utility in life. It is useless unless it leads to action. Mind is given to man to help him adapt himself to the world in which he finds himself: "We cannot escape our destiny, which is practical; and even our most theoretic faculties contribute to its working out."[32] A classical difficulty that constantly comes up against that way of reasoning is as follows: consciousness, when it has a biologically useful function, should have had already that function in order to be developed on the basis of its usefulness; and this it evidently cannot have. But let us listen to James. Whatever metaphysical insights we may have, whatever unapplicable esthetic perceptions or ethical sentiments, we can look upon them as an excess of function that necessarily accompanies the activity of all complicated machines.[33]

Every homeostatic level on which functions are stabilized signifies at the same time a higher level of "freedom" as we said above, and this seems now to agree with the ideas of James. The organism acquires new possibilities by stabilizing old ones. In principle it thus manifests its "riches," the possibility of being able to do more than is "necessary." By providing for its needs it develops virtues. The highest virtues flower finally upon the most elementary needs. Merleau-Ponty said the same thing in a more prosaic way in the text we have quoted.

13. I Myself; Mine

Has the significance of experience then not become beggarly? Does consciousness still preserve a fundamental function, namely, the *I-function*, when its traditional functions are transferred bit by bit to the body? Let us follow James' analysis of self-consciousness. What am I; what do I mean when I say "I"? James speaks of *self* in the broadest sense as: the whole of all that a man *can* call his own. Not only my body belongs to what is mine, but my psychic properties, my clothes, house, family and friends; my reputation and my work, the land and the horses that I own, my hunting and my bank account (I, 291).

If they are doing well and increase, I am happy; if they go down, I am downhearted. But we must distinguish between the various levels of the self. There is in the first place a *material* self, that is, the body. There is, moreover, the *social* self, that is wider than the material self, the being-recognized by my fellow men, the life in social relations, and here it appears, as a rule, that the social self is a multiplicity of selves. The boss at home, at the office; we know plenty of variations of that theme; but also, through our own direct experience, we know the difference in our own conduct and "character," when we move from one situation to another. Properly looked at, says James, a man has as many social selves as there are persons that have an image of him. I am myself not only in my body and my properties, but also as a function of my social relations. James in this connection makes a number of observations that preserve their actuality.

In the third place there is also the *spiritual self* that calls for our attention. James understands by this the inner self, subjectivity, the psychic powers or dispositions, taken concretely, not the principle of personal unity, the "pure I," for this, as spiritual self does not belong to the empirical "I." But what *is* that self? Must we not call it the *active* element of experience? There is something spiritual in us, from which something emanates:

> It is what welcomes or rejects. It presides over the perception of sensations, and by giving or witholding its assent it influences the movements they tend to arouse. It is the home of interest . . . It is the source of effort and attention, and the place from which appear to emanate the fiats of the will (I, 297 ff.) .

By that James does not mean a principle of personality about which we eventually suppose to be there; he does not mean a soul or spirit but an *experiencing,* itself an inner core that we *feel.* Can we not say more precisely what we feel? Here James becomes modest; he wants to speak only for himself, although he suggests that others will be able to confirm his own observations if not in respect to the content, at least in respect to the form.

Well, he says, it is difficult for me to discover any purely spiritual element. Every time I succeed in casting an introspective glance and turn with sufficient swiftness to my interior in order to catch those utterances of spontaneity in action, it is always one or other corporeal event that I become aware of; and it is chiefly an event that is localized in my head.

To direct my attention, to agree, to reject, to make an effort, all these are felt as movements of something in my head. Sometimes it concerns sensations in the muscles of my eyes, or in the muscles of my face, sometimes I feel something in my larynx. As to myself, says James, I must say that the central self, if I consider it carefully, consists of those corporeal feelings. The feeling of spiritual activity is therefore in reality a feeling of corporeal activities (I, 201 ff.).

To repeat once more: Every one of us is animated by an immediate feeling of respect for his own pure principles of individual existence (I, 318). But this does not lead to the discovery of a purely spiritual principle. The words "I" and "self," to the extent that they arouse feelings and have emotional significance, are *objective* indications that are related to all that is capable, in the stream of experience, to arouse excitations of a definite nature (I, 319). The most palpable being-self is the corporeal being-self. Our own body *is* the core of the stream of experience. It is "mine" par excellence: myself.

14. Myself: the Pure "I"

If James' analysis of the empirical "I" leaves us with a feeling of dissatisfaction it is because the "I," announced as the source of spontaneous activity, could be conceived only as an objectivity that is defined as to its content. And then the question inevitably comes up, *who* experiences the self, the "mine" as self. For the return upon oneself presupposes, at least logically, a duplication: *I* contemplate *myself,* and then do not find "I" but "mine." If we call the first "I" the pure "I," we can then ask the question whether I can contemplate and grasp myself. Can the pure "I" be an object of contemplation?

Here James accepts fully the ideas which Horwicz expressed concerning the matter.[34] He is even satisfied with simply quoting Horwicz (I, 325). Now the latter is unambiguously of the opinion that all self-consideration, all feelings and appreciations with regard to what is "mine," have a relation to objectivities. One may say also that everything to which a feeling and experience relates, *must* be grasped as object, in the widest sense of the word, as "Gegenstand," in virtue of an inner necessity. When experience returns to experience itself, it grasps the latter exclusively and necessarily as something that *is* experienced, and is to that extent a "content" of reflective experience. In other words, the pure "I" withdraws from all contemplation or observation that tries to grasp that "I" as such. The pure "I" is the final point of an endless regression. In the "I contemplate myself" I do not contemplate my pure "I" but an objectivated "myself."

If I then try to grasp that escaping "I" in: "I contemplate myself as an I that contemplates itself," the contemplating "I" escapes once more. We could go on and on endlessly and think logically about that reiterated regression. But *psychologically* we come rather quickly to the end. I can indulge in make-believe. I can pretend that I pretend; but pretend that I pretend that I pretend, is already something I cannot imagine.

If such iterations can be imagined and experienced, it is under one condition: *that a bipolarity be maintained in their formulation.* I think—something. I think—that I think something. I think—that I think something, namely that I think something. *There is no regression of the "I";* the same "I" experiences objects of increasing complexity. Duplications, complications and regressions do not appear in the "I-term," but in the object of the experience.

The fundamental structure of the intentionality remains that of: "I-am-something-conscious-of-something," however complicated the structure of that "something" may be. All complicated structures are variations of that unchangeable fundamental structure. We have here a phenomenological principle of major import. It makes superfluous the metaphysical constructions of a final "I" behind all empirically successive "I's." The soul "behind" the self, and the transcendental ego "behind" the soul are not new, real "I's," but *logical variants* of the one same "I-term." Personal identity is the identity of the one same person. It is interesting how James in principle arrives at the same conclusion.

15. The Experience of Personal Identity

In Chapter V, 2, we considered James' thesis that "I uninterruptedly experience myself." Thus was personal identity reintroduced. Not as *objective* identity, but as an *experiential* one. We must now look once more at that thesis and examine it a little more carefully.

Experiences are not loose; separate successive portions of experience do not replace one another; they interpenetrate and, what is more, belong together in a personal identity. This belonging-to is co-experienced in every experience. Every experience is capable of distinguishing the experiences that belong to its own "I" from among numerous other experiences in which it is involved (I, 331). The experiences that belong to the one same "I" possess a warmth and intimacy that is absent from the others. Experience recognizes its relatives.

In one experience I judge another experience as mine. What does this mean? Nothing but that there is question here of a judgment of similarity, that I experience experiences together; it is a case of subjective synthesis. We shall do well if we recall now what was said in Chapter V, 4, about the unity in the stream of experience. When I experience the inner relationship of my own experiences and can state that they belong to the one same stream of experience, such an experience is possible because of "a single pulse of subjectivity" (I, 278). The feeling of personal identity rests on the agreement noticed by one experience among diverse experienced things: I experience the identity of my present self with that of yesterday and say: "I am the same that I was yesterday" (I, 332).

James realizes fully how close his view is to the "I-theory" in association psychology. And yet, he thinks, it cannot be said that he agrees with association psychology when it says that "I," my personal identity is an aggregate of a series of permanently arising bodily sensations. But neither is it a substantive soul that functions as a bearer of the experiences. The "I" is always an actual "I," a now forthcoming experience that takes up past experiences in itself and orders them to itself. "I" means nothing more than that there is always an actual focus in the stream of experience. One can speak of an *appropriation* of earlier experiences by the actual.

At this moment, experiencing my continuity with my own past, I appropriate that past. The actual section of the stream of experience, the actual "thought" then represents my previous experiences. I experience *now* that I "am" the same as ten years ago. This I do now, or rather: the actual experience appropriates earlier experiences. This actual experience itself is never an object of and for oneself, but objectivates only what preceded it. In the next moment it will perhaps be objectivated itself.

The "I" is nothing else than the actual experience that appropriates the continuous stream of previous experiences: "The passing thought is the thinker" (I, 401). It is possible that the actual experience feels the actual experience of its own immediate existence, however difficult it is to verify in self-perception, but more than this immediate feeling of existence the actual experience does not give about itself; all knowledge about the now present experience can only be obtained by a subsequent experience, when the present one is past and the new appropriates this past one. *What then does that appropriation mean?* Evidently *not* that the actual experience appropriates the previous one to *itself,* for the actual experience has no explicit knowledge of itself; the actual experience appropriates the previous one to the most intimately experienced part of its object: *to the body.* The body is the core of the feeling of personal identity (I, 314). The body forms experientially the foundation of my self-experience. The continuous appropriation to the body in the experience of my previous experiences constitutes the feeling of personal identity.

16. Experience and Time

What we have said before means that the experience in all the transitions that may occur nevertheless makes itself a persisting stream, namely to the extent that it takes in retrospection. The actual experience seizes upon the earlier experience which in a certain sense is thereby protracted. This continuance, on the other hand, consists in this that the actual experience seizes upon the next experience, just as was already done by the un-actual, past experience. *"The knowledge of some other part of the stream, past or future, near or remote, is always mixed in with our knowledge of the present thing"* (*I*, 606) . It is only because of that that we can speak of a stream of experience.

But then *duration* is already a mark of the actual experience considered in itself. The present moment is not a *point* of time; it has *thickness:*

> In short, the practically cognized present is no knife-edge, but a saddle-back, with a certain breadth of its own on which we sit perched, and from which we look in two directions into time. The unit of composition of our perception of time is a *duration*, with a bow and a stern, as it were—a rearward—and a forward-looking end (I, 609) .

A succession of experiences is in itself not yet an experience of the succession. The past, in order that it may be experienced as "past," must be experienced *together with* the present and *during* the present moment (I, 682 ff.) ; the original image and source of all experience of time.

More interesting than the theory regarding the physiological processes of time that James now develops is the fact that he appears once more as a forerunner of Husserl in his formulation of his view. We read in Husserl that: every experience is in itself a flux of the "becoming"; it is what is, in an original production of an immutable type of being; a constant flow of retentions (memories) and protentions (anticipations) mediated through one self-flowing phase of originality, in which the living Now of experiences becomes conscious of its "before" and "after."[35]

Hence here also: the actual experience, as part of the stream of experience, possesses itself already a flowing character, and is actually characterized by retention and protention (anticipation) , by a going-back to what went before and an anticipation of coming experiences. It is in this fundamental structure of experience, continuous with retention and protention that Husserl, like James, sees the foundation of self-consciousness and reflection. Actual experience, said James, does not know about itself but it can know about the previous experience. Self-consciousness is accomplished in a retrospection. Husserl comes to the same conclusion in the contemplation of the original consciousness (the actual, now arising experience) and the possibility of reflection.

Retention, says Husserl,[36] is not a modification in which impressional data are really preserved, but a special kind of intentionality. When there is a new experience, the previous one is not lost but is "kept in our grasp." This makes possible a backward glance at what has gone before. It is true that retention is not yet a backward look, but because the past remains within my grasp, I *can* look back and achieve retention in a reflection. Hence it is the retention that makes possible a self-consciousness, a consciousness of our own experiences.[37] *Reflection is the fulfillment of the possibility pre-given in the retention, so that experience, grasping backward, experiences "itself."* And in this reflection is achieved the consciousness of one's personal identity.[38]

But the actual, backward grasping, reflection experience is *itself* an *actual* experience, *and as such is itself non-reflective.*[39] Here also James and Husserl agree: the actual experience is *never* reflectively conscious of itself but, at most, of the previous experience. Merleau-Ponty too understands Husserl in this sense: "The idea of a consciousness that is transparent to itself and whose existence comes down to having consciousness of its own existence is not so different from the notion of the unconscious."[40]

We saw that the achievement of retention in reflection was defined by James as "appropriation." We could ask both Husserl and James whether appropriation does not already presuppose consciousness. James foresaw that question:

> Some subtle reader will object that the Thought cannot call any part of its Object 'I' and knit other parts on to it, without first knitting that part on to *Itself;* and that it cannot knit it on to Itself without knowing Itself;—so that our supposition that the Thought may conceivably have no immediate knowledge of Itself is thus overthrown (I, 341 Note).

Experience that, in a retention-achieving-reflection appropriates retentional experiences to "its" body, discovers itself, grasping backwards, as "I."[41]

17. *Anticipation: Appropriation of Protentional Experiences*

If experience is really characterized by retention and protention (anticipation) is there not also an appropriation of protentional experiences, parallel with the appropriation of what is retentional? But how can one appropriate that which is still to come and hence is not yet there? This objection, however, is not acceptable. If we accept the protentional structure of experience, the being-before-toward, we also recognize the possibility of appropriating it reflectively which is called *anticipation*. And then the actual experience appropriates to itself coming experiences on the basis of protention.

This we have already met in principle in what James called "images- (representations) of-movement." For in order to perform a truly voluntary movement it is not enough that the person knows what he can do; or rather, this knowledge must not be a mere having-at-one's-disposal potentialities of movement in the motor organization of the body that can be actualized. We must have a pre-grasping and a having-at-our-disposal; in the feeling of "what can be done" there must pre-exist here and now movements to be executed in their course and end-result.

Thus when reaching for something, I see that "I can reach it," and thus I have it already in my grasp; so also before I jump I am already on the other side of the ditch; so likewise do I now direct myself to the ball which I shall catch immediately. To anticipate what is coming means that what is coming, the not-yet-fulfilled, running ahead of the fulfillment, is already active in my behavior. This protention, just like the retention, first comes about before all reflection, in the body-consciousness itself.[42] The body already "protends" (anticipates) toward that which will take place.

We saw until now how James argued that there must be first a "knowing" of one's ability (of the "I can"), a corporeal experience (II, 487), a store of images of movements that are based on experience (II, 488). These then have not merely a memory-value; they also enable us to feel beforehand a series of future sensations of movement (II, 521). James, after that, reached the conclusion that this pre-reflective ideomotor activity constitutes a sufficient foundation for the movement itself that simply flows from it (II, 522 ff.) .

"To act after a consideration," "to decide," "to will" in general must therefore be reduced to relations between ideas of movement that are coupled with a feeling of effort, a corporeal feeling that is the reality we ordinarily substantize as "to will," as a spiritual act. The will, according to James, like attention, is a phenomenon of struggle between representations. Ricoeur has given an extensive commentary on the difficulties in which James thus entangles himself.[43] We omit this and shall merely point out a solution that is contained in James' theory.

What is a representation of a movement as *representation?* James here uses the term *idea,* against which, as we have already fully shown, he has serious objections. Now, in using this term once more, we must note that James is not thinking of a "psychic content," but he uses it as a term for the experience of a situation. What the "current psychologies" call ideas are nothing but a portion of the total object of representations. All that we have simultaneously before the mind, irrespective of how complicated a context of things and relations it may be, is one object of experience. So "A-and-B-and their mutual irreconcilability-and-the-fact-that-only-one-of-them-can-be-true-and-be-realized-irrespec-tive-of-the-probability-or-desirability-of-both" could be one such complex object (II, 569) . The object of experience when we are considering things, or deliberating, or are hesitating, has that kind of structure and the transition to the decision is character-ized by the fact that, for instance, A is rejected and B is main-tained. We then have a feeling that we have made a choice.

But then we *have* truly *made* a choice. The choice may have been achieved pre-reflectively in body-consciousness; a "decision" has occurred; the experience that could go in diverse directions and foresaw them, went in *one* direction. The protention deter-mined itself in the object of experience. After our hesitation, there followed a behavior which we explain afterwards as follow-ing upon a *plan* of movement. But this plan was already, proten-tionally, the movement itself.

Blondel said the same thing: The "idea of the movement," the "plan of a movement" is already virtually a movement.[44] During the execution there can be a correction of the plan on the basis of factual sensations of movement, while, on the other hand, their course is once more regulated by the plan. But it is not only the body that "knows" that and how all this takes place. I can also have a *realization* of it; it is accessible to me in a reflection. I can consciously anticipate what will occur, that is, I can appropriate my protentional experiences before their fulfillment. I appropriate the future to myself, not as an empty time that still must appear, but as the coming movements-and-experiences that I foresee. It is in such a way that I become conscious of my coming movement and that I experience *"willing-now."* Human behavior is really permeated by the possibility of that reflection. *This reflection is the fulfillment of the possibilities pre-given in the protention (anticipation), so that experience, grasping forward, experiences "itself."*

But then, we find in this the solution of the problem of the activity of consciousness. If we admit that there is experience, we must also admit that it is *active* (II, 571), that it influences behavior, that it produces *effects*. In other words, there must be behaviors that are reflectively governed. But how is this possible if experience is really nothing but an "interiorization" of brain activity? Do we not say then that, ultimately, it is nevertheless the *brain* that "intelligently" governs behavior? (I, 79). We must then say that experience as such cannot be active.

Undoubtedly, we must not fall back into a dualism that postulates an interaction of mind and matter. Let us say then, rather, that reflective experience is the "interiorization" of a new dimension in the brain processes. Reflection means not only that things are experienced but that experience is experienced. And thus a new dimension has arisen in relation to things. Now immediate reaction and immediate experience can be "upheld"; we can "think before we act," that is, we can, by reflection make earlier experiences usable in reactions to actual situations. But this power presents itself differently under various complementary viewpoints. At one time it is as a modification in the intentionality of the experience, at another as a new property of the actual body.

18. Body Consciousness

Backward-grasping and forward-grasping, pre-figured in retention and protention, must be understood as the appropriation to "my" body, and not as a bending-back (re-flection) of "consciousness" upon itself. Retention and protention arise in the properties of the organism, in its spontaneous activity on the basis of its relative autonomy. *The body comes to itself in reflective experience,* discovers itself as source, as originator, as "I." It then, at the same time, discovers that its originality and spontaneity are already pre-given, and that they do not first arise through reflection. The body itself already had "consciousness," a pre-reflective consciousness, and (with respect to reflection) an implicit intentionality. The body, the *not-willed-through-reflection,* the involuntary, constitutes the foundation of reflection.[45]

The *being-able-to-move* must unambiguously be understood as an original intentionality according to Merleau-Ponty. "La conscience est originairement non pas un 'je pense que' mais un 'je peux'" (Consciousness, originally, is not a "I think that" but an "I can").[46] And he adds that the term is habitually used in the unpublished writings of Husserl. According to Husserl, a "practical horizon" belongs truly to every action, to every praxis,

> namely, a horizon of that which I can do in my horizon-conscious situation. This 'I-can' is not a matter of some reflection, inductive and from the outside, following inductively on my way of reacting to the unworldly, and that then 'objectively' determines my dispositions, my objective capabilities, historicities, etc. It is rather a question of the living capability-horizon in the given moment, of the conscious dominion-reach, of my power or capacity that is really conscious to me—but it is not conscious in the form of an act, but precisely in the form of a horizon, without which no act is an act, without which no praxis has the least meaning.[47]

It is a question of that inner horizon of James' "world of practical realities" (II, 293): the body. It is the body that primarily has "knowledge" of things; it is through the body that we learn movements, and "to move oneself" means: to have a view of things through the body, even without any "idea or representation" of those things.[48] It is the body-consciousness that lays the foundation for the reflective appropriations. It is the body that in its relation to the Life-world already pre-figures reflection. Although we often think that the body acts "blindly," does it not also often seem to us that the body shows insight, reflects, ponders, chooses and makes decisions? Is this not because, in the relative autonomy of the organism, the direct causal influence of internal and external processes is suspended or regulated? The organism maintains norms. It already has its own system of values, on the basis of which situations and events are "judged." It manifests spontaneous activity. It regulates its relations by retention and protention (anticipation). Between stimulus and reaction it introduces a phase of "inner activity" that is not found in lifeless nature, a phase of interior attuning by which it appears as subject.

All that appears once more in reflection, but now in a "seeing" way. For experience itself this is now an entirely new and original activity by which the "spirit" seems suddenly to rise above the "nature." But this spirit is pre-figured according to its nature in the behavior of the organism. The autonomy of the organism comes to itself in reflection as "spirit."

Perception of a thing comes about in the functioning of the body, as does also the perception of the body by itself.[49] Body consciousness is the primitive form and foundation of reflectivity. It is the body that "can," that "knows," and "wills," already before we know this once more in reflection.

19. The Body, Behavior and Reflection

One of James' opinions is that consciousness, if it is anything, is a means that is at the disposal of the organism so that it may adjust itself. We saw that that adaptation is not passive but active; that the organism is characterized by a relative autonomy which finds in homeostasis both its foundation and its expression. Homeostasis, by which norms are maintained, gives at the same time new possibilities. He who invents a language for practical purposes notices that he can also use it when he wishes to write poetry. Regulation and freedom are the two sides of homeostasis, they are aspects that call up one another. A new regulation leads to new freedom; new freedom demands new regulation if it wishes to be used. In what is typically human this process passes beyond a boundary.

If we come to the conclusion that behavior is in no way the result of a "spiritual activity" in the classical sense of the term, that perception and action, doxic confidence and habit, emotional reaction and "to will" all precede reflection and thus have no need of classical "consciousness," either in order to be achieved or in order to be explained; when we conclude that all behavior and the retentional and protentional experience that is implied in it arise from the body, we must note at the same time that a new dimension both of regulation and of freedom opens with the appearance of reflection. The body comes to itself in reflection and discovers itself as "I" in a continuity of previous experiences; in a stream of experience. The body discovers itself in a history.

The body discovers itself as an "I" that was already there, that has its origin in the past, which it can no longer appropriate, which reflection, looking backwards, cannot reach. It discovers itself toward a future which it is likewise unable to appropriate as an end for itself. Birth and death withdraw from its gaze, just as pre-reflective corporeity. But I can comprehend these boundaries *as boundaries*. In reflection I have a distance from "myself" which makes that possible. Thus are the potentialities of the beast essentially transcended.

I know about myself in the measure to which experience appropriates experiences to my body. Is not this the meaning of James' theory of emotions? In emotion (as experience) I experience what my body "experiences," the participation in the things and events that speak to that body in its organic structure and to which it is related; and with respect to which it takes a stand on the basis of its own, organic norms. No single "representation or idea" is necessary for that: the body is ready before I can imagine all the things that could occur. It knows its world, before "I" represent it to myself.

It is the body that orgininally thematizes *things* in a perception that takes place through the body. Hence the first perception can never be understood to be an "act of the mind"; the "thing-constitution" in its first meaning is not accessible to reflection, at least not in the way it is achieved. Doxic confidence, involved in and based on corporeity, cannot be reduced to a spiritual faith; it is on the contrary the foundation upon which reflective doxic modalities such as hesitation, agreement, doubt, negation and confirmation, etc. are founded. Doxic confidence itself is the way the body participates in the Life-world. It is the body that is with things, for its own interest.

But all that I *know*. In reflection I appropriate the experience to my body and come to myself. Not that I grasp myself as myself. In reflection, what is mine becomes accessible to me as mine, for experience. Thereby "I" becomes "seeing," and the sight which my body already had of things now appears to be blind. Experience is no longer exclusively something the body has acquired as familiar and habitual in its dealing with things; experience becomes the *knowing* of that familiarity, and of its connection with the situations in which it was acquired. In the reflective backward-grasping there opens a treasure of experience that can be applied at will. I can make use of that experience. I *think*. Experience lies no longer stored up in habitual patterns of behavior, but now it can be formulated.

I develop myself as my own psychologist, said James. I become my own onlooker and observer; I cannot even prevent myself from observing myself and noting what I, my body, does or what it is going to do. Retention and protention become transparent in reflection, in experience-that-appropriates. I see what I "can," I see what I "will," and I express that knowledge. My body speaks out in language.

In language I have the means by which I, together with others in my environment, fix meanings in the ever-flowing stream of experiences. We can fix these because we have become "seeing," because our own experience has appeared in sight through reflection; because I find agreements and identities in the residual retentionality of my memory, in my experience, beyond the immediate retention. I call things by name; the things that were preconstituted by the body become themselves, they become things that can be repeated; they become related things, samples of a kind, of a species. I reconstruct them in "general objects" (Allgemeingegenstände) ; I express their nature, I fix them in writing.

In direct experience, the body, still "speechless," speaks out its intentionality, its relatedness to things that concern it; the things that threaten it, that tempt it, the things that it needs, that are obstacles or helps for it, the things in which it participates through its life and to which it resounds in emotion. The body experiences those things, and this experience is a thematizing in a selectivity that is given in its organic character before all acts.

In reflection, the *stream of experience itself becomes* a field for new thematizations. What the organism already accomplished is now repeated on a higher level. An "interiority" arises; the experience of things in reflection becomes open for a new experience. I speak about "what takes place in me"; I *can* speak only because I experience that I experience. And in language I substantize my reflection as *I,* as my interiority, as my soul. I understand myself as "pure Ego," as a seeing mind that inhabits the blind body. The illusion of immanence is born, and the field is ripe for a philosophical fixation in an opposition between soul and body, mind and matter.

Why do I express myself that way in language? Because I speak *about* myself, and cannot "speak myself"? The reflective experience that appropriates the pre-reflective experience is itself fulfilled as pre-reflective. By grasping backward and grasping forward, experiences become accessible but they do not become "grasping." But how else can I formulate this than by saying that *I* (although I do not know anything about myself by "grasping") know about myself reflectively and similarly about my body? In reflection I divine a new originality, namely that of the pure I, because when I grasp backwards, I cannot simultaneously appropriate to the body the originality of the "backward grasping."

And yet I must acknowledge that that originality is founded on the originality of the body.

In this way a centuries-old tradition is attacked, the substantization of the "inner" that has been transmitted and become deposited in language. Phenomenology tries to rediscover the body as the source, by returning to the Life-world. In this it is in agreement with James.

But it would be a new error to refuse to estimate reflection according to its own value, and to consider it as being merely the mirroring of direct experience. James' way of considering things functionally is already unfavorable to such a view and is in fact opposed to it. Reflection, considered functionally, is a new homeostatic mechanism. As we have said already, it makes experience accessible and usable as experience. The insight into relations, the understanding that arises when the content of experience can be surveyed, enables the human organism to adapt itself in a new way to the environment—while maintaining its own norms. It enables us to confirm the relative autonomy as autonomy and to foster it by actively engaging ourselves in the environment.

A new autonomy is acquired; adaptation to the environment becomes, to some extent, a dominion over the environment. Bodily functions become substantized in, and in increasing measure transferred to, instruments and tools. The world of the machine opens; a world in which finally machines, constructed by us, maintain our organic norms for us. Are we not already living in such a time?

If we look at reflection as a new mechanism of regulation, we must then say also according to the rule of the reverse side that it also gives us a new freedom. The freedom of thought that does not *exclusively* serve the organism but seeks the truth, pursues the good *as* good, and realizes the beautiful for its own sake. This was not foreseen. It is, if you will, given into the bargain and is a gratuity. But we who possess that freedom cannot help looking at all things in the light of that freedom. And we are not totally wrong. For if the "higher" is built on the "lower" it is not exclusively a function of the "lower" although it is founded on it. On the contrary, it penetrates "with reverse power" into the "lower." The higher *governs* the lower. If we prefer, we can say also that higher forms are organization-forms of the lower. It remains true that even then, in the higher organized organism, the forms of organization which the higher ones have in common with the lower organisms now function in another context. In this way, human learning, also that of motor activities, is a degree richer than that of the animal because of reflection, and it is in this respect incomparable with it, in spite of all other relationships with the animal. Reflection that discovers values as values, penetrates back into the "solely corporeal." Human needs and urges, habits and emotions, perceptions and actions, are marked and stamped by reflection.

Hence, he who sees in reflection the properly human phenomenon is not wrong. And when he then says that human experience has a proper, irreducible view of things this is not wrong either. And from this it follows that human experience must and can be described and ordered on the basis of experience itself, and that human behavior can be understood on the basis of experience. But it does not follow that the mind has its own substantial existence. Human behavior and conduct can and must likewise be described and ordered on the basis of the viewpoint that they are functions of an organism.

NOTES

1. James, "The Experience of Activity," in *A Pluralistic Universe,* p. 392; *Essays,* p. 185.
2. James, "The Experience of Activity," in *A Pluralistic Universe,* pp. 377 ff.; *Essays,* pp. 187 ff.
3. F. J. J. Buytendijk, *Algemene Theorie der Menselijke Houding en Beweging,* (Utrecht, 1948), p. 434.
4. Merleau-Ponty, *Phénoménologie,* p. 210: "Je n'ai pas besoin de me représenter le mot pour le savoir et pour le prononcer. Il suffit que j'en possède l'essence articulaire et sonore comme l'une des modulations, l'un des usages possibles de mon corps."
5. James, *Talks to Teachers,* p. 38.
6. *Ibid.,* pp. 39 ff.
7. James, *Will to Believe,* p. 76.
8. Cf. James, *Principles,* vol. 1, p. 289: "One great splitting of the whole universe into two halves is made by each of us; and for each of us

almost all of the interest attaches to one of the halves; but we all draw the line of division between them in a different place. When I say that we all call the two halves by the same names and that those names are 'me' and 'not-me' respectively, it will at once be seen what I mean."

9. Cl. Bernard, *Leçons sur les Propriétés Physiologiques,* vol. 1, (Paris, 1859), pp. 9 ff.: "Cette sorte d'indépendance que possède l'organisme dans le milieu extérieur vient de ce que, chez l'être vivant, les tissus sont en realité soustraits aux influences extérieures directes et qu'ils sont protégés par une veritable milieu intérieur . . . ; . . . *l'indépendance du milieu extérieur et du milieu interne est telle, qu'on peut considérer ces êtres comme vivant dans un milieu organique propre.*"

10. W. B. Cannon, *The Wisdom of the Body,* (New York, 1932).

11. James, *Principles,* vol. 2, p. 383: "Instinct is usually defined as the ability to act in such a way that specific purposes are realized, without insight, and without previous exercise in the execution of them."

12. J. A. Bierens de Haan, *Die Tierischen Instinkte,* (Leiden, 1940), p. 229.

13. D. A. MacFarlane. "The Role of Kinesthesis in Maze Learning," *Univ. Cal. Publ. Psychol.,* vol. 4, 1930. Cf. F. J. J. Buytendijk, *Wege zum Verständnis der Tiere,* (Zürich, no year), pp. 178 ff., and *Traité de Psychologie Animale,* (Paris, 1952), pp. 197 ff., for a critique of the chain-reflex theory of behavior.

14. Cf. Buytendijk, *Algemene Theorie der Menselijke Houding en Beweging,* pp. 446 ff.

15. James, *Talks to Teachers,* pp. 174 ff.

16. Ch. Blondel, "Les 'Mouvements Volontaires,' " in G. Dumas, *Nouveau Traité de Psychologie,* T. 6, (Paris, 1939).

17. Buytendijk, *Wege zum Verständnis der Tiere,* p. 143: "Nirgends ist uns auch nur der geringste Anlass zu der Ansicht gegeben, dass jene Funktionen, dir wir die Psychischen nennen, in irgendeiner Lebensphase gleich einem Demon in den Korper fahren."

18. We follow here the explanation given in the *Principles.* James had already published that theory earlier, under the title "What is an Emotion," in *Mind,* vol. 9, 1884, pp. 188–205. Somewhat later there appeared, independently of James, a study by the Dane, Carl Lange, *Om Sindsbevoegelser,* 1885, translated as *Ueber Gemütsbewegungen,* (Leipzig, 1887), in which similar thoughts were expressed. That is why we speak of the James-Lange theory. Lange is quoted with approval in the *Principles.* James later returned to that problem in an article entitled: "The Physical Basis of Emotion," *Psych. Rev.,* vol. 1, 1894, pp. 516–529.

19. Cf. for the proper discussion of the theory, the article of Karl

304 On the Way Toward a Phenomenological Psychology

Stumpf, "Ueber den Begriff der Gemüthsbewegung," *Z. Psychol.*, vol. 21, 1899, pp. 47–49. The best critical explanation of the theory on the basis of experiments is found in W. B. Cannon, *Bodily Changes in Pain, Hunger, Fear and Rage,* (New York, 1920).

    20. E. B. Titchener, "An Historical Note on the James-Lange Theory of Emotion," *Amer. J. Psychol.*, vol. 25, 1914, pp. 427–447.

    21. Stumpf, "Ueber den Begriff der Gemüthsbewegung," p. 67. Regarding his own article which James had not yet read at that time, Stumpf wrote to James, September, 1899: "Merkwürdig ist mir mit Breutano gegangen. Ich dachte mit ihm in Hinsicht der Affecte ziemlich einstimmig zu sein und erhalte nun von ihm einen 7 Bogen langen Brief, worin er sich entschieden für *Ihre* Auffassung und gegen die meinige erklärt. Eine etwas beschämende Wirkung meiner Argumentationen! Ween er einmal an das Veröffentlichen seiner Arbeiten geht, werden Sie an ihm für die Affectlehre eine nicht zu verachtende Stütze haben;" Perry, *Thought*, vol. 2, p. 741.

    22. Perry, *Thought*, vol. 2, p. 89.

    23. R. H. Lotze, *Medicinische Psychologie*, (Leipzig, 1852), p. 518: "Wir haben andere Gedanken und Bestrebungen, wenn wir liegen, andere wenn wir stehen; eine erauringene zusammengedrängte Körperstellung dämpft unseren Muth, bequen und nachlässig gelagert vermögen wir schwerlich andächtig zu sein, und aller Zorn beruhigt sich durch die Ruhe des Körpers; die Hand, welche die Runzeln der Stirn glattet, beschwichtigt auch den Verdruss, der sich durch sie aussprach. Es würde schwer sein, die Grenzen dieses Einflusses zu bestimmen; aber er geht ohne Zweifel sehr weit . . ."

    Cf. there on the same page, the following passage: "Der heitere Genuss schöner Verhältnisse ist nicht blos diese abstracte *Freude,* sondern in dem lebhaftern, freieren Athmen, dem beschleunigten Herzschlage und der gediegenen Spannung der Muskerln fühlen wir unser eigenes Selbst davon gehaben und getragen; Reue und Bekümmerniss um Vergangenes ist nicht blos ein sittliches Verdammungsurtheil, das innerlich ausgesprochen, von der Seele neu vernommen wird; die Erschlaffung unserer Glieder, die mindere Grösse des Athmens, die Beklemmung der Brust, vielleicht im Aerger selbst die krampfaften Verengerungen der Bronchien und die aufwürgende Bewegung der Speiseröhre, die den Bissen im Munde stocken macht, zeigen, wie auch die leibliche Organisation symbolisch ein verschmähtes, unter dessen Drucke sie seufzt, auszustossen versucht." James' question, is the "leibliche Organisation" (corporeal organization) is not precisely what is primary, here does not seem a forced conclusion.

    24. Horwicz, *Psychologische Analysen auf Physiologischer Grundlage,* Bd. 2/1, p. 52.

    25. *Ibid.*, Bd. 2/2, pp. 58 ff.

26. The physical basis of emotion.

27. J. P. Sartre, in his *Esquisse d'une Théorie des Emotions*, (Paris, 1948), unjustly takes no account of this further development of James' theory. For after that modification, James' theory cannot be considered less phenomenological than that of Sartre.

28. James, *Talks to Teachers*, p. 229.

29. Cf. Hans Linschoten, "Algemene Functieleer," in M. J. Langeveld, ed., *Inleiding in de Psychologie*, (Groningen, 1957), pp. 163 ff.

30. Merleau-Ponty, *Phénoménologie*, p. 445: "Notre corps in tant qu'il se meut luimême, c'est-à-dire en tant qu'il est inséparable d'une vue du monde et qu'il est cette vue même réalisée, est la condition de possibilité, non seulement de la synthèse géométrique, mais encore de toutes les opérations expressives et de toutes les acquisitions qui constituent le monde culturel."

31. James, *Talks to Teachers*, p. 22.

32. *Ibid.*, p. 27.

33. *Ibid.*, p. 24.

34. Horwicz, *Psychologische Analysen auf Physiologischer Grundlage*, Bd. 2/2, pp. 260 ff.

35. Husserl, *Ideen*, vol. 1, p. 149: "Jedes Erlebnis ist in sich selbst ein Fluss des Werdens, es ist was es ist, in einer *ursprünglichen Erzeugung* von einem unwandelbaren Wesenstypus; ein beständiger Fluss von Retentionen und Protentionen vermittelt durch eine selbst fliessende Phase der Originalität, in der das lebedige Jetzt des Erlebnisses gegenuber seinem 'Vorhin' und 'Nachher' bewusst wird."

36. Edmund Husserl, "Vorlesungen zur Phanomenologie des Inneren Zeitbewusstsein," *Jb. Phil. Phenomenol. Forsch.*, 1928, pp. 147 ff.

37. Cf. *Ibid.*, p. 436: "Der Fluss des immanenten zeitkonstituierenden Bewusstseins *ist* nicht nur, sondern so merkwürdig und doch verständlich geartet ist er, dass in ihm notwendig eine Selbsterscheinung des Flusses bestehen und haber der Fluss selbst notwendig im Fliessen erfassbar sein muss."

38. Cf. Husserl, *Ideen*, vol. 1, p. 150: "Durch reflektiv *erfahrende* Akte allein wissen wir etwas vom Erlebnisstrom und von der notwendigen Bezogenheit desselben auf das reine Ich . . . ; dass all die Erlebnisse des Stromes die seinen sind eben insofern, als es auf sie hinblicken oder 'durch sie hindurch' auf anderes Ichfremdes blicken kann."

39. Cf. *Ibid.*, p. 150: "Wir können diese Modifikationen primär auf die unreflektiert bewussten aktuellen Erlebnisse beziehen, da sofort zu sehen ist, dass an diesen primären Modifikationen alle reflektiert bewussten eo ipso Anteil gewinnen müssen dadurch, dass sie als *Reflexionen* auf Erlebnisse, und in voller Konkretion genommen, selbst unreflektiert-bewusste Erlebnisse sind. . . ."

40. Merleau-Ponty, *Phénoménologie*, p. 436: "L'idée d'une con-

science qui serait transparente pour elle-même et dont l'existence se ramènerait à la conscience qu'elle a d'exister n'est pas si différente de la motion d'inconscient." Cf. Husserl, "Zeitbewusstsein," pp. 472 ff.

41. We shall not comment here on the differences between James and Husserl in respect to the "I." There are differences. But it does not seem impossible to reconcile the two views. Cf., as regards Husserl, *Ideen*, vol. 2, pp. 93-120.

42. Cf. Erwin Straus, *Vom Sinn der Sinne*, (Berlin, 1935), pp. 297 ff., and Buytendijk, *Algemene Theorie*, pp. 312 ff.

43. Paul Ricoeur, *Philosophie de la Volonté*, (Paris, 1949), pp. 167 ff.

44. Buytendijk, *Algemene Theorie*, pp. 437 ff.

45. Ricoeur, *Philosophie de la Volonté*, pp. 84 ff.

46. Merleau-Ponty, *Phénoménologie*, p. 160.

47. Edmund Husserl, *Geburt, Tod, Unbewusstsein*. Unpublished manuscript in the Husserl-Archives of Louvain, under signature A VI, 14. The quotation is found on p. 30 of the transcript.

48. Merleau-Ponty, *Phénoménologie*, p. 161: "La conscience est l'être à la chose par l'intermédiaire du corps. Un nouvement est appris lorsque le corps l'a compris, c'est-à-dire lorsqu'il l'a incorporé à son 'monde,' et mouvoir son corps c'est viser à travers lui les choses, c'est le laisser répondre à leur sollicitation qui s'exerce sur lui sans aucune représentation."

49. Edmund Husserl, "Die Welt der Lebendigen Gegenwart und die Konstitution der Ausserleiblichen Unwelt," *Phil. Phenomenol. Res.*, vol. 6, 1945-46, p. 341. "Im Funktionieren des Leibes findet die Dingwahrnehmung statt und auch die Wahrnehmung des Leibes durch sich selbst."

X CONCLUSION

1. On the Way to a Phenomenological Psychology

With the ideas expressed at the end of the last chapter, where we finish, begins a phenomenological psychology of the kind that was born during the last decade in the work of Buytendijk, Merleau-Ponty, Straus, and many others. In Husserl is found the methodological and systematic preparation that make possible that kind of psychology. But James was a forerunner of it. The coincidence is not fortuitous. James' psychology is phenomenological by intention and in its fundamental thoughts. Why did it not become so explicitly?

James, in his fight against the theory of representative knowledge, did not succeed in developing a clear concept of intentionality. Knowledge, involvement of experience in things, he considers to be a fundamental relation that must be acknowledged (I, 216) ; the cognitive character is a fundamental characteristic of the stream of experience (I, 271). But, he later tells us, the term "consciousness" signifies a kind of external relation,[1] namely between the existing man and the existing thing. Another formulation is also possible. When in a series of experiences one points to another, this means that the one functions as knower, and the other as object.[2] Here also it is a question of an external relation between experiences. He had already spoken in this vein ten years earlier.

What do we mean, when we say that we, here and now, know tigers in India?

> Most men would answer that what we mean by knowing the tigers is having them, however absent in body, become in some way present to our thought; or that our knowledge of them is known as presence of our thought to them. A great mystery is

usually made of this peculiar presence in absence; and the scholastic philosophy, which is only common sense grown pedantic, would explain it as a peculiar kind of existence, called *intentional inexistence,* of the tigers in our mind. At the very least, people would say that what we mean by knowing the tigers is mentally pointing towards them as we sit here.

But now what do we mean by *pointing,* in such a case as this? . . . The pointing of our thought to the tigers is known simply and solely as a procession of mental associates and motor consequences that follow on the thought, and that would lead harmoniously, if followed out, into some ideal or real context, or even into the immediate presence, of the tigers.[3]

James rejected Brentano's first definition of intentionality as intentional inexistence for he was afraid of any formulation that suggested immanence. On that account, James, at the critical moment, fell back upon an associationistic formula with a behavioristic tendency that defined knowledge once more as an outward relation.

Husserl was the first to define the concept of intentionality in a way that freed it from all outward and actual relations; namely he declared that it is truly characteristic of experience that it is the experience-of-something, and he warned against a psychological misinterpretation of the same.[4] Psychology *presupposes* that concept; it does *not* itself infer it. Now we have constantly met that concept in James as something that was presupposed. His whole analysis of the characteristics of the stream of experience rested on it, and so did his fight against association theory with all its implications. James' psychology was then already phenomenological although this term had not yet been invented.

His psychology was a descriptive doctrine of experience along lines that were already indicated in Brentano and were later formally elaborated by Husserl. James, like explicit phenomenology, encounters the problem of the Life-world. That Husserl, and after him Merleau-Ponty had an easier access to it is due to Husserl's purification of the concepts of intentionality and reduction.

And finally, James confronts us with a doctrine of experience of the body that in many essential points was anticipation of phenomenological psychology. And so the title of the present work is justified. James was on the way to a phenomenological psychology. We would, however, do him an injustice if we did not add that he was ahead of it with respect to a central point: namely, his integration of an objectivating psychology within the frame of reference of a descriptive psychology.

2. Nature and Reason

"This is no science. It is only the hope of a science." [5] These words express what James thought about the situation of psychology. Also about his own psychology. An essay, nothing more. And only an insight, some facts, but no systematic conception, no science. It was natural that James would reach that conclusion. He was not convinced that the development of unequivocal universal theoretical systems is meaningful. Suppose, he said, that we do attain it. Suppose for a moment that we have developed such a system of concepts, that we can reduce our world to a few simple ideas. Our universal conception has then rationalized the chaos of the concrete. Is the foundation of that rationality then itself rational? No, the foundations of our being remains logically transparent.[6]

Every systematic and rational conception of the whole is bound to fail. If philosophy had for its purpose to take possession of the whole of reality by the mind, the whole of immediate perception-experience alone would then constitute the object of philosophy, for only that experience finds the reality *itself*.[7] Hence there *can* not be a balanced conception of the whole.

There is another reason:

> While I talk and the flies buzz, a sea-gull catches a fish at the mouth of the Amazon, a tree falls in the Adirondack wilderness, a man sneezes in Germany, a horse dies in Tartary, and twins are born in France. What does that mean? Does the contemporaneity of these events with one another and with a million others as disjointed, form a rational bond between them, and unite them into anything that means for us a world?[8]

A system, if it wants to be a system, must be a *closed* system.[9] And why should all those events form one system? The world is a multiversum,[10] not a universum; a pluralistic "whole" of infinite diversity; a kaleidoscopic stream of varieties. No system can reduce it to one single principle.

And so James, one month before his death, gave a written instruction, on July 26, 1910, that his last work should bear as subtitle the words: *A Beginning of an Introduction to Philosophy*. In the world of the manifold, a philosopher remains a novice; he is one who hesitates in his wonderment, in his attempt to divest the concrete of its concrete by means of abstract conceptions; he is one who renounces such a system. And yet, he adds with touching inconsistency: "Say that I hoped by it to round out my system . . ." [11]

Before shaking our head, let us reflect on what is said by the Dictionary: *System:* "An assemblage of objects united by some form of regular interaction or interdependence." It is a whole composed of parts that are placed together. And James would say that it is a "reconnoitering" order by which we can feel at home in a given world.

> What is meant by coming 'to feel at home' in a new place, or with new people? It is simply that, at first, when we take up our quarters in a new room, we do not know what draughts may blow in upon our back, what doors may open, what forms may enter, what interesting objects may be found in cupboards and corners. When after a few days we have learned the range of all these possibilities, the feeling of strangeness disappears.[12]

And so philosophy, and scientific thought in general, is an attempt to feel at home in the multiversum. But this is only partially successful when we decide to confine ourselves to a one-sided view. We then choose some point of view from which we look at the phenomena and from which starting point we try to reduce them to only one formula. Now everyone does not choose *the same* point of view; and hence our formulas are likewise different.

Diverse viewpoints lead to diverse formulations. But does the one shut out the other? Must we not say rather that they complete one another? Must a mechanical interpretation of the world not be joined with a teleological one?[13] They *are* to be united when we realize that they are visions of the same Life-world, that "the deeper features of reality are found only in perceptual experience;" [14] that different viewpoints *must* see the phenomena in a different context or structure, that they *must* lead to different questions from which then different answers *must* result.

He who studies the work of William James is astonished when he quickly notices how unsystematic he is; and he may be annoyed by his inconsistency. So it was also with us when we followed James in his psychological considerations. And yet one cannot help being captivated by his originality, and we gradually develop also the feeling that James' seemingly unsystematic approach is an attempt to reach a more comprehensive system.

James' psychology is unusual because, unlike most psychologies, he does not choose between a view that explains things causally and another that describes things intentionally. James' psychology at first shows a methodological pluralism and hence a seeming confusion of heterogenous viewpoints and explanations. But the idea hidden behind it is the principle of complementarity. And this, in turn, can appear to its full advantage only when, like James, one realizes that the unity of the system is not based on "the one rational method" but on the unity of the pre-rational reality, on the one Life-world, the one original connection and context of divergent questions. And that connection and context is ordered by the body, by the bearer of life.

James is in search of that origin, the source from which the stream arises and beyond which it is not possible to go (backwards). The body is the place where the stream of experience arises.

The continuously flowing stream of experience has the capacity of reflection through retention and protention (anticipation). When the origin or source has attained reflection, it shows itself in a twofold manner: (1) as that which *is* experienced and can be understood only from experience; and (2) as that from which experience itself arises.

Here it is possible to choose two viewpoints; the description and analysis of experience and body in the context of intentionality, and the description and analysis of experience and body in the time-space context of experienced reality. The first leads to what is called *descriptive* psychology, the second to *explanatory* psychology. If the two are divorced, then there arises a "mental science" psychology and a "natural science" psychology; and these two, because they absolutize their individual viewpoints no longer understand one another and seem to exclude one another.

James desired to preserve their mutual connection. This presupposes a theory about that connection and coherence, a phenomenology of the Life-world, that was at least implicitly aimed at by James. Hence his seeming lack of system is in fact a consequence of a more profound, more comprehensive systematic view. It is this which caused him to say: "It is not that we are all nature but some point which is reason, but that all is nature and all is reason too. We shall see, damn it, we shall see. . ."[15]

NOTES

1. James, "Does 'Consciousness' Exist?", in *Essays*, p. 25.
2. James, "A World of Pure Experience," in *Essays*, p. 57.
3. James, "The Knowing of Things Together," pp. 109 ff.
4. Husserl, *Ideen,* vol. 1, p. 64.
5. James, *Psychology, Briefer Course,* p. 468.
6. James, *Will to Believe,* pp. 70 ff.
7. William James, *Some Problems of Philosophy,* (New York, 1911), pp. 96 ff.
8. James, *Will to Believe,* p. 119.
9. *Ibid.,* p. 13.
10. *Ibid.,* p. 43.
11. James, *Some Problems of Philosophy,* pp. vii ff.
12. James, *Will to Believe,* p. 78.
13. *Ibid.,* pp. 75 ff.
14. James, *Some Problems of Philosophy,* p. 97.
15. James, *Letters,* vol. 1, p. 153.

BIBLIOGRAPHY

Allport, F. H. *Theories of Perception and the Concept of Structure.* New York, Wiley, 1955.

Allport, G. W. "The Productive Paradoxes of William James," *Psychol. Rev.* 50 (1943), 95-120.

Amiel, H. F. *Fragments d'un journal intime.* Vol. I, E. Scheerer, ed. Geneva, Georg, 1919.

Angell, J. R. "The Province of Functional Psychology," *Psychol. Rev.*, 14 (1907), 61-91.

Bain, A. *The Emotions and the Will.* London, Longmans & Green, 1859.

Bassett, M. F. & Warne, C. J. "On Lapse of Verbal Meaning with Repetition," *Amer. J. Psychol.* 30 (1919), 415-418.

Berg, J. H. van den. "Het Gesprek," in: Berg, J. H. van den and Linschoten, H. *Persoon en Wereld.* Utrecht, Bÿjleveld, 1953, 136-154.

Bergson, H. *Essai sur les données immédiates de la conscience.* Paris, Presses universitaires de France, 1946.

Bergson, H. *Ecrits et paroles.* Paris, Presses universitaires de France, 1957.

Berkeley, G. *A Treatise Concerning the Principles of Human Knowledge.* London, Everyman's Library, 1910.

Berkeley, G. *Three dialogues Between Hylas and Philonous.* London, Everyman's Library, 1910.

Bernard, C. *Leçons sur les propriétés physiologiques et les altérations pathologiques des liquides de l'organisme.* Vol. I. Paris, 1859.

Bierens De Haan, J. A. *Die tierischen Instinkte und ihr Umbau durch Erfahrung.* Leiden, 1940.

Blondel, C. "Les 'mouvements volontaires,'" in G. Dumas, *Nouveau traité de psychologie.* T. VI. Paris, Alcan, 1939, 380-395.

Bohr, N. "Das Quantenpostulat und die neuere Entwicklung der Atomistik," *Naturwissenschaften,* 16 (1928), 245-257.

"Wirkungsquantum und Naturbeschreibung," *Naturwissenschaften,* 17 (1929), 483-486.

Boring, E. G. *A History of Experimental Psychology.* New York, Century, 1929.

314   On the Way Toward a Phenomenological Psychology

"Human Nature vs. Sensation," *Amer. J. Psychol.* 55 (1942), 310-327.

Brentano, F. *Psychologie vom empirischen Standpunkte.* Leipzig, 1874.

Burloud, A. *La pensée d'après les recherches expérimentales de H. J. Watt, de Messer et de Bühler.* Paris, 1927.

Buytendijk. F. J. J. *Wege zum Verständnis der Tiere.* Zürich, no year. *Algemene Theorie der Menselijke Houding en Beweging.* Utrecht, Het Spectrum, 1948. *Traîté de psychologie animale.* Paris, Presses universitaires de France, 1952.

Cannon, W. B. *Bodily Changes in Pain, Hunger, Fear and Rage.* New York, Appleton, 1920. *The Wisdom of the Body.* New York, Norton 1932.

Delfgaauw, B. "Verantwoording der Phänomenologische Psychologie," *Nederl. Tijdschr. Psychol.,* 9 (1954) , 78-83.

Descartes, R. *Oeuvres et Lettres.* Paris, Gallimard, 1949.

Dewey, J. "The Vanishing Subject in the Psychology of James," *J. Phil.* 37 (1940) , 589-599.

"The Principles," *Psychol. Rev.,* 50 (1943) , 121.

Don, V. J., & Weld, H. P. "Lapse of Meaning with Visual Fixation," *Amer. J. Psychol.,* 35 (1924) , 446-450.

Ebbinghaus, H. *Grundzüge der Psychologie.* Bd. I. Leipzig, Bühler, 1919.

Fink, E. *Zur ontologischen Frühgeschichte von Raum-Zeit-Bewegung.* The Hague, Nijhoff, 1957.

Freud, S. "Studien über Hysterie," in *Gesammelte Werke.* Bd. I. London, Imago, 1952, 75-312.

"Das Unbewusste," in *Gesammelte Werke.* Bd. X. London, Imago, 1946, 264-303.

"Die Verdrängung," in *Gesammelte Werke.* Bd. X. London, Imago, 1946, 247-261.

Gurwitsch, A. "On the Object of Thought," *Phil. phenomenol. Res.,* 7 (1946-1947) , 347-353.

The Field of Consciousness. Pittsburgh, Duquesne University Press, 1964.

Gusdorf, G. *La parole.* Paris, Presses universitaires de France, 1953.

Haering, T. *Philosophie der Naturwissenschaft.* München, Rösl, 1923.

Hall, G. Stanley. *Founders of Modern Psychology.* New York, Appleton, 1912.

Helmholtz, H. von. "Uber die Erhaltung der Kraft," *Wissenschaftliche Abhandlungen.* Bd. I. Leipzig, Engelmann, 1882, 12-75.

"Uber das Ziel und die Fortschritte der Naturwissenschaft," *Vorträge und Reden.* Bd. I. Braunschweig, Vieweg, 1884, 333-363.

Hering, E. "Grundzüge der Lehre vom Lichtsinn," in Graefe-Saemisch,

Handbuch der gesamten Augenheilkunde. Bd. III. Berlin, 1925, Kap. XII.

Heymans, G. *Inleiding tot de Speciale Psychologie.* Haarlem, 1948.

Hobbes, T. *Leviathan.* H. Morley, ed. London, 1886.

Horwicz, A. *Psychologische Analysen auf Physiologischer Grundlage.* Bd. II/I. Halle.

Hume, D. *A Treatise on Human Nature.* T. H. Green & T. H. Grose, ed., 2 Vols. London, Longmans & Green, 1909.

Husserl, E. *Logische Untersuchungen.* Bd. II. Halle, Niemeyer, 1901. Bd. II/I. Halle, Niemeyer, 1922.

Ideen zu einer Reinen Phanomenologie und Phanomenologischen Philosophie. Bd. I. The Hague, 1950. Bd. II. The Hague, 1952. Bd. III. The Hague, 1952.

"Vorlesungen zur Phänomenologie des Inneren Zeitbewusstaeins," *Jb. Phil. phänomenol. Forsch.,* 9 (1928), 367-496.

Geburt, Tod, Unbewusstsein. Unpublished manuscript. Husserl Archives, Louvain, A VI 14, ± 1930.

"Die Frage nach dem Ursprung der Geometrie als Intentional-historisches Problem," *Rev. int. Phil.,* 1 (1939), 203-225.

"Die Welt der Lebendigen Gegenwart und die Konstitution der Ausserleiblichen Umwelt," *Phil. phenomenol. Res.,* 6 (1945-1946), 323-343.

Erfahrung und Urteil. Hamburg, Claassen & Goverts, 1948.

Die Krisis der Europäischen Wissenschaften und die Transzendentale Phänomenologie. The Hague, 1954.

"Persönliche Aufzeichnungen" (published by Biemel), *Phil. phenomenol. Res.,* 16 (1955-1956), 293-302.

In Commemoration of William James. B. Blanshard & H. Schneider, ed. New York, Columbia University Press, 1942.

James, H., ed. *The Letters of William James.* 2 Vol. Boston, Little & Brown, 1920.

"Remarks on the Occasion of the Centenary of William James," in *In Commemoration,* 3-10.

James, W. "The Sentiment of Rationality," *Mind,* 4 (1879), 317-346. Also in *Will to Believe,* 63-110.

"The Feeling of Effort," *Anniv. Mem. Boston Soc. nat. Hist.* Boston, 1880.

"Le sentiment de l'effort," *Critique philos.,* 9, 2 (1880), 123-135, 145-148, 200-208, 220-231, 289-291.

"The Sense of Dizziness in Deaf-mutes," *Amer. J. Otol.,* 4 (1882).

"On Some Omissions of Introspective Psychology," *Mind,* 9 (1884), 1-26.

"What is an Emotion?", *Mind,* 9 (1884), 188-205.

The Principles of Psychology. 2 Vols. London, Macmillan, 1890.
"A Plea for Psychology as a 'Natural Science,' " *Philos. Rev.,* 1
(1892) .
Psychology, Briefer Course. New York, Holt, 1893.
"The Physical Basis of Emotion," *Psychol. Rev.,* 1 (1894) , 516-529.
"The Knowing of Things Together," *Psychol. Rev.,* 2 (1895) ,
105-124. Reprinted under the title: "The Tigers in India," in
The Meaning of Truth, 1909. See: *Pragmatism,* 1943 ed., 361-368.
The Will to Believe. New York, Longmans & Green, 1897.
Talks to Teachers. London, 1920.
The Varieties of Religious Experience (1902) . New York, Modern
Library, 1902.
"Does 'Consciousness' exist?", *J. Phil.,* 1 (1904) , 477-491. Also in
Essays, 1-38.
"A World of Pure Experience," *J. Phil.,* 1 (1904) , 533-543. Also in
Essays, 39-91.
"The Thing and Its Relations," *J. Phil.,* 2 (1905) , 29-41. Also in *A
Pluralistic Universe,* 347-369, in *Essays,* 92-122.
"How Two Minds Can Know One Thing," *J. Phil.,* 2 (1905) ,
176-181. Also in *Essays,* 123-136.
"The Place of Affectional Facts in a World of Pure Experience," *J.
Phil.,* 2 (1905) , 281-287. Also in *Essays,* 137-154.
"The Experience of Activity," *Psychol. Rev.,* 12 (1905) , 1-17. Also in
A Pluralistic Universe, 370-394, in *Essays,* 155-189.
"La notion de conscience," *Arch. Psychol.,* 5 (1905) , 1-12. Also in
Essays, 206-233.
Pragmatism. London, Longmans & Green, 1943. Added to this edi-
tion (1907) are four essays from *The Meaning of Truth.* New
York, Longmans & Green, 1909.
A Pluralistic Universe (1909 ed.) . New York, 1928. Published in one
volume with *Essays,* New York, 1958.
Some Problems of Philosophy. New York, Longmans & Green, 1911.
Essays in Radical Empiricism. London, Longmans & Green, 1912.
"A List of the Published Writings of William James," H. James, Jr. &
E. Holt, ed. *Psychol. Rev.,* 18 (1911) , 157-165.
Jaspers, K. *Allgemeine Psychopathologie.* Berlin, 1948.
Kantor, J. R. "Jamesian Psychology and the Stream of Psychological
Thought," in *In Commemoration,* 143-156.
Koffka, K. *Principles of Gestalt Psychology.* London, 1935.
Kopfermann, H. "Psychologische Untersuchungen über die Wirkung
zweidimensionaler Darstellungen körperlicher Gebilde," *Psychol.
Forsch.,* 13 (1930) , 293-364.
Kouwer, B. J. & Linschoten, H. *Inleiding tot de Psychologie.* Assen, 1958.
Kuhn, H. "The Phenomenological Concept of 'Horizon,' " in

M. Farber, ed., *Philosophical Essays in Memory of E. Husserl.* Cambridge, Mass., Harvard University Press, 1940, 106-123.

Lacan, J. "Fonction et champ de la parole et du langage en psychanalyse," *La psychanalyse. I. Sur la parole et le langage.* Paris, 1956, 81-166.

Ladd, G. T., "Psychology—a So-called 'Natural Science,' " *Philos. Rev.,* 1 (1892).

Lashley, K. S. "The Behavioristic Interpretation of Consciousness," *Psychol. Rev.,* 30 (1923), 237-272, 329-353.

Lewin, K. *Principles of Topological Psychology.* New York, McGraw-Hill, 1936.

Linschoten, H. "Logische en Phenomenologische Analyse van de Bewegingsverschijnselen," *Tijdschr. Phil.,* 12 (1950), 668-728.

Postscript, in J. H. van den Berg & J. Linschoten, *Persoon en Wereld.* Utrecht, Bijleveld, 1953, 244-253.

"Uber das Einschlafen," *Psychol. Beitr.,* 2 (1955-1956), 70-97, 266-298.

Strukturanalyse der Binokularen Tiefenwahrnehmung. Groningen, 1956.

"Algemene Functieleer," in M. J. Langeveld, ed., *Inleiding in de Psychologie.* Groningen, 1957, 54-207.

"A Gentle Force." Beschouwingen over het Associatiebegrip. Groningen, 1957.

"Anthropologische Fragen zur Raumproblematik," *Studium Generale,* 11 (1958), 86-99.

"Geschiedenis der Psychologie," in Langeveld, ed., *Inleiding in de Psychologie.* Groningen, 1957.

Locke, J. *An Essay Concerning Human Understanding* (1690). A. S. Pringle-Pattison, ed. Oxford, Clarendon, 1928.

Lotze, R. H. *Medicinische Psychologie.* Leipzig, Weidmann, 1852.

McDougall, W. *Body and Mind.* London, Methuen, 1920.

MacFarlane, D. A. "The role of Kinesthesis in Maze Learning," *Univ. Calif. Publ. Psychol.,* 4 (1930), 277-305.

Mach, E. *Die Analyse der Empfindungen.* Jena, 1906.

Marcel, G. *Etre et avoir.* Paris, Aubier, Editions Montaigne, 1935.

Merleau-Ponty, M. *Phenomenologie de la perception.* Paris, Gallimard, 1945.

Metzger, A. "William James and the Crisis of Philosophy," in *In Commemoration,* 209-222.

Metzger, A. *Gesetze des Sehens.* Frankfurt a. M., Kramer, 1953. *Psychologie.* Darmstadt, Steinkopff, 1954.

Mill, J. *Analysis of the Phenomena of the Human Mind* (1829). J. S. Mill, ed. Vol. I. London, Longmans & Green, 1869.

Mill, J. S. *A System of Logic.* Vol. I. London, Longmans & Green, 1862.

Müller, J. *Zur Vergleichenden Physiologie des Gesichtssinnes des Menschen und der Thiere.* Leipzig, 1826.

Handbuch der Physiologie des Menschen. Bd. II/2. Koblenz, 1838.

Nogué, J. *L'activité primitive du moi.* Paris, 1936.

Packard, V. *The Hidden Persuaders.* New York, McKay, 1957.

Perry, R. B. *The Thought and Character of William James.* Vol. I Boston, Little & Brown, 1935. Vol. 11. Boston, Little & Brown, 1936. *Briefer Version,* in one volume, New York, Braziller, 1954. *In the Spirit of William James.* New Haven, Yale University Press, 1938. "James the Psychologist," *Psychol. Rev.,* 50 (1943), 122-124.

Pos, H. J., "Betekenis als Taalkundig en als Wijsgerig Fenomeen," in *Taal, Mens, en Cultuur.* Assen, 1957, 179-186.

Ricoeur, P. *Philosophie de la volonté.* Paris, Aubier, 1949.

Roback, A. A. *History of American Psychology.* New York, Library, 1952.

Rothschuh, K. E. *Geschichte der Physiologie.* Berlin, 1953.

Santayana, G. *Character and Opinion in the United States.* New York, 1921.

Sartre, J. P. *La nausée.* Paris, 1948.

Esquisse d'une théorie des émotions. Paris, Hermann, 1948.

Schütz, A. "On Multiple Realities," *Phil. phenomenol. Res.,* 5 (1944-1945), 533-576.

"Common-sense and Scientific Interpretation of Human Action," *Phil. phenomenol. Res.,* 14 (1953-1954), 1-38.

"Symbol, Reality and Society," in L. Bryson, ed., *Symbols and Society.* New York, 1955.

Severance, E. & Washburn, M. F. "The Loss of Associative Power in Words after Long Fixation," *Amer. J. Psychol.,* 18 (1907), 182-186.

Souriau, P. "La conscience de soi," *Rev. philos.,* 22 (1886), 449-472.

Stern, W. *Allgemeine Psychologie.* The Hague, Nijhoff, 1950.

Sterne, L. *The Life and Opinions of Tristram Shandy, Gentleman* (1759). Vol. I. London, 1900.

Stirner, M. *Der Einzige und Sein Eigentum.* Berlin, 1924.

Straus, E. *Vom Sinn der Sinne.* Berlin, 1935.

"Der Archimedische Punkt," in *Rencontre-Encounter-Begegneung* (Fesstbundel Buytendijk). Utrecht, Het Spectrum, 1957, 472-491.

Stumpf, K. "Uber den Begriff der Gemüthsbewegung," *Z. Psychol.,* 21 (1899), 47-99. *Erschinungen und Psychische Funktionen.* Berlin, 1907.

William James nach Seinen Briefen. Berlin, Heise, 1928.

Taine, H. *Histoire de la littérature anglaise.* T. IV. Paris, 1911.

Tilquin, A. *Le Behaviorisme.* Paris, Vrin, 1950.

Titchener, E. B. "An Historical Note on the James-Lange Theory of Emotion," *Amer. J. Psychol.,* 25 (1914), 427-447.

"Functional Psychology and the Psychology of Act, I," *Amer. J. Psychol.*, 32 (1921).

Verplanck, W. S. "A Glossary of Some Terms Used in the Objective Science of Behavior," *Psychol. Rev. Suppl.*, 64 (1957), No. 6, Part 2.

Volkelt, H. "Grundbegriffe," *Neue psychol. Stud.*, 12 (1934), H. 1, 1-45.

Watson, J. B. "Psychology as the Behaviorist Views it," *Psychol. Rev.*, 20 (1913), 158-177.

Behavior. An Introduction to Comparative Psychology. New York, Holt, 1914.

Psychology from the Standpoint of a Behaviorist. Philadelphia, Lippincott, 1924.

Behaviorism. New York, Norton, 1925.

The Ways of Behaviorism. New York, Harper, 1928.

Weinmann, R. *Die Lehre von den spezifischen Sinnesenergien.* Hamburg, 1895.

Wells, H. G. *The New Machiavelli.* Baltimore, 1946.

Werner, H. "Untersuchungen über Empfindung und Empfinden," *Z. Psychol.*, 114 (1930), 152-166.

Einführung in die Entwicklungspsychologie. Leipzig, Barth, 1926.

Wundt, W. *Grundzüge der Physiologischen Psychologie.* Leipzig, Engelmann, 1874, 1 Bd. 1880, 2 Bde. 1887, 2 Bde. 1908/11, 3 Bde.

"Uber Psychische Causalität und das Princip des Psychophysischen Parallelismus," *Philos. Stud. (Wundt)*, 10 (1894), 1-124.

Grundriss der Psychologie. Leipzig, Kröner, 1922.